W9-CGY-226

HAMMOND

LARGE TYPE

WORLD ATLAS

G.K.HALL &CO.
Boston, Massachusetts
1991

Library of Congress Cataloging-in-Publication Data

Hammond Incorporated.
    Hammond large type world atlas.

        p.   cm.

    Includes gazetteer and indexes.
    ISBN 0-8161-4701-9
    1. Atlases.   2. Large type books.   I. Title: Large
type world atlas.
G1021.H2727   1990   (G&M)
912--dc20   90-22658
                                                 CIP
                                                 MAP

CONTENTS

28.95

931622

Gazetteer-Index of the World   6-13

The World   14-15

North America   16-17
Canada   18-19
United States   20-21
New England States   22-23
Middle Atlantic States   24-25
Southeastern United States   26-27
North Central United States   28-29
South Central United States   30-31
Northwestern United States   32-33
Southwestern United States   34-35
Mexico   36-37
Central America   38-39
The West Indies   40-41

South America   42-43
Colombia, Venezuela and the Guianas   44-45
Peru and Ecuador   46-47
Brazil and Bolivia   48-49
Argentina, Chile, Paraguay and Uruguay   50-51

Europe   52-53
United Kingdom and Ireland   54-55
Scandinavia   56-57
Germany   58-59
Belgium, Netherlands and Luxembourg   60-61
France   62-63
Spain and Portugal   64-65
Italy   66-67   (Continued)

CONTENTS

Switzerland and Liechtenstein   68-69

Austria, Czechoslovakia and Hungary   70-71

The Balkans   72-73

Poland   74-75

Union of Soviet Socialist Republics   76-77

Asia   78-79

The Near and Middle East   80-81

Turkey, Syria, Lebanon and Cyprus   82-83

Israel and Jordan   84-85

Iran and Iraq   86-87

Southern Asia   88-89

Indochinese and Malayan Peninsulas   90-91

China and Mongolia   92-93

Japan and Korea   94-95

Republic of the Philippines   96-97

Southeast Asia   98-99

Australia and New Zealand   100-101

Pacific Ocean   102-103

Africa   104-105

Western Africa   106-107

Northeastern Africa   108-109

Central Africa   110-111

Southern Africa   112-113

Antarctica   114-115

Index of the World   116-144

A NOTE REGARDING THE INDEXES

The Gazetteer-Index of the World on the following pages provides a quick reference index for countries and other important areas with their capitals and includes a conveniently arranged statistical comparison of area and population.

The index of the World appearing on pages 116-144 contains an alphabetical listing of all of the features appearing in the atlas, with the exception of those political or geographical entities included in the Gazetteer-Index.

Entries are generally indexed to the map having the largest scale but, in the case of those which have equal coverage or are important to surroundings on more than one map, more than one reference may be given.

With the exception of some outlying islands and certain features not necessarily having a political affiliation, each entry includes the political division or continent in which it is located. The page number then appears before the diagonal line, and the key reference on the appropriate map follows the diagonal line.

GAZETTEER-INDEX OF THE WORLD

This alphabetical list contains continents, countries, states, colonial possessions and other major geographical areas. It provides a quick reference to their area, population, capital or chief town, map page number and index key thereon. The population figures used in each case are the latest reliable figures obtainable. The index key indicates the square on the respective page in which the name may be found. The asterisk before the name designates a member of the United Nations.

COUNTRY	AREA (SQUARE MILES)	POPULATION	CAPITAL OR CHIEF TOWN	REF.
*Afghanistan	250,775	16,363,000	Kabul	88
Africa	11,707,000	484,000,000	....	104-105
Alabama, U.S.A.	51,705	3,893,978	Montgomery	26/B3
Alaska, U.S.A.	591,004	401,841	Juneau	20/B3
*Albania	11,100	2,590,600	Tirane	73/A2
Alberta, Canada	255,285	2,237,724	Edmonton	18/C2
*Algeria	919,591	18,666,000	Algiers	106/C2
American Samoa	77	32,297	Pago Pago	103/D3
Andorra	188	39,940	Andorra la Vella	63/C4
*Angola	481,351	7,262,000	Luanda	112/A2
Antarctica	5,500,000	....	...........,..........	114-115
*Antigua & Barbuda	171	75,000	St. John's	41/D2
*Argentina	1,072,070	28,438,000	Buenos Aires	50-51
Arizona, U.S.A	114,000	2,718,425	Phoenix	35/D3
Arkansas, U.S.A.	53,187	2,286,419	Little Rock	31/D2
Armenian S.S.R., U.S.S.R.	11,506	3,031,000	Erivan	76/C3
Aruba	75	55,148	Oranjestad	41/C3
Asia	17,128,500	2,688,000,000	....	78-79
*Australia	2,966,136	14,576,330	Canberra	100-101
Australian Capital Territory	927	221,609	Canberra	101/D3
*Austria	32,375	7,555,338	Vienna	70/B2
Azerbaidzhan S.S.R., U.S.S.R.	33,436	6,028,000	Baku	76/C3
*Bahamas	5,382	209,505	Nassau	41/B1
*Bahrain	240	358,857	Manama	80/B2
*Bangladesh	55,126	87,052,024	Dhaka	89/C2
*Barbados	166	248,983	Bridgetown	41/D3
*Belgium	11,781	9,848,647	Brussels	61
*Belize	8,867	145,353	Belmopan	38/B1
*Benin	43,483	3,338,240	Porto-Novo	107/C4
Bermuda	21	67,761	Hamilton	17/F3
*Bhutan	18,147	1,301,000	Thimphu	89/C2
*Bolivia	424,163	5,755,000	La Paz, Sucre	48/B3
*Botswana	224,764	936,600	Gaborone	112/B3

COUNTRY	AREA (SQUARE MILES)	POPULATION	CAPITAL OR CHIEF TOWN	REF.
*Brazil	3,284,426	119,098,992	Brasília	48-49
British Columbia, Canada	366,253	2,744,467	Victoria	18/B2
British Indian Ocean Terr.	29	2,000	Victoria (Seychelles)	79/C5
*Brunei	2,226	192,832	Bandar Seri Begawan	98/B2
*Bulgaria	42,823	8,890,000	Sofia	72/B1
*Burkina Faso	105,869	7,094,000	Ouagadougou	107/B3
*Burma	261,789	33,640,000	Rangoon	90/A1
*Burundi	10,747	4,028,420	Bujumbura	111/D3
*Byelorussian S.S.R. (White Russian S.S.R.), U.S.S.R.	80,154	9,560,543	Minsk	76/B3
California, U.S.A.	158,706	23,667,837	Sacramento	34/B2
*Cambodia	69,898	5,756,141	Phnom Penh	91/B2
*Cameroon	183,568	8,503,000	Yaoundé	110/B2
*Canada	3,851,787	24,343,181	Ottawa	18-19
*Cape Verde	1,557	296,093	Praia	14/H4
Cayman Islands	100	18,000	Georgetown	40/A2
*Central African Republic	242,000	2,284,000	Bangui	110/C2
Central America	197,480	22,000,000	....	38-39
*Chad	495,752	4,309,000	N'Djamena	104/C3
Channel Islands	75	129,000	....	55/C4
*Chile	292,257	11,275,440	Santiago	50-51
*China (People's Rep.)	3,691,000	1,008,175,288	Beijing	92-93
China (Republic of)	13,971	18,029,798	Taipei	93/D2
*Colombia	439,513	28,776,000	Bogotá	44
Colorado, U.S.A.	104,091	2,889,735	Denver	35/F2
*Comoros	719	345,000	Moroni	105/E4
*Congo	132,046	1,537,000	Brazzaville	110/B3
Connecticut, U.S.A.	5,018	3,107,576	Hartford	23/A4
Cook Islands	91	17,754	Avarua	103/E3
Coral Sea Islands Territory, Australia	8.5	....	(Norfolk Isl.)	101/D2
*Costa Rica	19,575	2,271,000	San José	38/C3
*Cuba	44,206	9,706,369	Havana	40/A2
*Cyprus	3,473	637,000	Nicosia	82/B2
*Czechoslovakia	49,373	15,364,000	Prague	70/B1
Delaware, U.S.A.	2,044	594,317	Dover	25/D4
*Denmark	16,629	5,118,000	Copenhagen	57/A3
District of Columbia, U.S.A.	69	638,432	Washington	25/C4
*Djibouti	8,880	386,000	Djibouti	109/D3
*Dominica	290	74,089	Roseau	41/D3
*Dominican Republic	18,704	5,647,977	Santo Domingo	41/C2
*Ecuador	109,483	8,644,000	Quito	46

COUNTRY	AREA (SQUARE MILES)	POPULATION	CAPITAL OR CHIEF TOWN	REF.
*Egypt	386,659	43,465,000	Cairo	108/B2
*El Salvador	8,260	4,748,000	San Salvador	38/B2
England, U.K.	50,516	46,220,995	London	55
*Equatorial Guinea	10,831	244,000	Malabo	105/C3
Estonian S.S.R., U.S.S.R.	17,413	1,466,000	Tallinn	76/B3
*Ethiopia	471,776	31,065,000	Addis Ababa	109/C4
Europe	4,057,000	690,000,000	....	52-53
Falkland Islands & Dependencies	6,918	1,813	Stanley	51/B5
*Fiji	7,055	645,000	Suva	103/D3
*Finland	130,128	4,812,150	Helsinki	56-57
Florida, U.S.A.	58,664	9,746,421	Tallahassee	27/C4
*France	210,038	53,963,000	Paris	62-63
French Guiana	35,135	73,022	Cayenne	45
French Polynesia	1,544	150,000	Papeete	103/E3
*Gabon	103,346	555,000	Libreville	110/D3
*Gambia	4,127	601,000	Banjul	107/A3
Georgia, U.S.A.	58,910	5,463,087	Atlanta	27/C3
Georgian S.S.R., U.S.S.R.	26,911	5,015,000	Tbilisi	76/C3
*Germany	137,753	78,278,587	Berlin	58-59
*Ghana	92,099	11,450,000	Accra	107/B4
Gibraltar	2.28	29,648	Gibraltar	64/B2
Gilbert Islands (Kiribati)	291	56,213	Bairiki	102/C2
*Great Britain & Northern Ireland (United Kingdom)	94,399	55,638,495	London	54-55
*Greece	50,944	9,740,417	Athens	73/B1
Greenland	840,000	51,000	Nuuk (Godthåb)	16/H1
*Grenada	133	103,103	St. George's	41/D3
Guadeloupe & Dependencies	687	328,400	Basse-Terre	41/D2
Guam	209	105,979	Agaña	102/B2
*Guatemala	42,042	6,043,559	Guatemala	38/B2
*Guinea	94,925	5,143,284	Conakry	107/A3
*Guinea-Bissau	13,948	810,000	Bissau	107/A3
*Guyana	83,000	793,000	Georgetown	45
*Haiti	10,694	5,053,792	Port-au-Prince	40/B2
Hawaii, U.S.A.	6,471	964,691	Honolulu	20/C3
*Honduras	43,277	3,955,000	Tegucigalpa	38/C2
Hong Kong	403	4,986,560	Victoria	93/C2
*Hungary	35,919	10,702,000	Budapest	71/C2
*Iceland	39,768	231,000	Reykjavík	56/A1

COUNTRY	AREA (SQUARE MILES)	POPULATION	CAPITAL OR CHIEF TOWN	REF.
Idaho, U.S.A.	83,564	944,038	Boise	32/D2
Illinois, U.S.A.	56,345	11,427,414	Springfield	29/D3
*India	1,269,339	685,184,692	New Delhi	88-89
Indiana, U.S.A.	36,185	5,490,260	Indianapolis	29/E3
*Indonesia	788,430	147,490,260	Jakarta	98/B3
Iowa, U.S.A.	56,275	2,913,808	Des Moines	28/C3
*Iran	636,293	37,447,000	Tehran	87/C2
*Iraq	172,476	12,767,000	Baghdad	86/B2
*Ireland (Eire)	27,136	3,443,405	Dublin	55
*Israel	7,847	3,980,000	Jerusalem	84
*Italy	116,303	56,243,935	Rome	66-67
*Ivory Coast (Côte d'Ivoire)	124,504	7,920,000	Yamoussoukro	107/B4
*Jamaica	4,411	2,184,000	Kingston	40/B2
*Japan	145,730	117,060,396	Toyko	94-95
*Jordan	35,000	2,152,273	Amman	84-85
Kalaallit Nunaat (Greenland)	840,000	51,000	Nuuk (Godthåb)	16/H1
Kansas, U.S.A.	82,277	2,364,236	Topeka	28/B4
Kazakh S.S.R., U.S.S.R.	1,048,300	14,684,000	Alma-Ata	76/D3
Kentucky, U.S.A.	40,409	3,660,257	Frankfort	26/B2
*Kenya	224,960	15,327,061	Nairobi	111/D2
Kirgiz S.S.R., U.S.S.R.	76,641	3,529,000	Frunze	76/D3
Kiribati	291	56,213	Bairiki	102/C2
Korea, North	46,540	18,317,000	Pyongyang	94
Korea, South	38,175	37,448,836	Seoul	94
*Kuwait	6,532	1,355,827	Al Kuwait	80/B2
*Laos	91,428	3,811,000	Vientiane	90/B2
Latvian S.S.R., U.S.S.R.	24,595	2,521,000	Riga	76/B3
*Lebanon	4,015	2,688,000	Beirut	82/B3
*Lesotho	11,720	1,339,000	Maseru	113/C3
*Liberia	43,000	1,873,000	Monrovia	107/B4
*Libya	679,358	3,096,000	Tripoli	108/A2
Liechtenstein	61	25,220	Vaduz	69/D1
Lithuanian S.S.R., U.S.S.R.	25,174	3,398,000	Vilna	76/B3
Louisiana, U.S.A.	47,752	4,206,098	Baton Rouge	31/D3
*Luxembourg	999	364,606	Luxembourg	61/C3
Macau	6	261,680	Macau	93/C2
*Madagascar	226,657	8,955,000	Antananarivo	113/D2
Maine, U.S.A.	33,265	1,125,030	Augusta	22/C2
*Malawi	45,747	6,123,000	Lilongwe	105/D4
Malaya, Malaysia	50,806	11,138,227	Kuala Lumpur	91/B3
*Malaysia	128,308	13,435,588	Kuala Lumpur	98/B2

COUNTRY	AREA (SQUARE MILES)	POPULATION	CAPITAL OR CHIEF TOWN	REF.
*Maldives	115	157,000	Male	79/C4
*Mali	464,873	7,160,000	Bamako	107/B3
*Malta	122	366,000	Valletta	67/C3
Man, Isle of	227	64,000	Douglas	55/B3
Manitoba, Canada	250,999	1,026,241	Winnipeg	18/D2
Marquesas Islands, Fr. Polynesia	492	5,419	Atuona	103/F3
Martinique	425	328,566	Fort-de-France	41/D3
Maryland, U.S.A.	10,460	4,216,941	Annapolis	25/C4
Massachusetts, U.S.A.	8,284	5,737,081	Boston	23/A3
*Mauritania	419,229	1,681,000	Nouakchott	104/B3
*Mauritius	790	971,000	Port Louis	79/B5
*Mexico	761,601	67,395,826	Mexico City	36-37
Michigan, U.S.A.	58,527	9,262,070	Lansing	29/E2
Micronesia, Fed. States of	——		Kolonia	102/B2
Minnesota, U.S.A.	84,402	4,075,970	St. Paul	28/C2
Mississippi, U.S.A.	47,689	2,520,631	Jackson	26/A3
Missouri, U.S.A.	69,697	4,916,759	Jefferson City	28/C4
Moldavian S.S.R., U.S.S.R.	13,012	3,947,000	Kishinev	76/B3
Monaco	368 acres	26,000	Monaco	63/D4
*Mongolia	606,163	1,732,000	Ulaanbaatar	92-93
Montana, U.S.A.	147,046	786,690	Helena	32/E2
*Morocco	172,414	20,646,000	Rabat	113/C2
*Mozambique	303,769	12,130,000	Maputo	105/D4
Namibia	317,827	1,009,000	Windhoek	112/A3
Nauru	7.7	7,254	Yaren (dist.)	102/C3
Nebraska, U.S.A.	77,355	1,569,825	Lincoln	28/A3
*Nepal	54,663	15,020,451	Kathmandu	89/C2
*Netherlands	15,892	14,306,000	The Hague, Amsterdam	60-61
Netherlands Antilles	308	183,000	Willemstad	41/C3
Nevada, U.S.A.	110,561	800,493	Carson City	34/C2
New Brunswick, Canada	28,354	696,403	Fredericton	18/E2
New Caledonia	7,335	143,000	Noumea	102/C4
Newfoundland, Canada	156,184	567,681	St. John's	18/F2
New Hampshire, U.S.A.	9,279	920,610	Concord	23/B3
New Hebrides (Vanuatu)	5,700	112,596	Vila	102/C3
New Jersey, U.S.A.	7,787	7,365,011	Trenton	25/D3
New Mexico, U.S.A.	121,593	1,303,445	Santa Fe	35/F3
New South Wales, Australia	309,498	5,126,217	Sydney	101/D3
New York, U.S.A.	49,108	17,558,072	Albany	24/C2
*New Zealand	103,736	3,175,737	Wellington	101/E3
*Nicaragua	45,698	2,732,000	Managua	38/C2

COUNTRY	AREA (SQUARE MILES)	POPULATION	CAPITAL OR CHIEF TOWN	REF.
*Niger	489,189	4,994,000	Niamey	107/C3
*Nigeria	357,000	82,643,000	Lagos	107/C4
North America	9,363,000	376,000,000	....	16-17
North Carolina, U.S.A.	52,669	5,881,385	Raleigh	26/D3
North Dakota, U.S.A.	70,702	652,717	Bismarck	28/A2
Northern Ireland, U.K.	5,452	1,507,065	Belfast	55
Northern Marianas (U.S.)	184	16,780	Capitol Hill	102/B2
Northern Territory, Australia	519,768	123,324	Darwin	100/C2
Northwest Territories, Canada	1,304,896	45,741	Yellowknife	18-19
*Norway	125,053	4,111,000	Oslo	56-57
Nova Scotia, Canada	21,425	847,442	Halifax	18/E2
Oceania	3,292,000	23,000,000	....	102-103
Ohio, U.S.A.	41,330	10,797,624	Columbus	29/F3
Oklahoma, U.S.A.	69,956	3,025,495	Oklahoma City	30/C2
*Oman	120,000	919,000	Muscat	81/B2
Ontario, Canada	412,580	8,625,107	Toronto	18/D2
Oregon, U.S.A.	97,073	2,633,149	Salem	32/B3
*Pakistan	310,403	83,782,000	Islamabad	88
*Panama	29,761	1,830,175	Panamá	39/D3
*Papua New Guinea	183,540	3,010,727	Port Moresby	99/D3
*Paraguay	157,047	3,026,165	Asunción	50/C2
Pennsylvania, U.S.A.	45,308	11,864,751	Harrisburg	24/B3
*Peru	496,222	17,031,221	Lima	46-47
*Philippines	115,707	48,098,460	Manila	96-97
Pitcairn Islands	18	54	Adamstown	103/F4
*Poland	120,725	36,062,309	Warsaw	74-75
*Portugal	35,549	9,784,200	Lisbon	64
Prince Edward Island, Canada	2,184	122,506	Charlottetown	18/E2
Puerto Rico	3,515	3,196,520	San Juan	41/C2
*Qatar	4,247	248,000	Doha	80/B2
Quebec, Canada	594,857	6,438,403	Québec	18/D2
Queensland, Australia	666,872	2,295,123	Brisbane	101/C2
Rhode Island, U.S.A.	1,212	947,154	Providence	23/B4
*Romania	91,699	22,400,000	Bucharest	72/B1
Russian S.F.S.R., U.S.S.R.	6,592,812	137,551,000	Moscow	76-77
*Rwanda	10,169	5,046,000	Kigali	110/C3
Sabah, Malaysia	29,300	1,002,608	Kota Kinabalu	98/B2
*Saint Kitts & Nevis	104	44,404	Basseterre	41/D2
*Saint Lucia	238	115,783	Castries	41/D3
Saint-Pierre & Miquelon	93.5	6,041	Saint-Pierre	119/F2
*Saint Vincent & the Grenadines	150	124,000	Kingstown	41/D3

COUNTRY	AREA (SQUARE MILES)	POPULATION	CAPITAL OR CHIEF TOWN	REF.
San Marino	23.4	21,000	San Marino	66/C2
*São Tomé and Príncipe	372	86,000	São Tomé	107/C4
Sarawak, Malaysia	48,202	1,294,753	Kuching	98/B2
Saskatchewan, Canada	251,699	968,313	Regina	18/C2
*Saudi Arabia	829,995	9,319,000	Riyadh	80/B2
Scotland, U.K.	30,414	5,117,146	Edinburgh	54
*Senegal	75,954	5,703,000	Dakar	106/A3
*Seychelles	145	63,000	Victoria	111/E3
*Siam (Thailand)	198,455	44,278,000	Bangkok	90/B2
*Sierra Leone	27,925	3,571,000	Freetown	107/A4
*Singapore	226	2,413,945	Singapore	91/B3
*Solomon Islands	11,500	221,000	Honiara	102/B3
*Somalia	246,200	4,895,000	Mogadishu	111/E2
*South Africa	455,318	23,771,970	Cape Town, Pretoria	112/B3
South America	6,875,000	246,000,000		42-43
South Australia, Australia	379,922	1,285,033	Adelaide	100/C3
South Carolina, U.S.A.	31,113	3,122,814	Columbia	26/C3
South Dakota, U.S.A.	77,116	690,768	Pierre	28/A2
South-West Africa (Namibia)	317,827	1,009,000	Windhoek	112/A3
*Spain	194,881	37,746,260	Madrid	64-65
*Sri Lanka	25,332	14,850,001	Colombo	89/C4
*Sudan	967,494	18,681,000	Khartoum	108/B3
*Suriname	55,144	354,860	Paramaribo	45
*Swaziland	6,705	585,000	Mbabane	105/D5
*Sweden	173,665	8,328,000	Stockholm	56-57
Switzerland	15,943	6,365,960	Bern	68-69
*Syria	71,498	9,172,000	Damascus	83/C3
Tadzhik S.S.R., U.S.S.R.	55,251	3,801,000	Dushanbe	76/D4
Tahiti, French Polynesia	402	150,000	Papeete	103/E3
*Tanzania	363,708	17,982,000	Dar es Salaam	111/D3
Tasmania, Australia	26,178	418,957	Hobart	101/D4
Tennessee, U.S.A.	42,144	4,591,120	Nashville	27/B3
Texas, U.S.A.	266,807	14,227,574	Austin	30/C3
*Thailand	198,455	44,278,000	Bangkok	90/B2
Tibet, China	463,320	1,790,000	Lhasa	92/B2
*Togo	21,622	2,702,945	Lomé	107/C4
Tonga	270	99,000	Nuku'alofa	103/D4
*Trinidad & Tobago	1,980	1,067,108	Port-of-Spain	41/D3
*Tunisia	63,378	6,392,000	Tunis	106/C1
*Turkey	300,946	46,312,000	Ankara	82-83
Turkmen S.S.R., U.S.S.R.	188,455	2,759,000	Ashkhabad	76/C4

COUNTRY	AREA (SQUARE MILES)	POPULATION	CAPITAL OR CHIEF TOWN	REF.
Turks & Caicos Islands	166	7,436	Cockburn Town	41/C2
Tuvalu	10	7,349	Fongafale	103/C3
*Uganda	91,076	12,630,076	Kampala	111/D2
*Ukrainian S.S.R., U.S.S.R.	233,089	49,754,642	Kiev	76/B3
*Union of Soviet Socialist Republics	8,649,490	268,800,000	Moscow	76-77
*United Arab Emirates	32,278	1,043,225	Abu Dhabi	81/B2
*United Kingdom	94,399	55,638,495	London	54-55
*United States of America	3,623,420	226,549,448	Washington	20-21
*Upper Volta (Burkina Faso)	105,869	7,094,000	Ouagadougou	107/B3
*Uruguay	72,172	2,947,000	Montevideo	50/C3
Utah, U.S.A.	84,899	1,461,037	Salt Lake City	35/E2
Uzbek S.S.R., U.S.S.R.	173,591	15,391,000	Tashkent	76/D3
*Vanuatu	5,700	112,596	Vila	102/C3
Vatican City	108.7 acres	733	....	67/B2
*Venezuela	352,143	14,570,085	Caracas	44-45
Vermont, U.S.A.	9,614	511,456	Montpelier	23/A3
Victoria, Australia	87,876	3,832,443	Melbourne	101/C4
*Vietnam	128,405	52,741,766	Hanoi	90/B2
Virginia, U.S.A.	40,767	5,346,797	Richmond	26/D2
Virgin Islands (British)	59	12,000	Road Town	41/C2
Virgin Islands (U.S.A.)	132	96,569	Charlotte Amalie	41/C2
Wake Island	2.5	302	Wake Islet	102/C2
Wales, U.K.	8,017	2,790,462	Cardiff	55
Washington, U.S.A.	68,139	4,132,204	Olympia	32/B2
Western Australia, Australia	975,096	1,273,624	Perth	100/B2
Western Sahara	102,703	165,000	....	106/A2
*Western Samoa	1,133	158,130	Apia	103/D3
West Virginia, U.S.A.	24,231	1,950,258	Charleston	26/C2
*White Russian S.S.R. (Byelorussian S.S.R.), U.S.S.R.	80,154	9,560,543	Minsk	76-77
Wisconsin, U.S.A.	56,153	4,705,642	Madison	29/D3
World	57,970,000	4,508,000,000	....	14-15
Wyoming, U.S.A.	97,809	469,557	Cheyenne	33/F3
*Yemen	188,321	8,486,189	San'a	80/B3
*Yugoslavia	98,766	22,690,000	Belgrade	72/A1
Yukon Territory, Canada	207,075	23,153	Whitehorse	18/B1
*Zaire	905,063	26,377,000	Kinshasa	110/C3
*Zambia	290,586	5,679,808	Lusaka	112/B2
*Zimbabwe	150,803	7,539,000	Harare (Salisbury)	112/B2

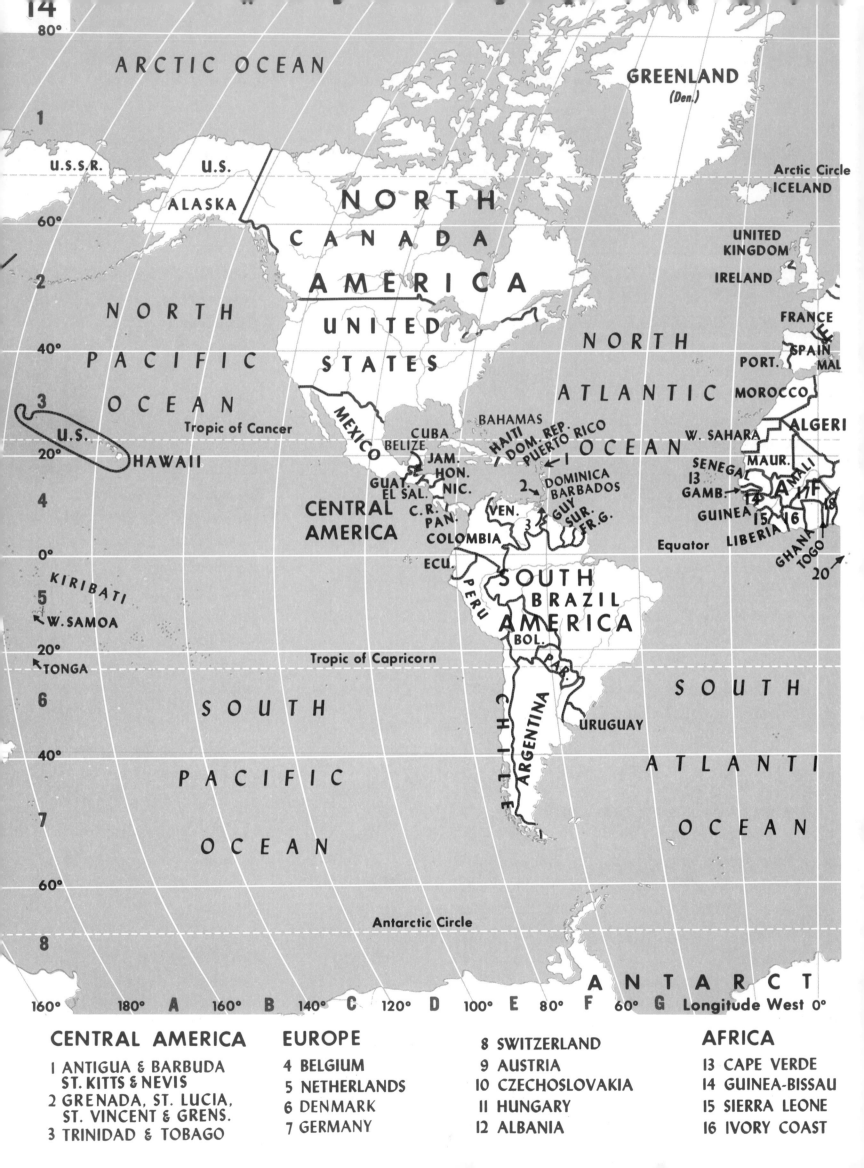

ARCTIC OCEAN

GREENLAND
(Den.)

1

U.S.S.R.   U.S.   Arctic Circle
                                                                                          ICELAND
60°   ALASKA

NORTH   NORTH   UNITED
                                                                              KINGDOM
2   C A N A D A   IRELAND

NORTH   A M E R I C A
                                                                                          FRANCE
40°   PACIFIC   UNITED   NORTH   PORT.   SPAIN
                          STATES   MAL
                                                                      MOROCCO
OCEAN   ATLANTIC
3   ALGERI
Tropic of Cancer   BAHAMAS   W. SAHARA
     U.S.   MEXICO   CUBA   HAITI DOM. REP.   MAUR.
20°   BELIZE   PUERTO RICO   OCEAN   SENEGA
          HAWAII   JAM.   1   13   M A L I
                          GUAT. HON.   DOMINICA   GAMB   14
4   EL SAL. NIC.   2 BARBADOS   GUINEA   15 16
                    CENTRAL C.R.   VEN.   GUY   LIBERIA
                    AMERICA PAN.   SUR.   GHANA TOGO
                          COLOMBIA   3   FR.G.   Equator   20
0°   ECU.
                                    SOUTH
KIRIBATI   BRAZIL
5   AMERICA
  W. SAMOA   PERU
20°   BOL.
  TONGA   Tropic of Capricorn   SOUTH

6   SOUTH   PAR.
                                    CHILE
40°   ARGENTINA URUGUAY ATLANTI
          PACIFIC
7
                                                              OCEAN
          OCEAN
60°

                    Antarctic Circle
8
                                                        A N T A R C T

160°   180° A 160° B 140° C 120° D 100° E 80° F 60° G Longitude West 0°

CENTRAL AMERICA

1 ANTIGUA & BARBUDA
  ST. KITTS & NEVIS
2 GRENADA, ST. LUCIA,
  ST. VINCENT & GRENS.
3 TRINIDAD & TOBAGO

EUROPE

4 BELGIUM
5 NETHERLANDS
6 DENMARK
7 GERMANY

8 SWITZERLAND
9 AUSTRIA
10 CZECHOSLOVAKIA
11 HUNGARY
12 ALBANIA

AFRICA

13 CAPE VERDE
14 GUINEA-BISSAU
15 SIERRA LEONE
16 IVORY COAST

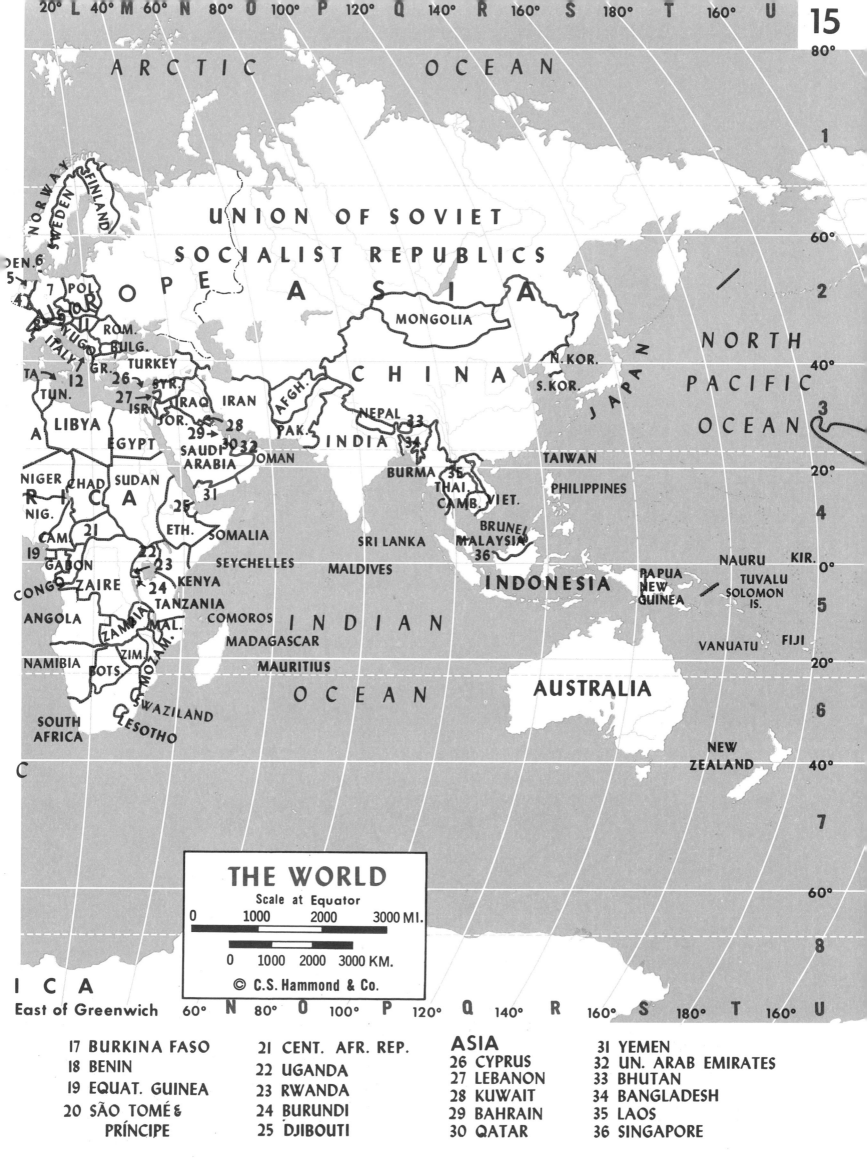

80°
1
60°
2
40°
3
20°
4
0°
5
20°
6
40°
7
60°
8

ARCTIC OCEAN

NORWAY SWEDEN FINLAND

DEN. 6
5
4
7 POL
UR
YUGO
ROM.
BULG.
ITALY GR. TURKEY
TA TUN.
12 26 SYR.
27 ISR JOR. IRAQ IRAN
28
LIBYA EGYPT 29 30 32 OMAN
A SAUDI ARABIA
NIGER CHAD SUDAN 31
RICA
NIG. ETH. SOMALIA
21 22 SEYCHELLES
CAM. 23 KENYA
19 GABON 24
CONGO ZAIRE TANZANIA
ANGOLA ZAMBIA MAL. COMOROS MADAGASCAR
NAMIBIA ZIM. MOZAM. MAURITIUS
BOTS
SWAZILAND
SOUTH AFRICA LESOTHO
C
I C A

UNION OF SOVIET
SOCIALIST REPUBLICS
E U R O P E A S I A

MONGOLIA

CHINA

N. KOR.
S. KOR.
JAPAN

NORTH

PACIFIC

OCEAN

AFGH.
NEPAL 33
PAK. INDIA 34
TAIWAN
BURMA 35
THAI.
CAMB. VIET.
PHILIPPINES
SRI LANKA
MALDIVES
BRUNEI
MALAYSIA
36
INDONESIA
NAURU KIR.
TUVALU
PAPUA NEW GUINEA SOLOMON IS.
VANUATU FIJI

INDIAN

OCEAN

AUSTRALIA

NEW ZEALAND

THE WORLD
Scale at Equator
0 1000 2000 3000 MI.

0 1000 2000 3000 KM.
© C.S. Hammond & Co.

17 BURKINA FASO	21 CENT. AFR. REP.	**ASIA**
18 BENIN	22 UGANDA	26 CYPRUS
19 EQUAT. GUINEA	23 RWANDA	27 LEBANON
20 SÃO TOMÉ &	24 BURUNDI	28 KUWAIT
PRÍNCIPE	25 DJIBOUTI	29 BAHRAIN
		30 QATAR

31 YEMEN
32 UN. ARAB EMIRATES
33 BHUTAN
34 BANGLADESH
35 LAOS
36 SINGAPORE

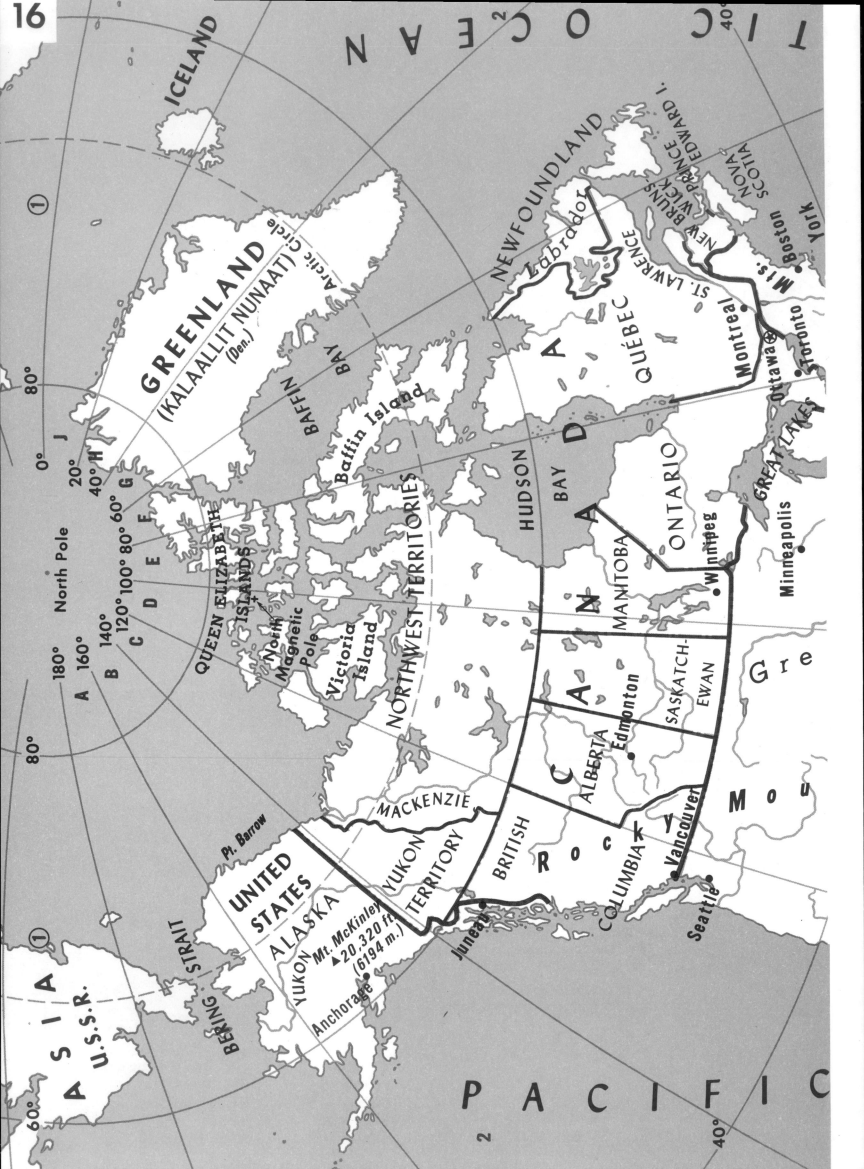

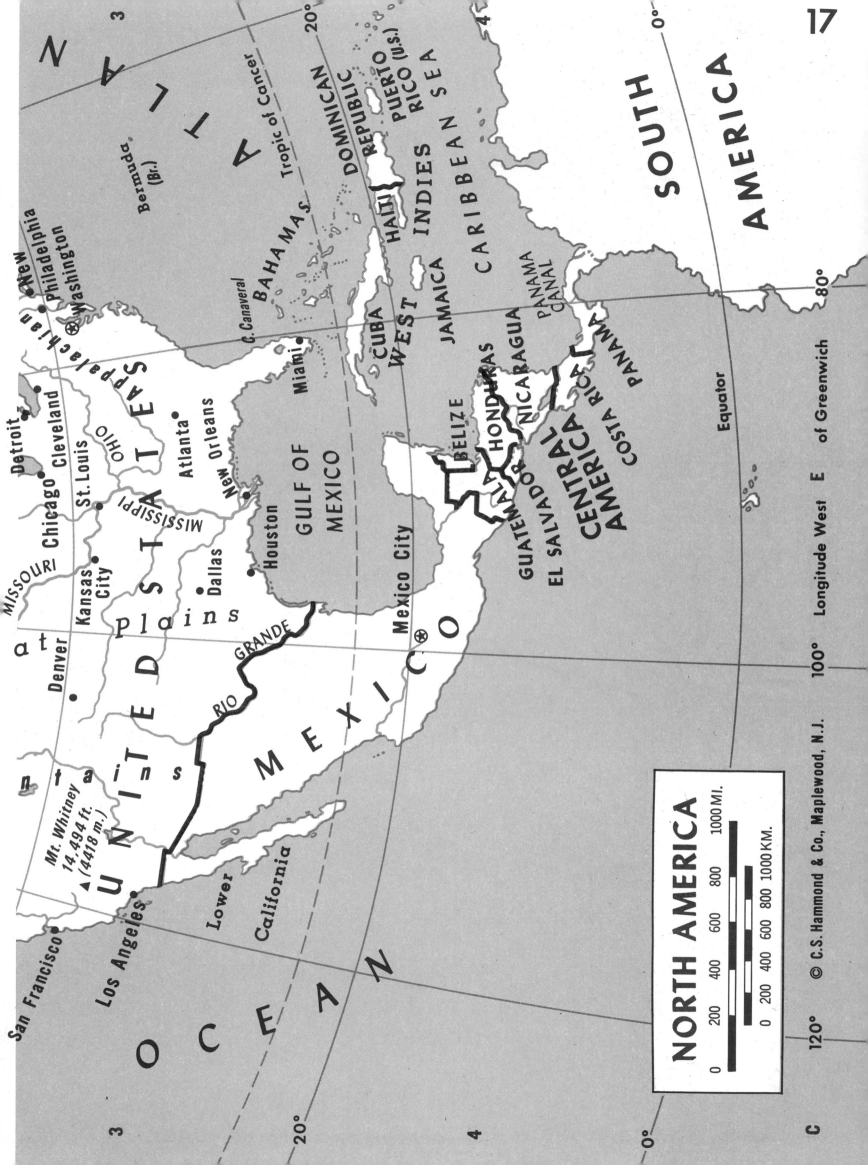

NORTH AMERICA

SOUTH AMERICA

ATLANTIC

Bermuda (Br.)

New
Philadelphia
Washington

Detroit
Cleveland
Chicago
St.Louis
Appalachian
OHIO
Atlanta
New Orleans
MISSOURI
Kansas City
Denver
Dallas
Houston
Plains
at
RIO GRANDE
RIO
Mt. Whitney 14,494 ft. (4418 m.)
UNITED STATES
n t a i n s
San Francisco
Los Angeles
Lower California
MEXICO
Mexico City

Tropic of Cancer
BAHAMAS
C. Canaveral
Miami
GULF OF MEXICO

CUBA
HAITI
DOMINICAN REPUBLIC
PUERTO RICO (U.S.)
WEST INDIES
JAMAICA
CARIBBEAN SEA
BELIZE
GUATEMALA
HONDURAS
EL SALVADOR
NICARAGUA
PANAMA CANAL
CENTRAL AMERICA
COSTA RICA
PANAMA

OCEAN

Equator

20°
3
20°

80°

Longitude West   E   of Greenwich

100°

120°

4

0°

C

0°

© C.S. Hammond & Co., Maplewood, N.J.

0   200   400   600   800   1000 MI.
0   200   400   600   800   1000 KM.

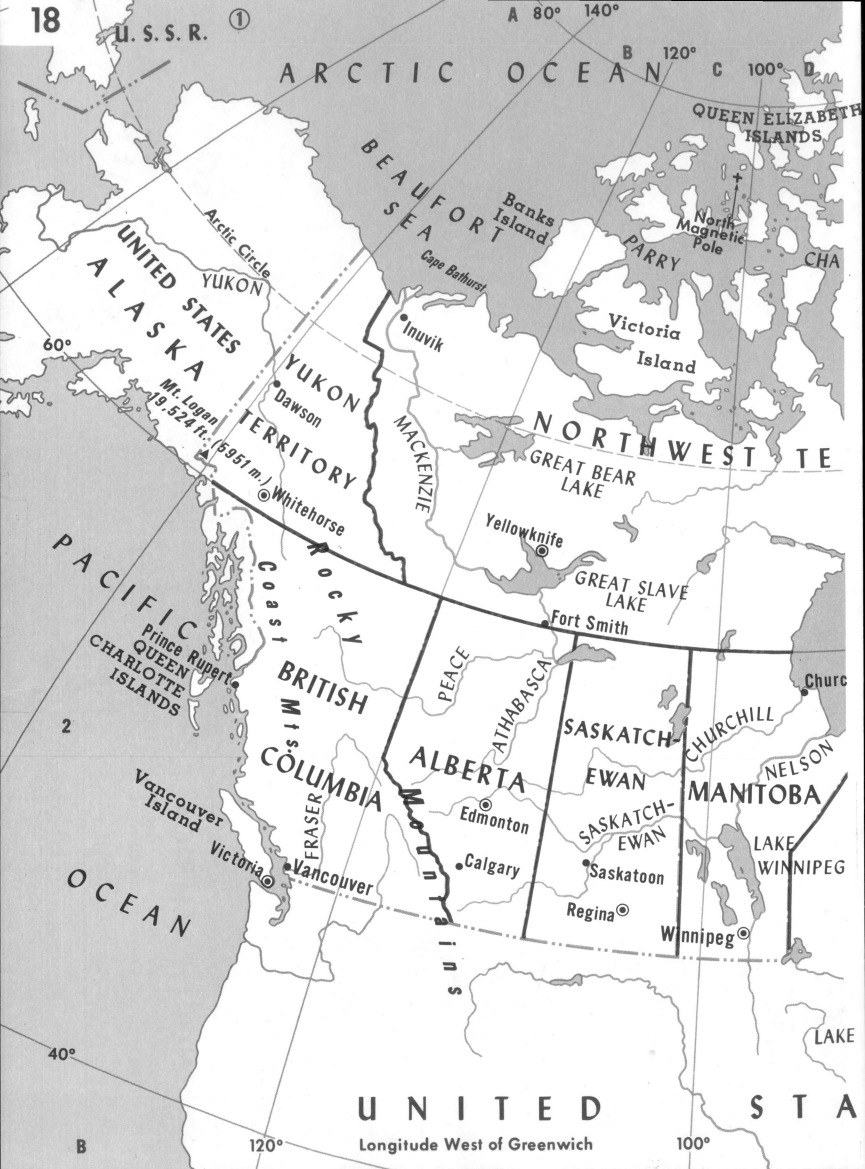

U.S.S.R. ①

ARCTIC OCEAN

QUEEN ELIZABETH ISLANDS

BEAUFORT SEA

Banks Island

PARRY

CHA

North Magnetic Pole

Cape Bathurst

Victoria Island

Arctic Circle

YUKON

• Inuvik

UNITED STATES

ALASKA

60°

Mt. Logan
19,524 ft. (5951 m.)

YUKON

• Dawson

TERRITORY

MACKENZIE

NORTHWEST TE

GREAT BEAR LAKE

⊚ Whitehorse

• Yellowknife

GREAT SLAVE LAKE

PACIFIC

Rocky

Coast

Prince Rupert

QUEEN CHARLOTTE ISLANDS

2

BRITISH

Mts.

COLUMBIA

Fort Smith

PEACE

ATHABASCA

SASKATCH-

Churc

CHURCHILL

NELSON

EWAN

MANITOBA

Vancouver Island

FRASER

Victoria ⊚

• Vancouver

Mountains

ALBERTA

• Edmonton ⊚

• Calgary

SASKATCH-
EWAN

• Saskatoon

LAKE WINNIPEG

OCEAN

Regina ⊚

Winnipeg ⊚

40°

UNITED

STA

LAKE

B

120°

Longitude West of Greenwich

100°

A 80° 140°

B 120°

C 100° D

80° F 80°
60°
E
80° 60°

Ellesmere Island

Devon
Island

NNEL

BAFFIN

BAY

G R E E N L A N D

(KALAALLIT NUNAAT)

(Denmark)

60°

CANADA

0   200   400   600 MI.

0   200   400   600 KM.

Baffin

Island

DAVIS STRAIT

RRITORIES

HUDSON STRAIT

LABRADOR

SEA

ATLANTIC

Ungava

HUDSON

Peninsula

NEWFOUNDLAND

Labrador

2

hill

BAY

Schefferville

JAMES
BAY

QUÉBEC

Newfoundland

Gander

Saint John's

Cape Race

GULF OF

St. Pierre & Miquelon
(Fr.)

ONTARIO

NEW
BRUNS-
WICK

ST. LAWRENCE

PRINCE EDWARD
ISLAND

Charlottetown

Thunder
Bay

Timmins

Québec

LAWRENCE

Fredericton

Halifax

Sudbury

MONTRÉAL

ST.

NOVA SCOTIA

OCEAN

40°

SUPERIOR

Ottawa

TORONTO

ST.

LAKE
ONTARIO

LAKE
MICHIGAN

LAKE
HURON

Hamilton

Windsor   LAKE ERIE

80°

E   F
D

A   120°   B   110°   C   100°

CANADA

PACIFIC

WASHINGTON
Seattle
Olympia
COLUMBIA
Portland
Salem
OREGON

Great
Falls
MONTANA
Helena

MISSOURI

**NORTH
DAKOTA**
Bismarck

**SOUTH
DAKOTA**
Pierre

R
O
C
K
Y

IDAHO
Boise
SNAKE

WYOMING

Black
Hills

1

40°

Sierra Nevada
Coast Ranges

G r e a t

NEVADA
Carson
City

B a s i n

GREAT
SALT
LAKE

Salt Lake
City

UTAH

M
o
u
n
t
a
i
n
s

Cheyenne

NEBRASKA

PLATTE

Om

Lincoln

Sacramento
San
Francisco

Mt. Whitney
14,494 ft.▲ (4418 m.)

Las
Vegas

Pikes Peak
14,110 ft.▲ (4301 m.)

Denver

COLORADO   ARKANSAS

KANSAS

Top

Wichita

2

CALIFORNIA

Los Angeles

COLORADO

ARIZONA

San
Diego

Phoenix
GILA

Tucson.

Albuquerque

Sante Fe

NEW   MEXICO

RED

Oklahoma
City
OKLAH

O C E A N

© C.S. Hammond & Co., Maplewood, N.J.

El Paso

M   E   X   I   C   O

RIO   GRANDE

Ft. Worth

TEXAS

Austin

Hou
San Antonio

30°

180° ARCTIC 160°   Pt. Barrow 140° OCEAN 70°

U.S.S.R.

3

BERING

SEA

ALEUTIAN
IS.

ALASKA
YUKON   Fairbanks
Mt. McKinley
20,320 ft.▲ (6194 m.)
Anchorage

Arctic Circle

CANADA

60°

60°

Juneau

ALASKA

0   200   400   600 MI.

0   200 400 600 KM.

160°

H
A
W
A
I

Kauai

Oahu
Honolulu

Molokai
Lanai

PACIFIC ▼ OCEAN

20°

HAWAII

160°   0   50   100 150 KM.

Maui

20°

Mauna Loa
▲ 13,677 ft.
(4169 m.)

Hawaii

156°

0   50   100   150 MI.

D 90° E 80° F 70° G

N A D A

ST. LAWRENCE

MINNESOTA

L. SUPERIOR

M I C H I G A N

S.

MAINE

⊙ Augusta

Montpelier ⊙

VT. N.H. ⊙ Concord

NEW YORK

L. ONTARIO

Albany ⊙

MASS. ⊙ Boston

Providence R.I. ⊙

Buffalo CONN.

Hartford ⊙

St. Paul

WISCONSIN

Minneapolis

Milwaukee

MISSISSIPPI

L. HURON

Detroit

Lansing ⊙

L. MICHIGAN

L. ERIE

Cleveland

PENNSYLVANIA

Harrisburg ⊙

Pittsburgh ⊙

N.J. NEW YORK

Trenton ⊙

40°

Philadelphia

IOWA

Madison ⊙

Des Moines ⊙

Chicago

ILLINOIS

Springfield ⊙

MISSOURI

Columbus ⊙

OHIO

Indianapolis ⊙

Cincinnati ⊙

INDIANA

Louisville

OHIO

WEST

VIRGINIA

Baltimore

MD.

Dover ⊙ DEL.

Washington Annapolis ⊙

Charleston ⊙

VIRGINIA

aha

eka ⊙

Kansas City

Jefferson City ⊙

Topeka

MISSOURI

St. Louis

Frankfort ⊙

KENTUCKY

Nashville ⊙

Richmond ⊙

Norfolk

NORTH

Raleigh ⊙

Cape Hatteras

Ozark

Tulsa

Mts.

ARKANSAS

TENNESSEE

CAROLINA

Charlotte ⊙

OMA

Little Rock ⊙

Memphis

Birmingham ⊙

Atlanta ⊙

SOUTH

Columbia ⊙

CAROLINA

Dallas

LOUISIANA

Jackson ⊙

MISSISSIPPI

ALABAMA

Montgomery ⊙

GEORGIA

Savannah

BRAZOS

ston

Baton Rouge ⊙

New Orleans

Tallahassee ⊙

Jacksonville

FLORIDA

C. Canaveral

A T L A N T I C O C E A N

2

30°

Tampa

GULF OF MEXICO

Miami

B A H A M A S

3

STRAITS OF FLORIDA

Tropic of Cancer

UNITED STATES

0   100   200   300   400 MI.

0   100   200   300   400 KM.

C U B A

D 90° Longitude West of Greenwich 80° F

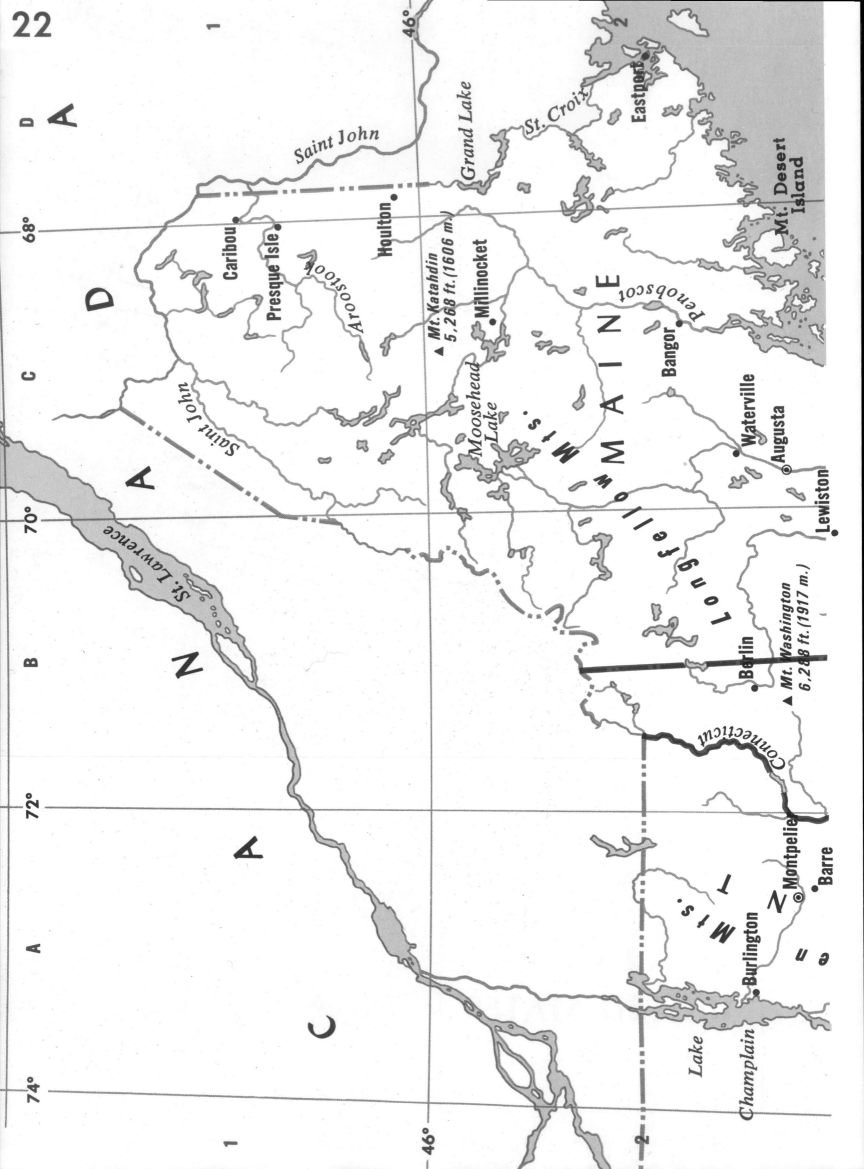

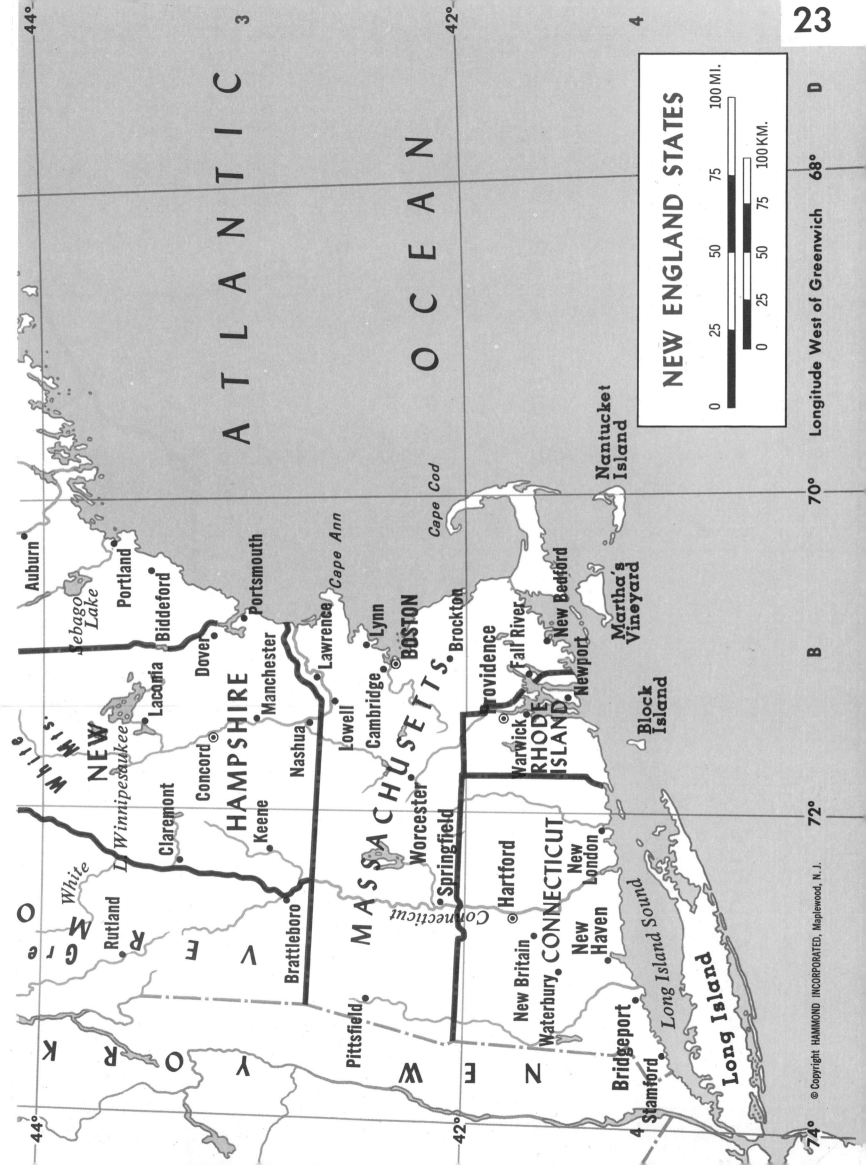

NEW ENGLAND STATES

100 MI.
75
50
25
0

100 KM.
75
50
25
0

Longitude West of Greenwich

68°
70°
72°
74°

44°
42°

D
B
W
E
N

© Copyright HAMMOND INCORPORATED, Maplewood, N. J.

ATLANTIC

OCEAN

Auburn
Portland
Sebago Lake
Biddeford
Portsmouth
Cape Ann
Lawrence
Lynn
BOSTON
Cambridge
Cape Cod
Brockton
Nantucket Island
Martha's Vineyard
New Bedford
Newport
Fall River
Providence
Block Island
Warwick
RHODE ISLAND
Laconia
Dover
NEW
HAMPSHIRE
Manchester
Nashua
Lowell
MASSACHUSETTS
Worcester
Springfield
Concord
Keene
Claremont
Winnipesaukee
White Mts.
Rutland
White
Gre
Mre
N
VE
Brattleboro
Pittsfield
Hartford
Connecticut
New Britain
Waterbury
CONNECTICUT
New London
New Haven
Bridgeport
Stamford
Long Island Sound
Long Island
YORK
NEW

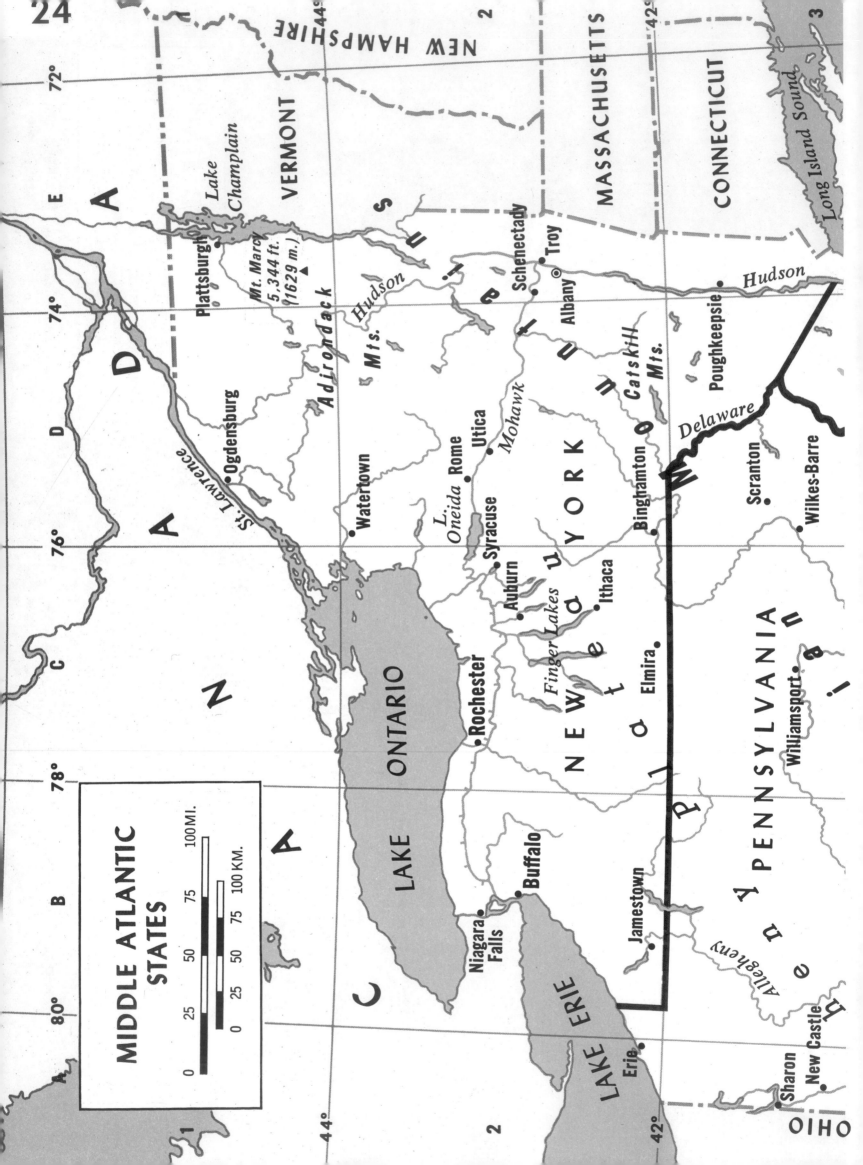

MIDDLE ATLANTIC STATES

0 25 50 75 100 MI.

0 25 50 75 100 KM.

NEW HAMPSHIRE

VERMONT

Lake Champlain

Plattsburgh

Mt. Marcy 5,344 ft. (1629 m.) ▲

Adirondack Mts.

Hudson

Ogdensburg

St. Lawrence

C A N A D A

Watertown

L. Oneida

Rome

Utica

Mohawk

Schenectady

Troy

Albany ◉

MASSACHUSETTS

CONNECTICUT

Long Island Sound

Hudson

Catskill Mts.

Poughkeepsie

Delaware

Scranton

Wilkes-Barre

Binghamton

N E W   Y O R K

Syracuse

Auburn

Ithaca

Finger Lakes

Elmira

Williamsport

P l a t e a u

A l l e g h e n y

PENNSYLVANIA

Allegheny

Rochester

LAKE   ONTARIO

Buffalo

Niagara Falls

LAKE   ERIE

Jamestown

Erie

Sharon

New Castle

OHIO

72°

74°

76°

78°

80°

44°

42°

48°

44°

42°

E

D

C

B

A

1

2

3

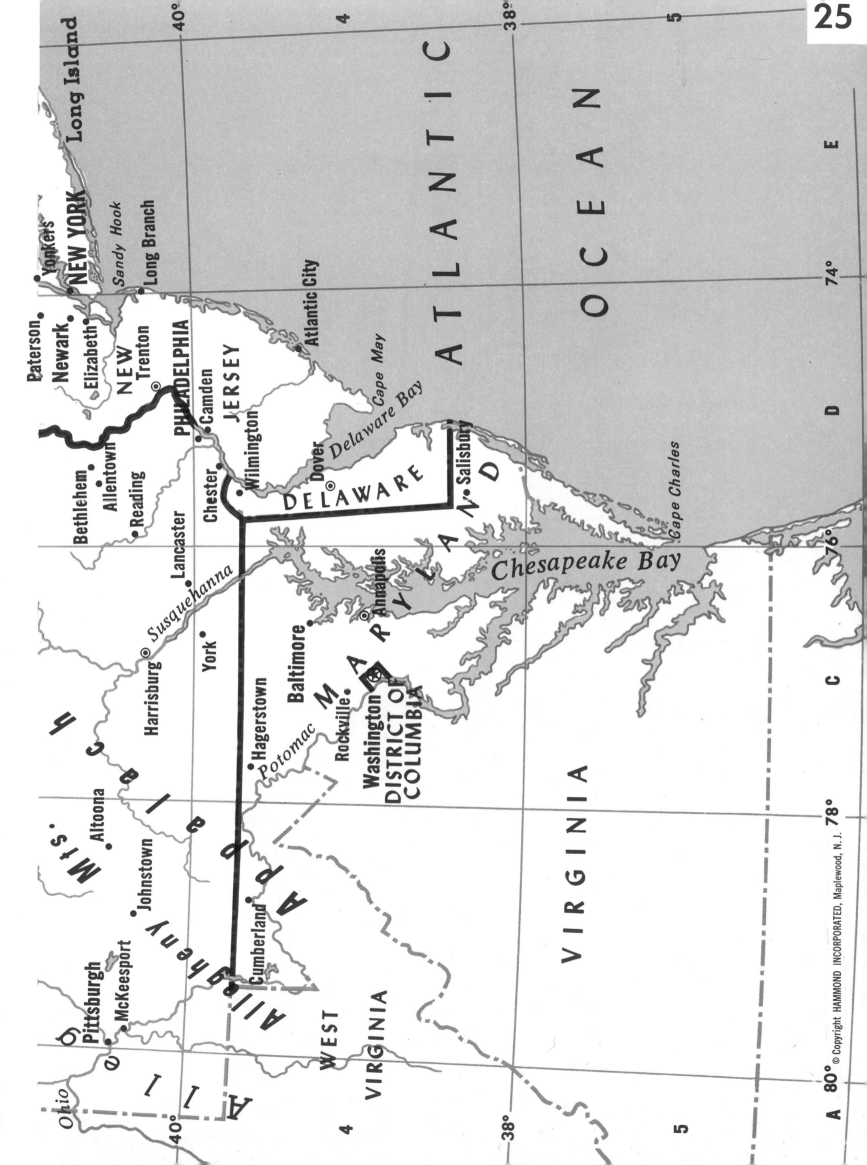

ATLANTIC OCEAN

Long Island

NEW YORK

Yonkers

Paterson
Newark
Elizabeth
NEW JERSEY
Trenton

Sandy Hook
Long Branch

Atlantic City

PHILADELPHIA
Camden

Bethlehem
Allentown
Reading

Wilmington
Chester

Lancaster

Susquehanna

Harrisburg

York

Hagerstown

Altoona

Johnstown

Pittsburgh
McKeesport

Ohio

Cumberland

APPALACHIAN

Allegheny Mts.

Potomac

Rockville

Baltimore

Washington
DISTRICT OF
COLUMBIA

Annapolis

MARYLAND

DELAWARE

Dover

Cape May

Delaware Bay

Salisbury

Chesapeake Bay

Cape Charles

WEST
VIRGINIA

VIRGINIA

VIRGINIA

40°
4
38°
5
E
74°
D
76°
C
78°
80°
38°
4
5
40°
A

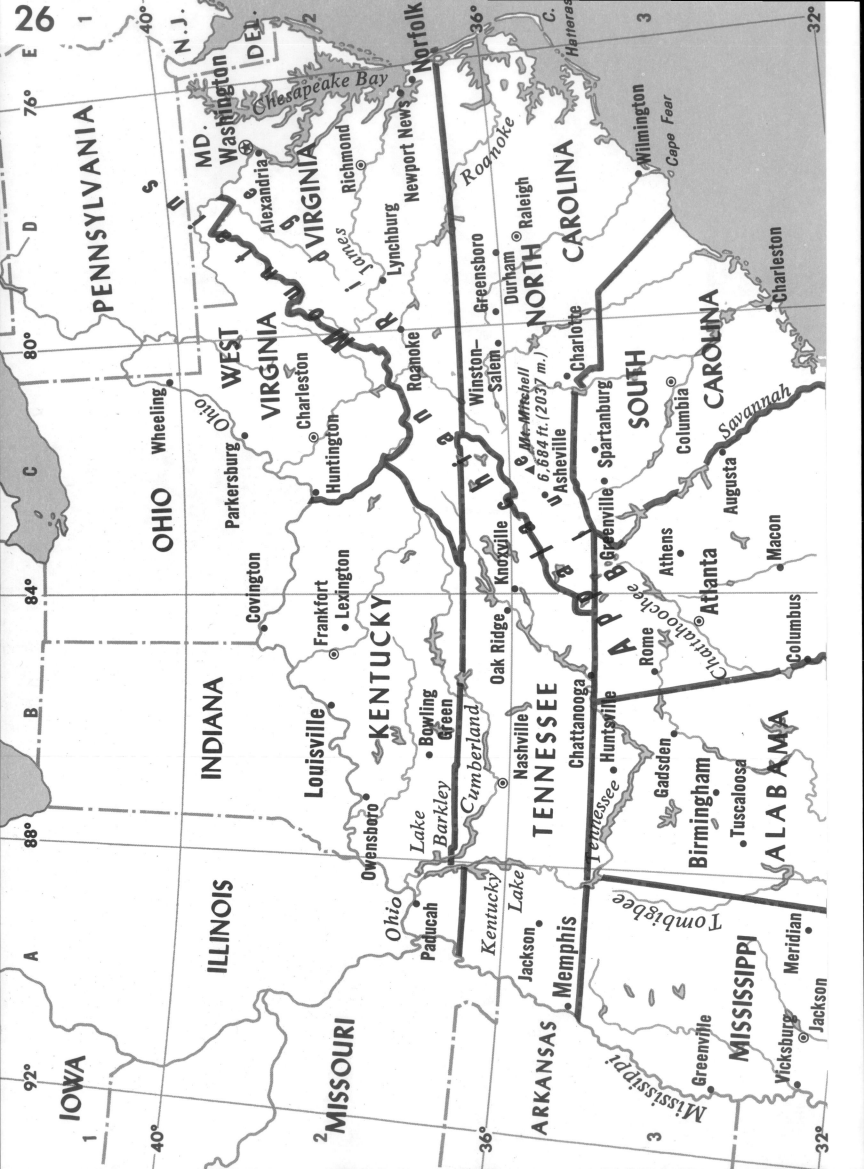

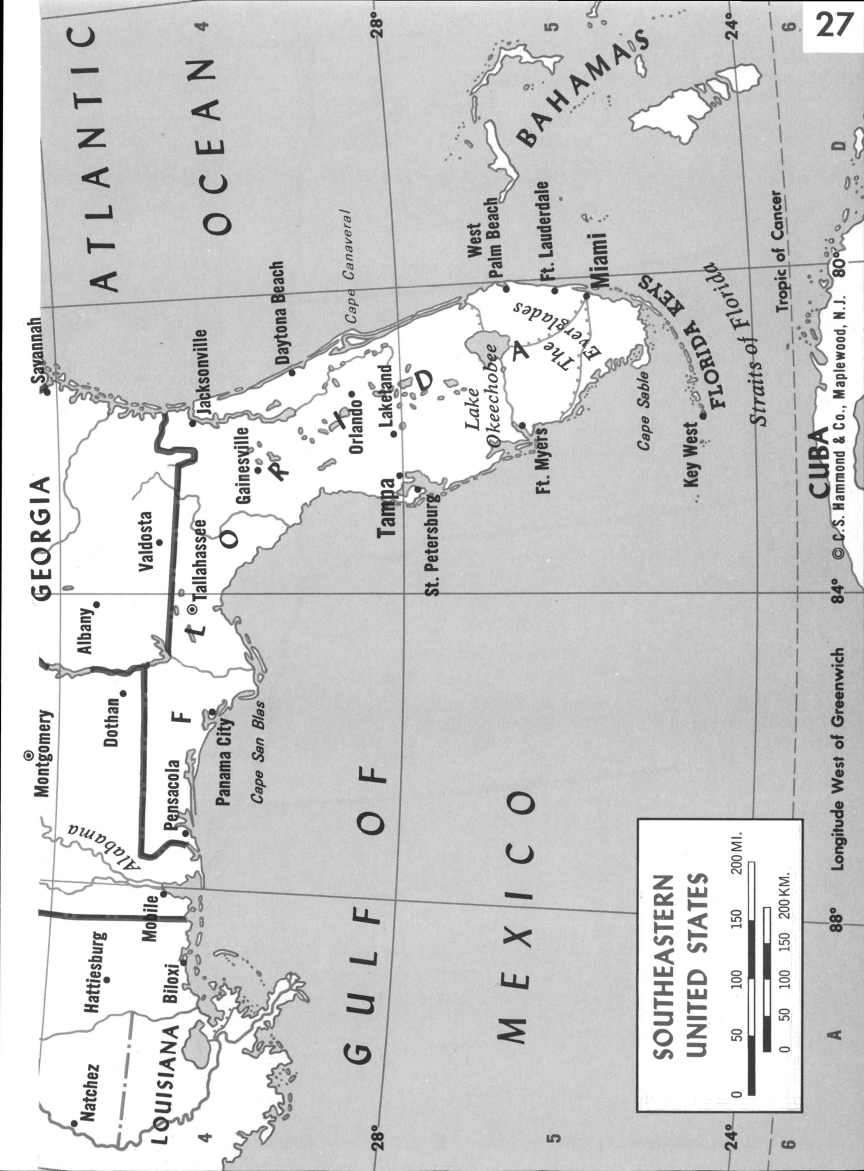

ATLANTIC

OCEAN

BAHAMAS

GEORGIA

Savannah

Jacksonville

Cape Canaveral

Daytona Beach

West Palm Beach

Ft. Lauderdale

Miami

Gainesville

Orlando

Lakeland

Lake Okeechobee

The Everglades

Valdosta

Tallahassee

FLORIDA

Tampa

St. Petersburg

Ft. Myers

Cape Sable

Key West

FLORIDA KEYS

Straits of Florida

Tropic of Cancer

CUBA

Albany

Montgomery

Dothan

Panama City

Cape San Blas

GULF OF

MEXICO

Pensacola

Alabama

Natchez

Hattiesburg

Mobile

Biloxi

LOUISIANA

28°

24°

28°

24°

80°

84°

88°

Longitude West of Greenwich

© C.S. Hammond & Co., Maplewood, N.J.

SOUTHEASTERN
UNITED STATES

0   50   100   150   200 MI.

0   50 100 150 200 KM.

CANADA

92° C D 88° E 84° F 80° 48°

① NORTH CENTRAL
UNITED STATES

0   50   100   150   200 MI.

0   50   100   150   200 KM.

2

Isle Royale

LAKE SUPERIOR

Superior

Croix

Marquette

Sault Ste. Marie

Georgian
Bay

LAKE HURON

M
I
C
H
I
G
A
N

C
A
N
A
D
A

WISCONSIN

Eau Claire

Appleton

Green
Bay

Traverse City

44°

Oshkosh

LAKE MICHIGAN

La Crosse

Wisconsin

Saginaw

Flint

Milwaukee

Grand Rapids

Pontiac

Madison ◉

Racine

Lansing ◉

LAKE ERIE

Dubuque

Ann
Arbor

DETROIT

CANADA

Rockford

Kalamazoo

pids

CHICAGO

Cleveland

PA.

3

Davenport

Joliet

Gary

South Bend

Toledo

Akron

Rock
Island

Fort Wayne

Lima

Canton

Moines

Peoria

INDIANA

OHIO

40°

ILLINOIS

Muncie

Springfield

Columbus ◉

Quincy

Decatur

Indianapolis ◉

Dayton

Springfield ◉

WEST
VIRGINIA

Columbia

Alton

Wabash

Terre
Haute

Cincinnati

Ohio

4

St. Louis

Mississippi

Evansville

New Albany

O U R I

Ohio

KENTUCKY

VIRGINIA

Cape Girardeau

36°

N SAS

TENN.

D   88°   Longitude West of Greenwich   84°   F

96°   D   92°   E   88°   F

1

MISSOURI

Mississippi

ILL.

36°

Ozark

Blytheville

TENNESSEE

Mts.

Tulsa

OMA Muskogee

Arkansas

⊚ Oklahoma
City

n

Fort
Smith

ARKANSAS

⊚ Little Rock

Canadian

Hot Sprs.
Nat'l Park

Pine
Bluff

2

*Lake
Texoma*

Mississippi

ALABAMA

Red

Texarkana

El Dorado

Dallas

Sabine

Shreveport

Monroe

MISSISSIPPI

32°

ort
orth

Trinity

Waco

Brazos

*Sam Rayburn
Res.*

*Toledo
Bend
Res.*

Red

ustin

Alexandria

LOUISIANA

onio

Colorado

Lake Charles

⊚ Baton Rouge

Beaumont

Lafayette

HOUSTON

New
Orleans

3

Galveston

*Mississippi
Delta*

28°

GULF   OF   MEXICO

Padre

Island

le

SOUTH CENTRAL
UNITED STATES

0   50   100   150   200 MI.

4

0   50   100   150   200 KM.

96°   D   92°

© Copyright HAMMOND INCORPORATED, Maplewood, N.J.

128° **A** 124° **B** 120° **C** 116°

1

Vancouver Island

C **A** **N**

Strait of Juan de Fuca

48°

Cape Flattery

Bellingham

PACIFIC

Olympic Mts.

Everett

GRAND COULEE

Kali

DAM

Puget

Spokane

Seattle

Sd.

WASHINGTON

Tacoma

Olympia ⊙

2

Mt. Rainier ▲

14,410 ft.

(4392 m.)

Yakima

Snake

Columbia

Walla

Lewiston

Walla

Bitte

Vancouver

Columbia

Portland ▲ Mt. Hood

Pendleton

11,239 ft.

(3426 m.)

Corvallis

Salem ⊙

44°

Salmon

Willamette

Eugene

OCEAN

Bend

IDA

OREGON

Cape

Blanco

3

Boise

⊙

Medford

Klamath Falls

Snake

Owyhee

Twin Falls

Coast Range

Cascade Range

Columbia Plateau

40°

CALIFORNIA

NEVADA

4

B

120° Longitude West of Greenwich 116°

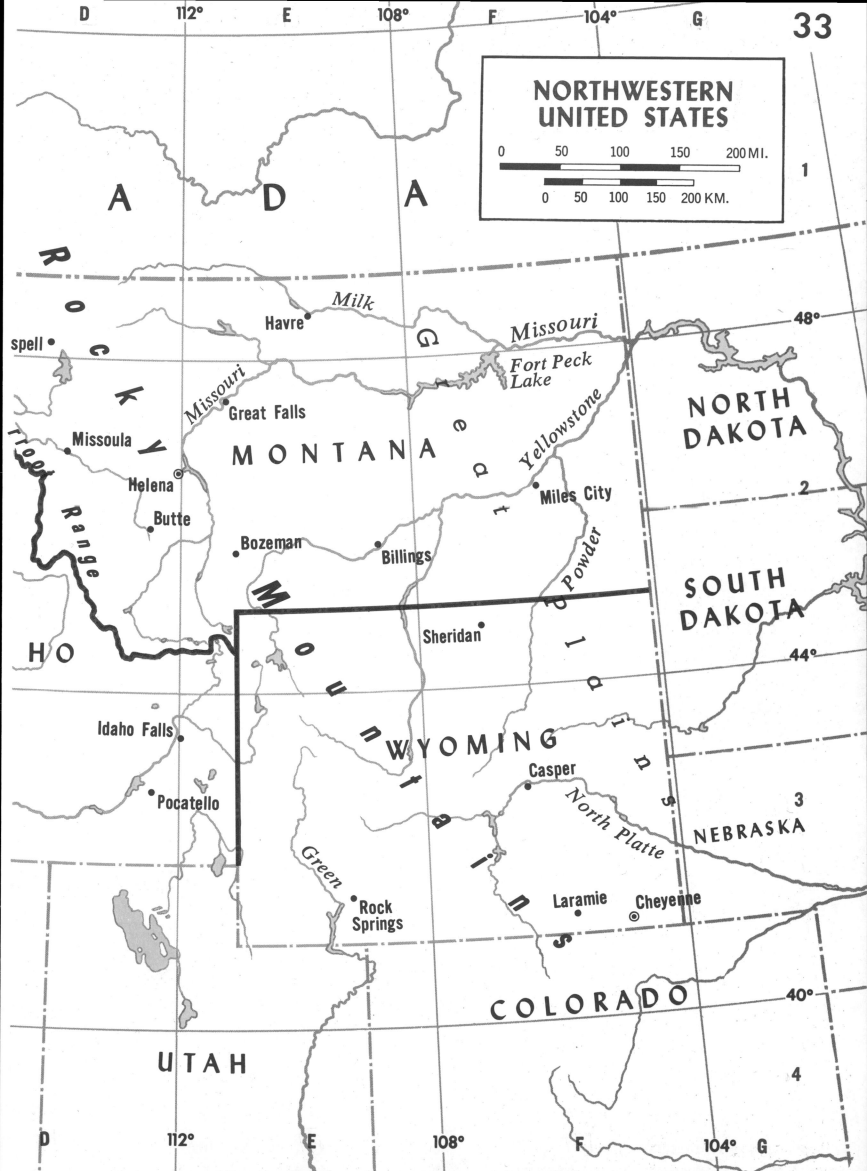

NORTHWESTERN
UNITED STATES

0   50   100   150   200 MI.

0   50   100   150   200 KM.

D   112°   E   108°   F   104°   G

C A   N   A   D   A

R
o
c
k
y   Milk   Havre

Missouri

spell

Great Falls

Missouri   Fort Peck
Lake

Missouri

G
r
e
a
t

Yellowstone

NORTH
DAKOTA

Missoula

Helena   M O N T A N A

Butte   Miles City

Bozeman

Billings

P
l
a
i
n
s   SOUTH
DAKOTA

Idaho Falls   M
o
u
n
t
a
i
n
s   Sheridan   Powder

HO   48°

44°

Pocatello   W Y O M I N G

Green

Rock
Springs   Casper

North Platte   Laramie   Cheyenne   NEBRASKA

U T A H   C O L O R A D O   40°

D   112°   E   108°   F   104°   G

1

2

3

4

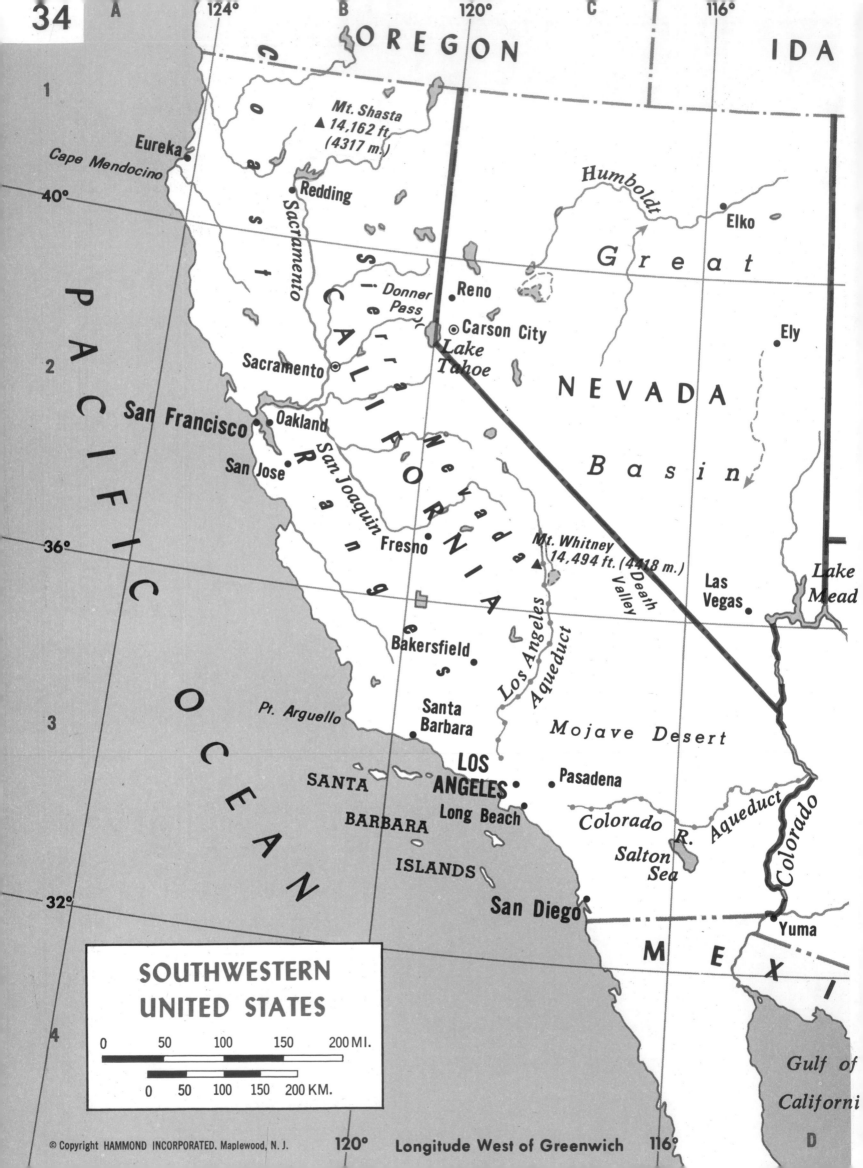

OREGON

IDA

124°

120°

116°

A

B

C

1

Mt. Shasta
▲ 14,162 ft
(4317 m.)

Humboldt

Eureka

Cape Mendocino

40°

Redding

Elko

Great

Sacramento

Donner
Pass

Reno

Ely

◎ Carson City

Lake
Tahoe

2

Sacramento ◎

NEVADA

San Francisco

Oakland

Basin

San Jose

San Joaquin

36°

Fresno

Mt. Whitney
14,494 ft. (4418 m.)
▲

Death
Valley

Las
Vegas

Lake
Mead

Bakersfield

Los Angeles Aqueduct

Pt. Arguello

3

Santa
Barbara

Mojave Desert

SANTA

LOS
ANGELES

Pasadena

BARBARA

Long Beach

Colorado R. Aqueduct

Colorado

ISLANDS

Salton
Sea

32°

San Diego

Yuma

MEXI

SOUTHWESTERN
UNITED STATES

0   50   100   150   200 MI.

0   50   100   150   200 KM.

Gulf of

California

© Copyright HAMMOND INCORPORATED, Maplewood, N.J.

120°   Longitude West of Greenwich   116°

D

PACIFIC OCEAN

CALIFORNIA

Sierra Nevada

Coast

D | 112° | E | 108° | F | 104° | G

HO

WYOMING

NEBRASKA

1

Great Salt Lake

• Logan

• Ogden

⊙ Salt Lake City

• Provo

UTAH

Green

Colorado

Ft. Collins •

Greeley •

40°

Boulder •

⊙ Denver

KANSAS

Colorado

Grand Junction •

Pikes Peak ▲ Colorado Springs
14,110 ft. (4301 m.)

COLORADO

Arkansas

2

Pueblo •

Lake Powell

San Juan

Durango •

Farmington •

36°

Santa Fe ⊙

R
o
c
k
y

M
o
u
n
t
a
i
n
s

G
r
e
a
t

P
l
a
i
n
s

OKLA.

Plateau

• Flagstaff

Prescott •

Albuquerque •

ARIZONA

NEW MEXICO

Clovis •

3

Phoenix ⊙

Salt

Roswell •

Pecos

• Mesa

Gila

Gila

Hobbs •

Carlsbad •

32°

• Tucson

Las Cruces •

Rio

Grande

TEXAS

CO

4

112° | E | 108° | F | 104°

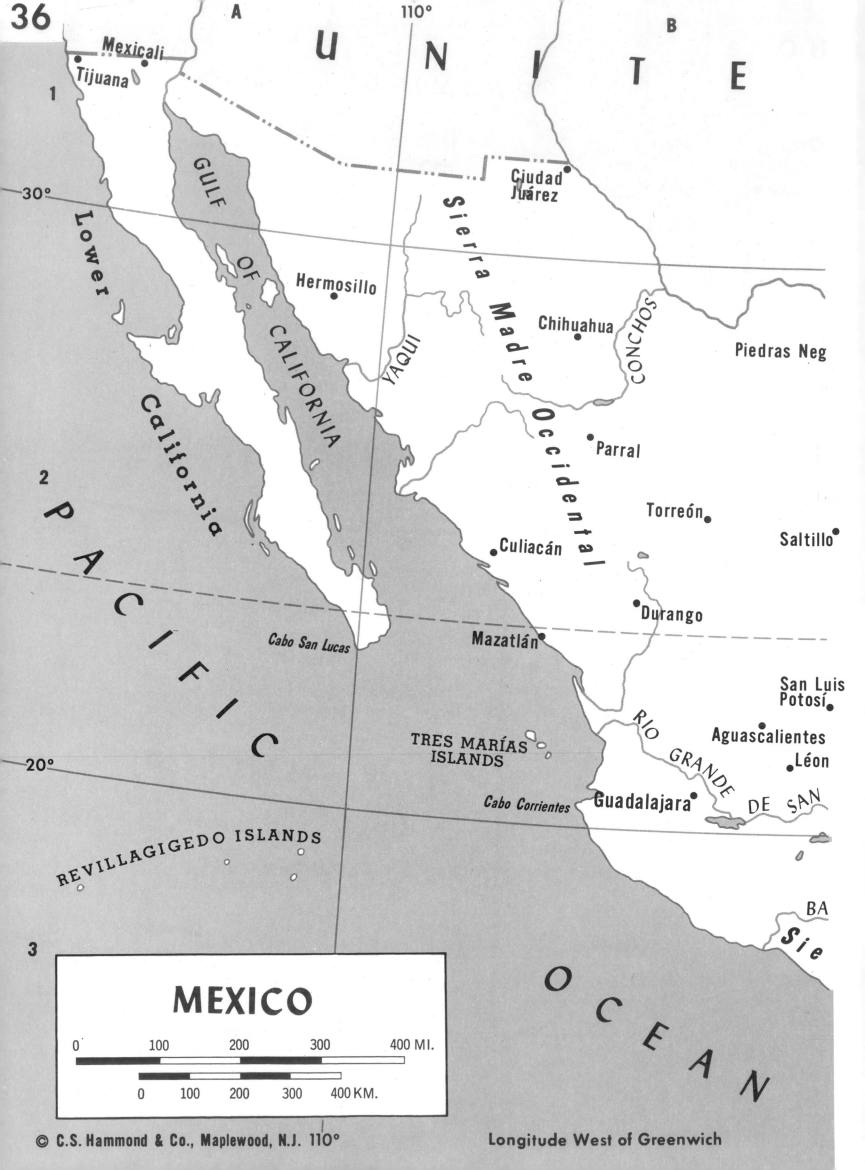

A 110° B

U N I T E

U N I T E

Mexicali
Tijuana

1

30°

GULF

Lower

OF

Ciudad
Juárez

Hermosillo

CALIFORNIA

Sierra Madre Occidental

Chihuahua

CONCHOS

Piedras Neg

California

YAQUI

Parral

2

Torreón

Saltillo

Culiacán

P A C I F I C

Durango

Cabo San Lucas

Mazatlán

San Luis
Potosí

TRES MARÍAS
ISLANDS

RIO

Aguascalientes
Léon

GRANDE

20°

Cabo Corrientes

Guadalajara

DE SAN

REVILLAGIGEDO ISLANDS

BA

Sie

3

O C E A N

MEXICO

| 0 | 100 | 200 | 300 | 400 MI. |

| 0 | 100 | 200 | 300 | 400 KM. |

Longitude West of Greenwich

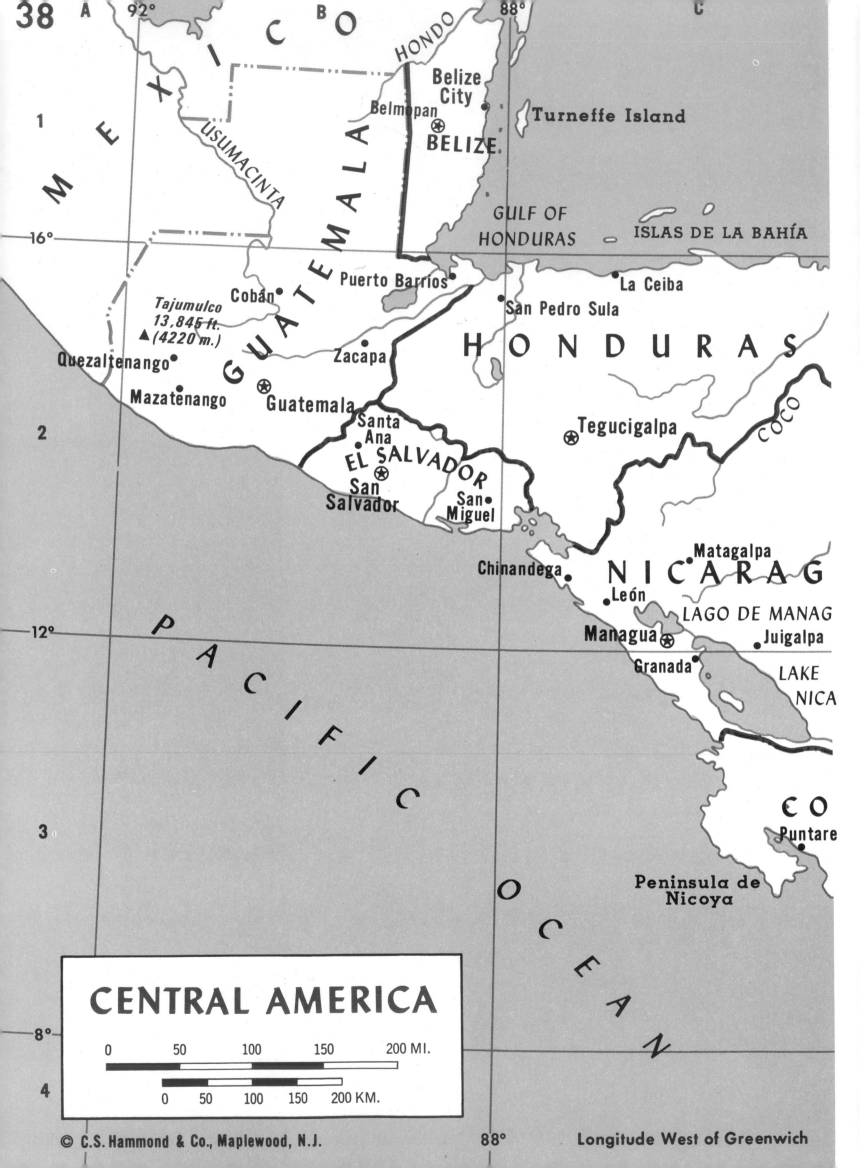

CENTRAL AMERICA

A 92° B 88° C

1

MEXICO

CABO HONDO

Belize City
Belmopan
⊛ BELIZE

Turneffe Island

GUATEMALA

USUMACINTA

16°

GULF OF HONDURAS

ISLAS DE LA BAHÍA

Cobán
Puerto Barrios

La Ceiba
San Pedro Sula

HONDURAS

Tajumulco
13,845 ft.
▲ (4220 m.)

Zacapa

Quezaltenango

Mazatenango
⊛ Guatemala

COCO

Santa
Ana

⊛ Tegucigalpa

2

EL SALVADOR
⊛
San
Salvador

San
Miguel

Matagalpa

Chinandega

NICARAG

León

LAGO DE MANAG

Juigalpa

PACIFIC

12°
Managua ⊛

Granada

LAKE
NICA

CO

3

Puntare

Peninsula de
Nicoya

OCEAN

CENTRAL AMERICA

0   50   100   150   200 MI.

0   50   100   150   200 KM.

8°

4

88°   Longitude West of Greenwich

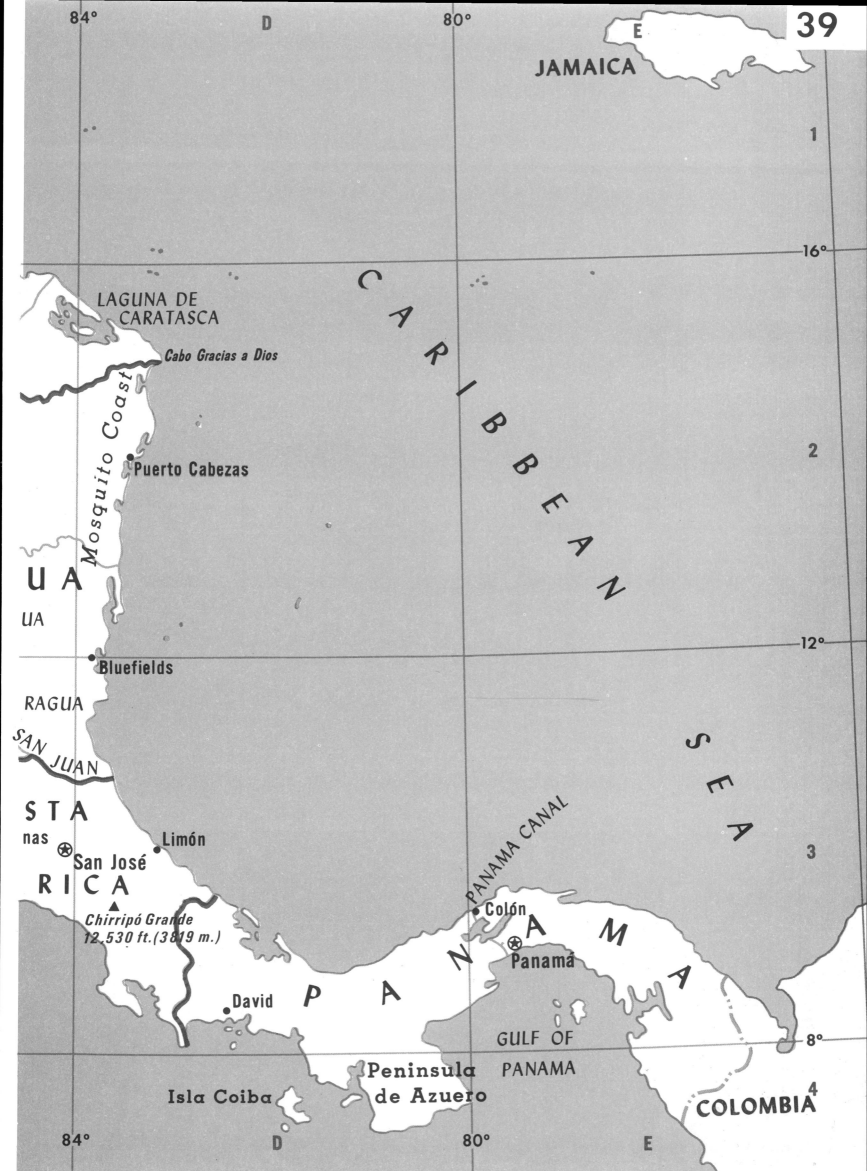

84°   D   80°   E

JAMAICA

1

16°

C
A
R
I
B
B
E
A
N

LAGUNA DE
CARATASCA

Cabo Gracias a Dios

Mosquito Coast

Puerto Cabezas

2

U A

UA

12°

Bluefields

RAGUA

SAN JUAN

S E A

3

STA

nas ⊛

Limón

San José

PANAMA CANAL

RICA

Colón

▲
Chirripó Grande
12.530 ft.(3819 m.)

P A N ⊛ A M A

Panamá

David

P A N A M A

GULF OF

8°

Peninsula
de Azuero

PANAMA

Isla Coiba

COLOMBIA

4

84°   D   80°   E

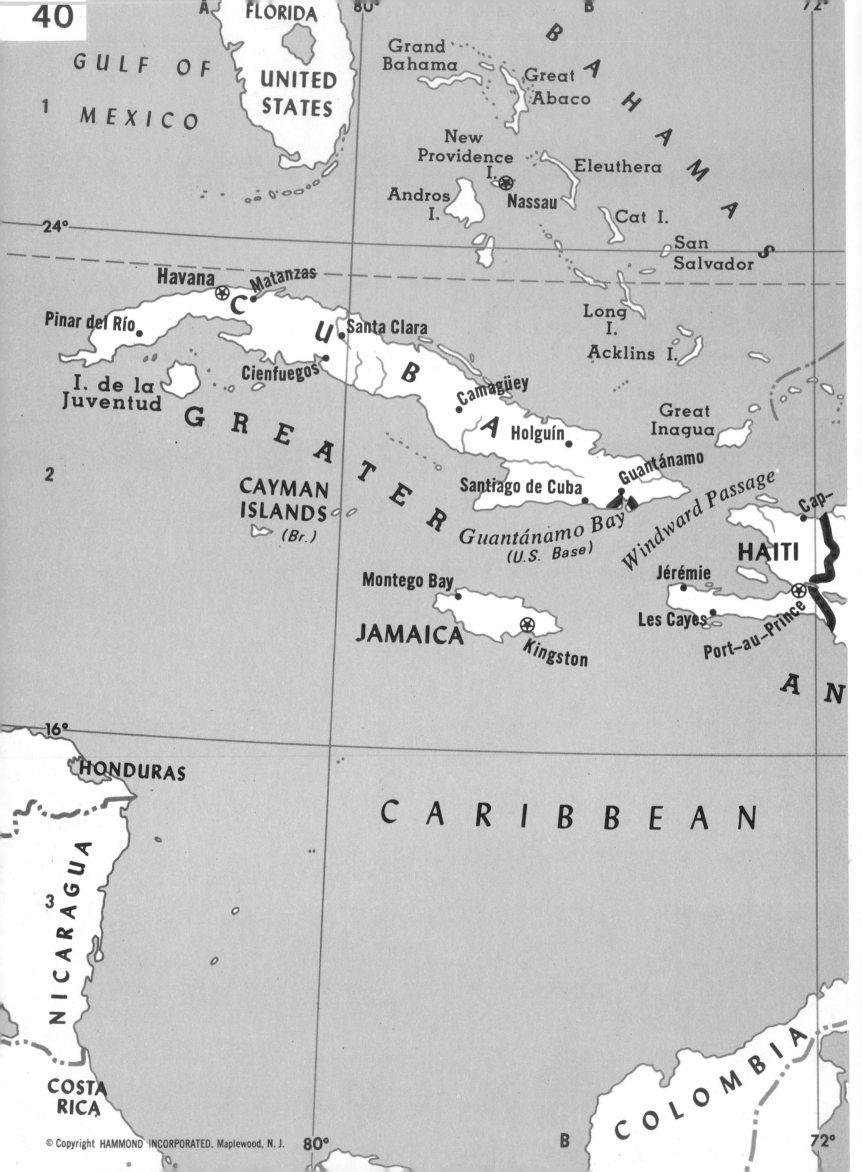

GULF OF
MEXICO

1

FLORIDA

UNITED
STATES

Grand
Bahama

Great
Abaco

B A H A M A S

New
Providence
I.

Eleuthera

Andros
I.

Nassau

Cat I.

San
Salvador

24°

Havana   Matanzas

Long
I.

Pinar del Río

C

Santa Clara

U

Acklins I.

Cienfuegos

B

I. de la
Juventud

Camagüey

A

G R E A T E R

Holguín

Great
Inagua

2

CAYMAN
ISLANDS

Santiago de Cuba

Guantánamo

(Br.)

Guantánamo Bay
(U.S. Base)

Windward Passage

Cap–

HAITI

Jérémie

Montego Bay

Les Cayes

JAMAICA

Kingston

Port–au–Prince

A N

16°

HONDURAS

C A R I B B E A N

N I C A R A G U A

3

C O L O M B I A

COSTA
RICA

80°   72°

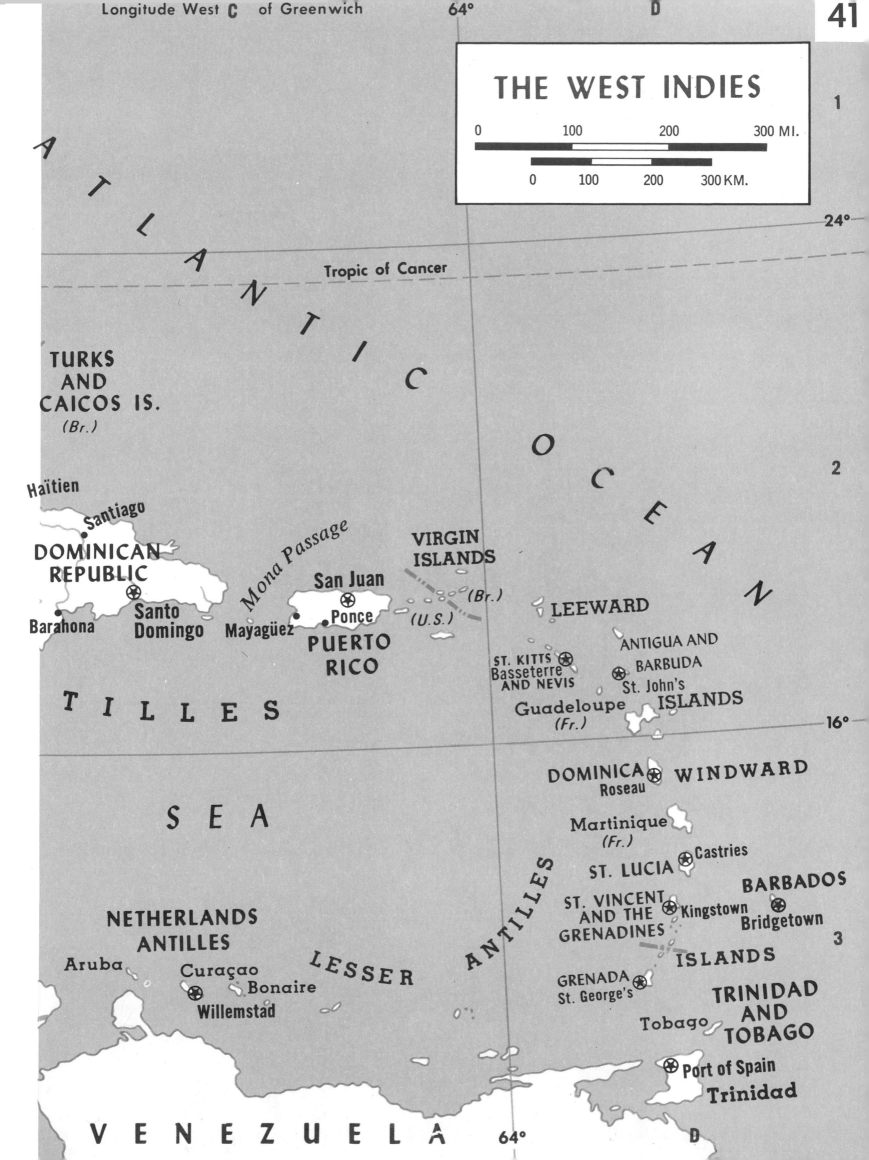

Longitude West **C** of Greenwich 64° **D** **41**

┌─────────────────────────────────┐
│ THE WEST INDIES │
│ 0   100   200   300 MI. │
│ 0   100   200   300 KM. │
└─────────────────────────────────┘

1

24°

Tropic of Cancer

A
T
L
A
N
T
I
C

O
C
E
A
N

2

TURKS
AND
CAICOS IS.
(Br.)

Haïtien
Santiago
DOMINICAN
REPUBLIC
Barahona
Santo
Domingo
Mayagüez

Mona Passage

San Juan
Ponce
PUERTO
RICO

VIRGIN
ISLANDS
(Br.)
(U.S.)

LEEWARD

ANTIGUA AND
BARBUDA
St. John's

ST. KITTS
Basseterre
AND NEVIS

Guadeloupe
(Fr.)

ISLANDS

16°

T I L L E S

S E A

DOMINICA   WINDWARD
Roseau

Martinique
(Fr.)

ST. LUCIA   Castries

A
N
T
I
L
L
E
S

NETHERLANDS
ANTILLES

Aruba
Curaçao
Bonaire
Willemstad

LESSER   ANTILLES

ST. VINCENT
AND THE
GRENADINES   Kingstown

BARBADOS

Bridgetown

ISLANDS

3

GRENADA
St. George's

TRINIDAD
AND
TOBAGO

Tobago

Port of Spain
Trinidad

V E N E Z U E L A   64°   **D**

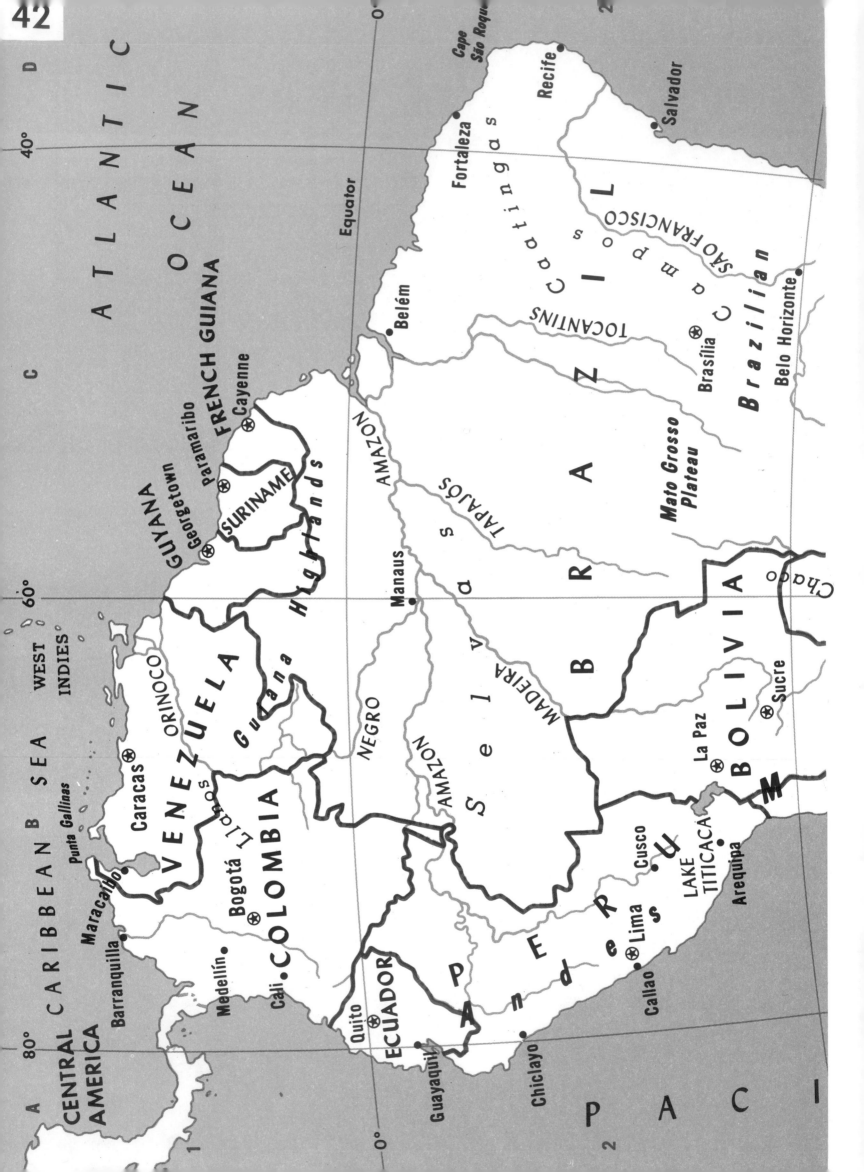

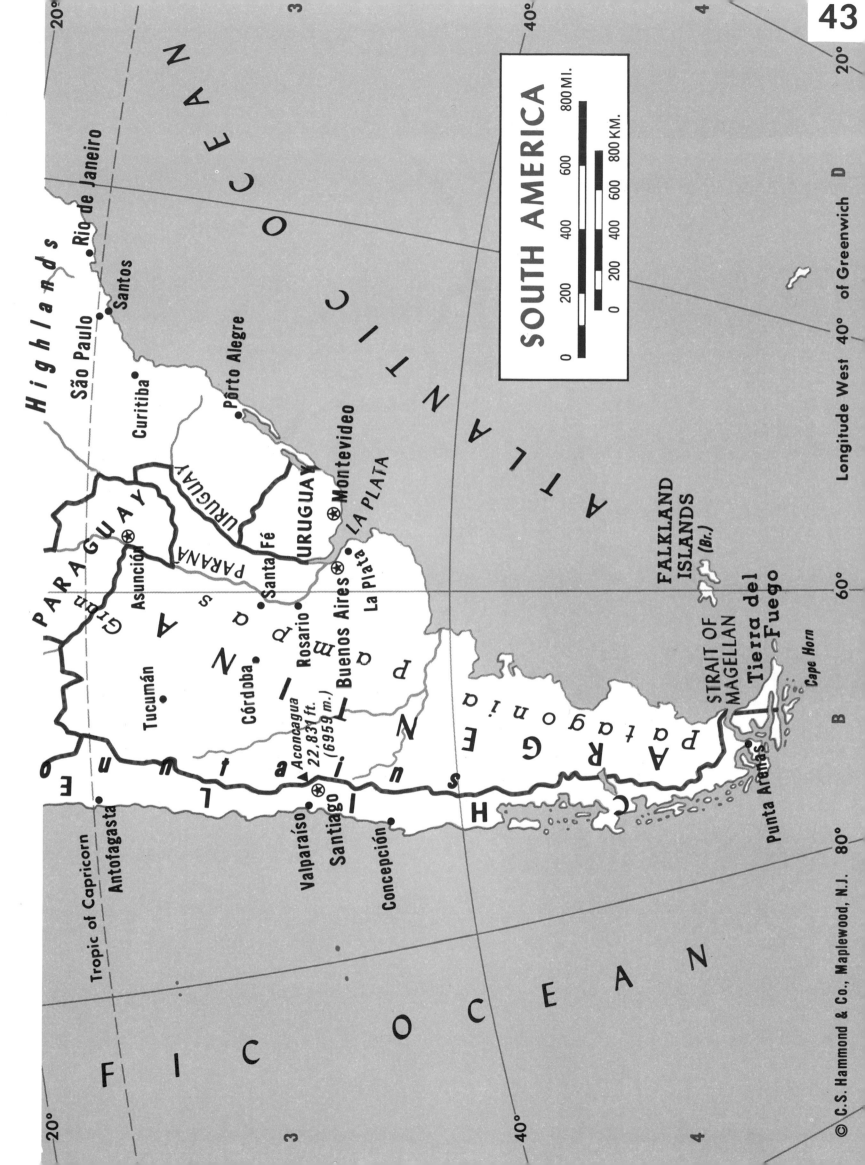

SOUTH AMERICA

800 MI.
600
400
200
0

800 KM.
600
400
200
0

PACIFIC OCEAN

ATLANTIC OCEAN

Highlands

Rio de Janeiro

Santos

São Paulo

Curitiba

Pôrto Alegre

PARAGUAY

Asunción

Gran Chaco

Santa Fé

URUGUAY

Montevideo

LA PLATA

PARANA

Rosario

Córdoba

Buenos Aires

La Plata

Tucumán

A R G E N T I N A

▲ Aconcagua
22,831 ft.
(6959 m.)

C H I L E

Valparaíso

Santiago

Concepción

Antofagasta

Tropic of Capricorn

Patagonia

FALKLAND
ISLANDS

(Br.)

STRAIT OF
MAGELLAN

Tierra del
Fuego

Punta Arenas

Cape Horn

Longitude West 40° of Greenwich

© C.S. Hammond & Co., Maplewood, N.J.

C 60° ST. LUCIA D 52°

BARBADOS

A N T I L L E S

ST. VINC.
& GRENS.

SSER ANTILLES GRENADA

A T L A N T I C

Isla de
Margarita

Carúpano TRINIDAD
AND
TOBAGO

Cumaná

elona O C E A N

Maturín Delta of the
Orinoco

El Tigre

A

Ciudad Bolívar 8°

Cuyuni Georgetown

New Amsterdam

Angel
Fall G U Y A N A Paramaribo

Devil's I.

Mt. Roraima
9,094 ft.
(2772 m.) Cayenne

G
u SURINAME FRENCH
i GUIANA
a
n
a

H

i
Essequibo g

h

l

Branco a

n

d Oyapock

s

B R A Z I L

tor

Negro

0°

Amazon

**COLOMBIA, VENEZUELA
AND THE GUIANAS** 3

| 0 | 100 | 200 | 300 MI. |

| 0 | 100 | 200 | 300 KM. |

nwich C 60° D 52°

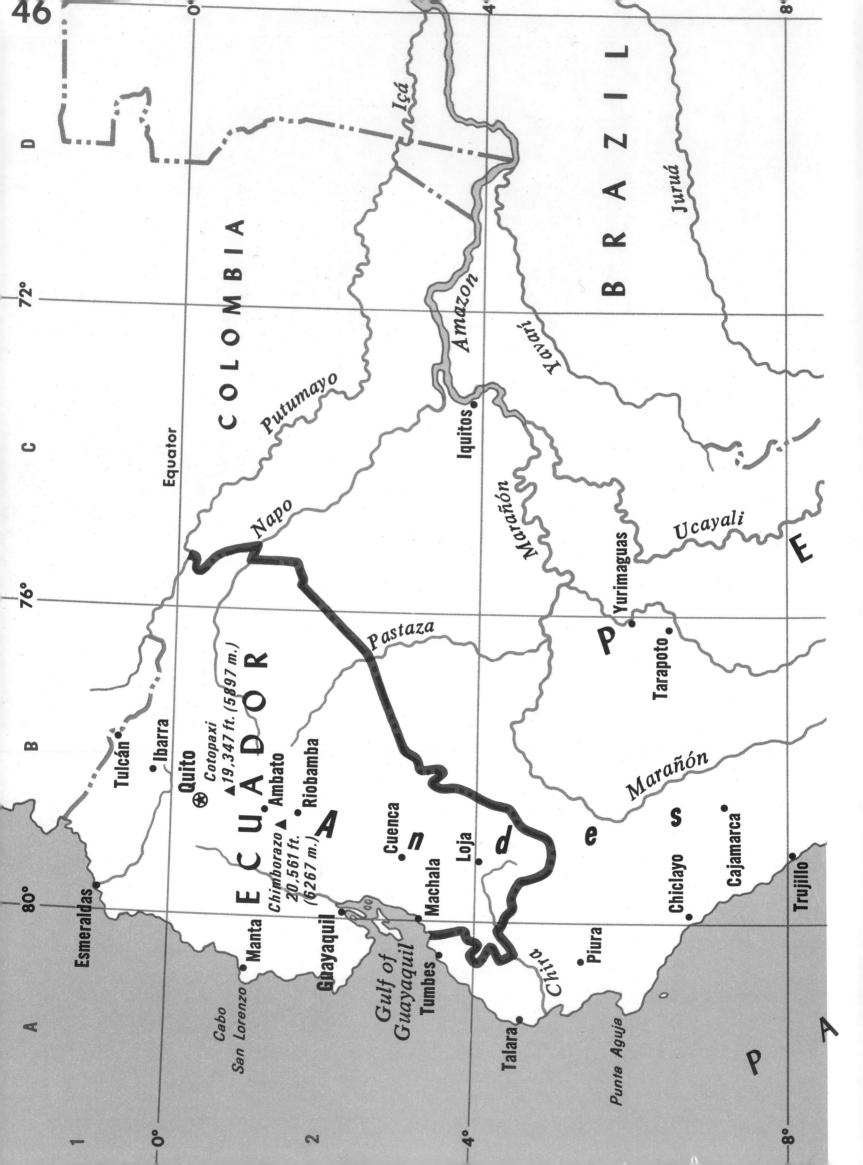

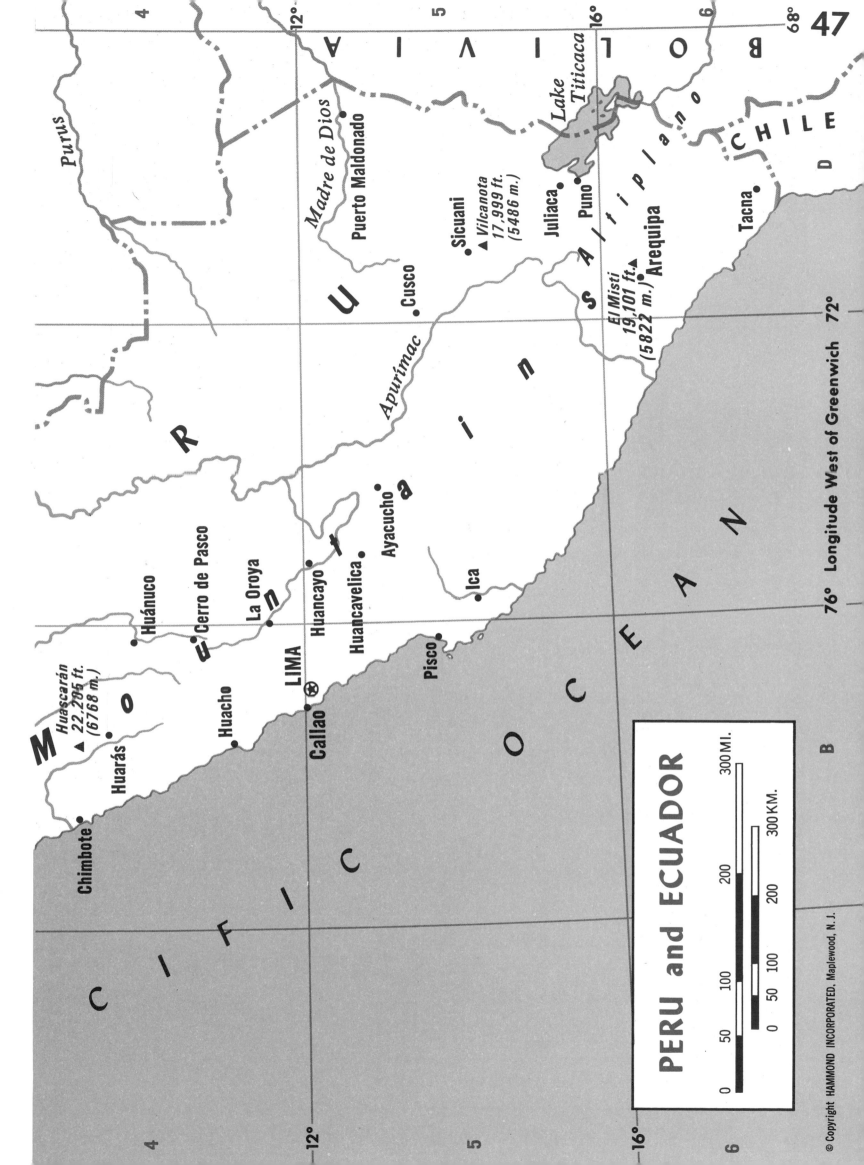

PERU and ECUADOR

300 MI.

300 KM.

| 0 | 50 | 100 | 200 | 300 MI. |
| 0 | 50 | 100 | 200 | 300 KM. |

72° Longitude West of Greenwich

76°

BOLIVIA

CHILE

Lake Titicaca

Altiplano

Madre de Dios

Purus

Puerto Maldonado

Sicuani

▲Vilcanota 17,999 ft. (5486 m.)

Juliaca

Puno

Cusco

Apurímac

El Misti 19,101 ft. (5822 m.)▲

Arequipa

Tacna

Ayacucho

Ica

Cerro de Pasco

Huánuco

La Oroya

Huancayo

Huancavelica

Pisco

LIMA

Callao

Huacho

Huarás

Huascarán ▲ 22,205 ft. (6768 m.)

Chimbote

PACIFIC OCEAN

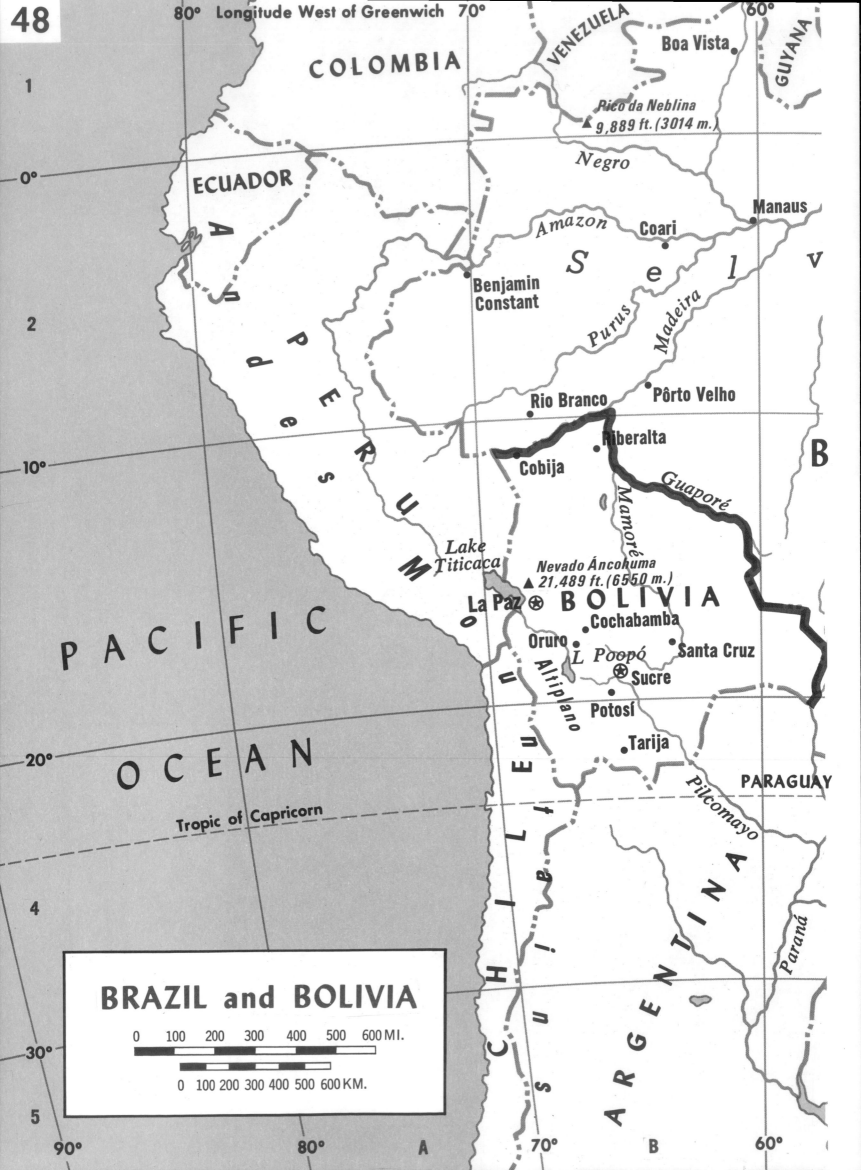

80° Longitude West of Greenwich 70°

1

COLOMBIA

VENEZUELA

Boa Vista

GUYANA

60°

Pico da Neblina
▲ 9,889 ft. (3014 m.)

0°

ECUADOR

Negro

Manaus

Coari

A

Amazon

S

e

l

v

Benjamin
Constant

Purus

Madeira

2

P

e

r

u

M

Rio Branco

Pôrto Velho

Riberalta

Cobija

Guaporé

B

10°

Mamoré

Lake
Titicaca

Nevado Áncohuma
▲ 21,489 ft. (6550 m.)

La Paz ⊛

BOLIVIA

PACIFIC

Cochabamba

Oruro

Santa Cruz

L. Poopó

Altiplano

⊛ Sucre

OCEAN

Potosí

C

Tarija

20°

PARAGUAY

h

i

l

e

Pilcomayo

Tropic of Capricorn

Paraná

4

A
R
G
E
N
T
I
N
A

BRAZIL and BOLIVIA

0   100   200   300   400   500   600 MI.

30°

0 100 200 300 400 500 600 KM.

5

90°   80°   A   70°   B   60°

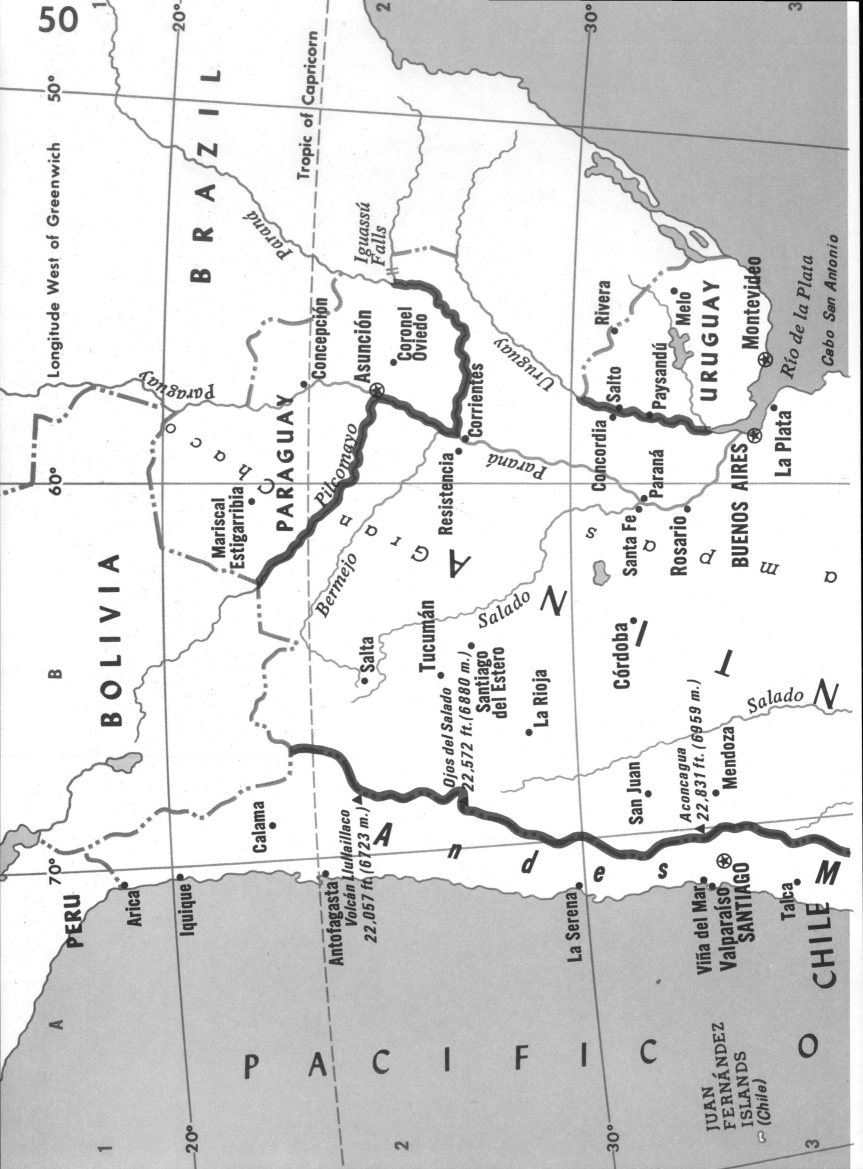

BRAZIL

BOLIVIA

PERU

PARAGUAY

Longitude West of Greenwich

Tropic of Capricorn

Paraná

Iguassú Falls

Paraguay

Paraguay

Concepción

Asunción

Coronel Oviedo

Corrientes

Mariscal Estigarribia

Pilcomayo

Bermejo

Resistencia

Rivera

Melo

URUGUAY

Montevideo

Río de la Plata

Cabo San Antonio

Uruguay

Salto

Paysandú

Concordia

Paraná

Santa Fe

Rosario

BUENOS AIRES

La Plata

Salta

Tucumán

Ojos del Salado 22,572 ft. (6880 m.)

Santiago del Estero

La Rioja

Córdoba

Salado

Aconcagua 22,831 ft. (6959 m.)

San Juan

Mendoza

Salado

Calama

Antofagasta Volcán Llullaillaco 22,057 ft. (6723 m.)

A n d e s

La Serena

Viña del Mar Valparaíso SANTIAGO

Talca

CHILE

Arica

Iquique

JUAN FERNÁNDEZ ISLANDS (Chile)

PACIFIC

OCEAN

ARGENTINA

B

A

50°

60°

70°

20°

30°

20°

30°

1

2

3

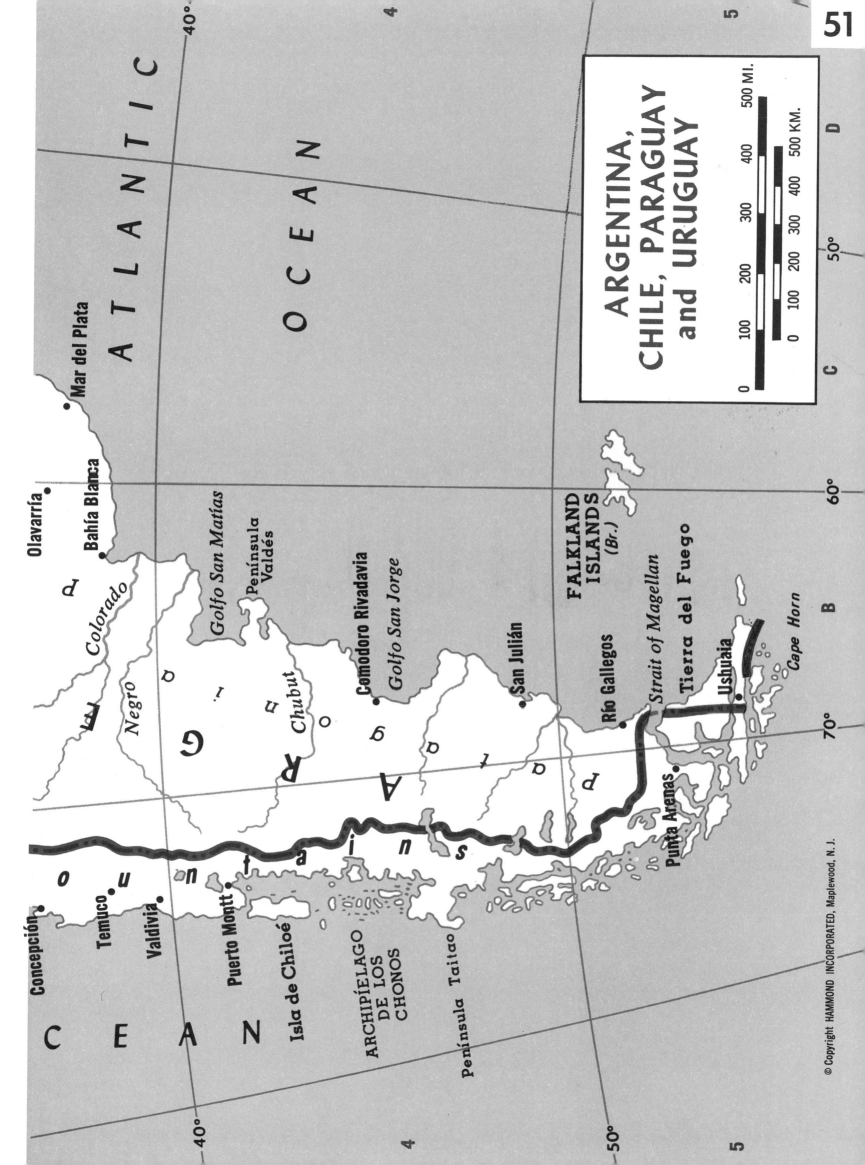

ARGENTINA,
CHILE, PARAGUAY
and URUGUAY

100   200   300   400   500 MI.

0   100   200   300   400   500 KM.

ATLANTIC

OCEAN

Mar del Plata

Olavarría

Bahía Blanca

Colorado

Río

Golfo San Matías

Península
Valdés

Comodoro Rivadavia

Golfo San Jorge

San Julián

Río Gallegos

FALKLAND
ISLANDS
(Br.)

Strait of Magellan

Tierra del Fuego

Ushuaia

Cape Horn

Punta Arenas

P a t a g o n i a

A n d e s   M o u n t a i n s

Negro

Chubut

Concepción

Temuco

Valdivia

Puerto Montt

Isla de Chiloé

ARCHIPIÉLAGO
DE LOS
CHONOS

Península Taitao

O C E A N

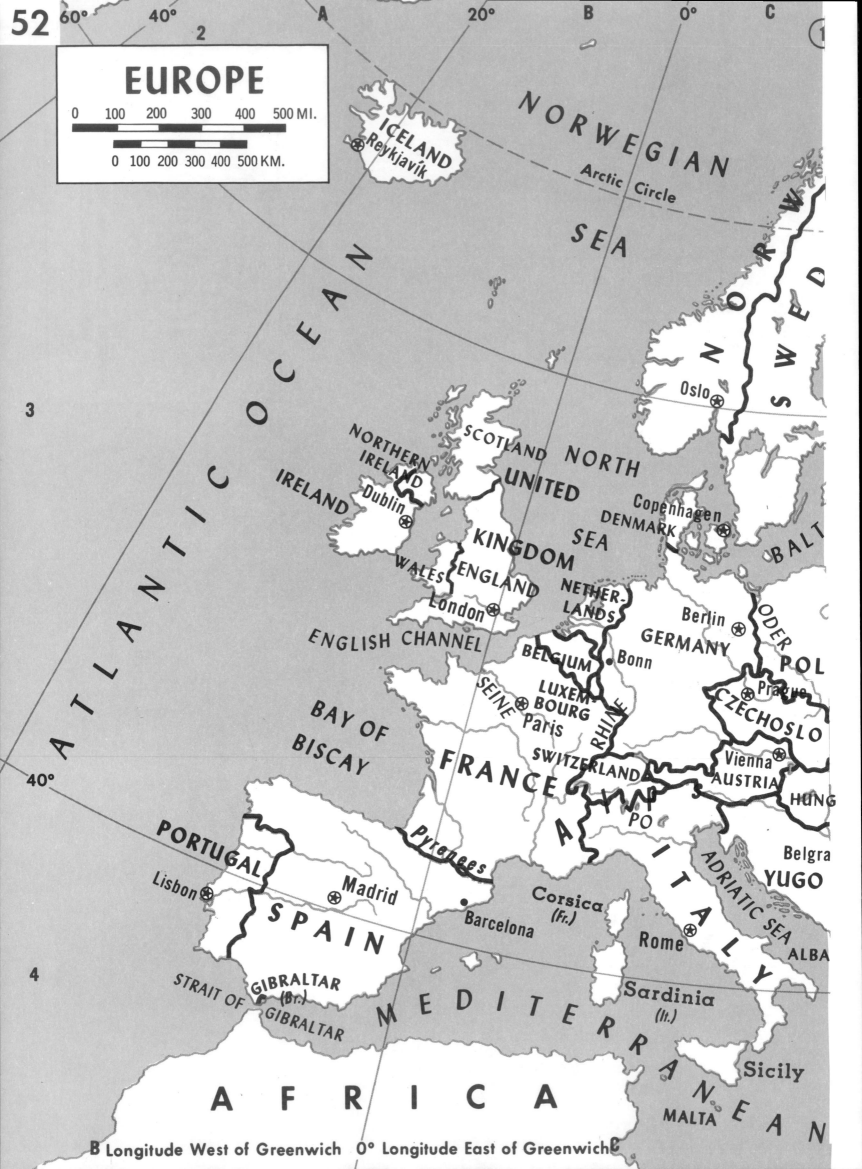

EUROPE

0 100 200 300 400 500 MI.

0 100 200 300 400 500 KM.

60° 40° A 20° B 0° C

2

NORWEGIAN

SEA

Arctic Circle

ICELAND
Reykjavík

ATLANTIC OCEAN

3

NORTHERN
IRELAND

SCOTLAND NORTH

IRELAND

Dublin

UNITED

Oslo

N O R W

S W E D

KINGDOM

SEA

Copenhagen
DENMARK

BALT

WALES ENGLAND

London

NETHER-
LANDS

Berlin

GERMANY

ODER

POL

ENGLISH CHANNEL

BELGIUM

Bonn

BAY OF

BISCAY

SEINE

LUXEM-
BOURG

Paris

Prague

CZECHOSLO

RHINE

SWITZERLAND

Vienna

FRANCE

AUSTRIA

40°

PO

HUNG

PORTUGAL

Pyrenees

Corsica
(Fr.)

Belgra

YUGO

Lisbon

Madrid

SPAIN

Barcelona

ADRIATIC SEA

Rome

ALBA

4

STRAIT OF

GIBRALTAR
(Br.)
GIBRALTAR

M E D I T E R R

Sardinia
(It.)

A N E A N

Sicily

A F R I C A

MALTA

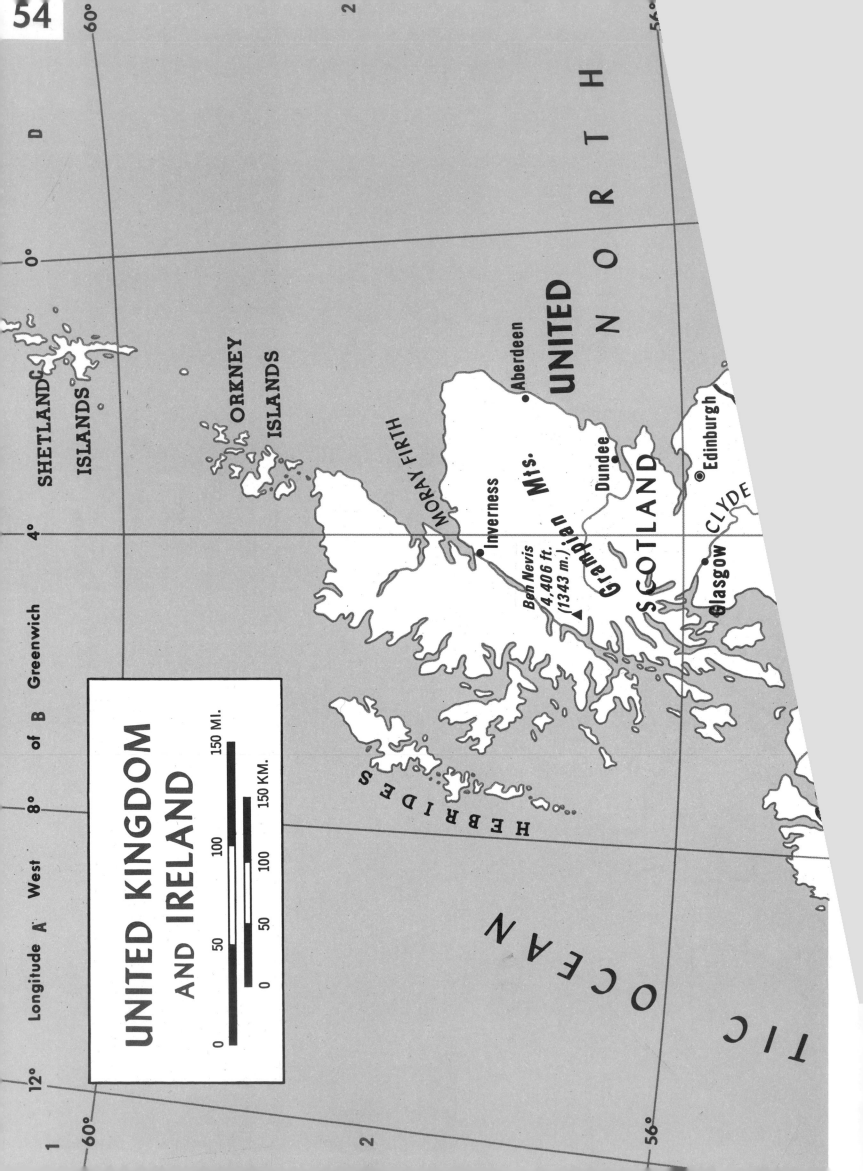

UNITED KINGDOM
AND IRELAND

50   0   50   100   150 MI.

0   50   100   150 KM.

SHETLAND
ISLANDS

ORKNEY
ISLANDS

MORAY FIRTH

Aberdeen

UNITED

N O R T H

Inverness

Ben Nevis
4,406 ft.
(1343 m.)
▲

Grampian

Mts.

Dundee

SCOTLAND

Edinburgh

CLYDE

Glasgow

H E B R I D E S

A T L A N T I C   O C E A N

North Sea

Longitude   A   West   8°   of   B   Greenwich

12°   D   0°   4°   8°   60°

1   60°   2   56°

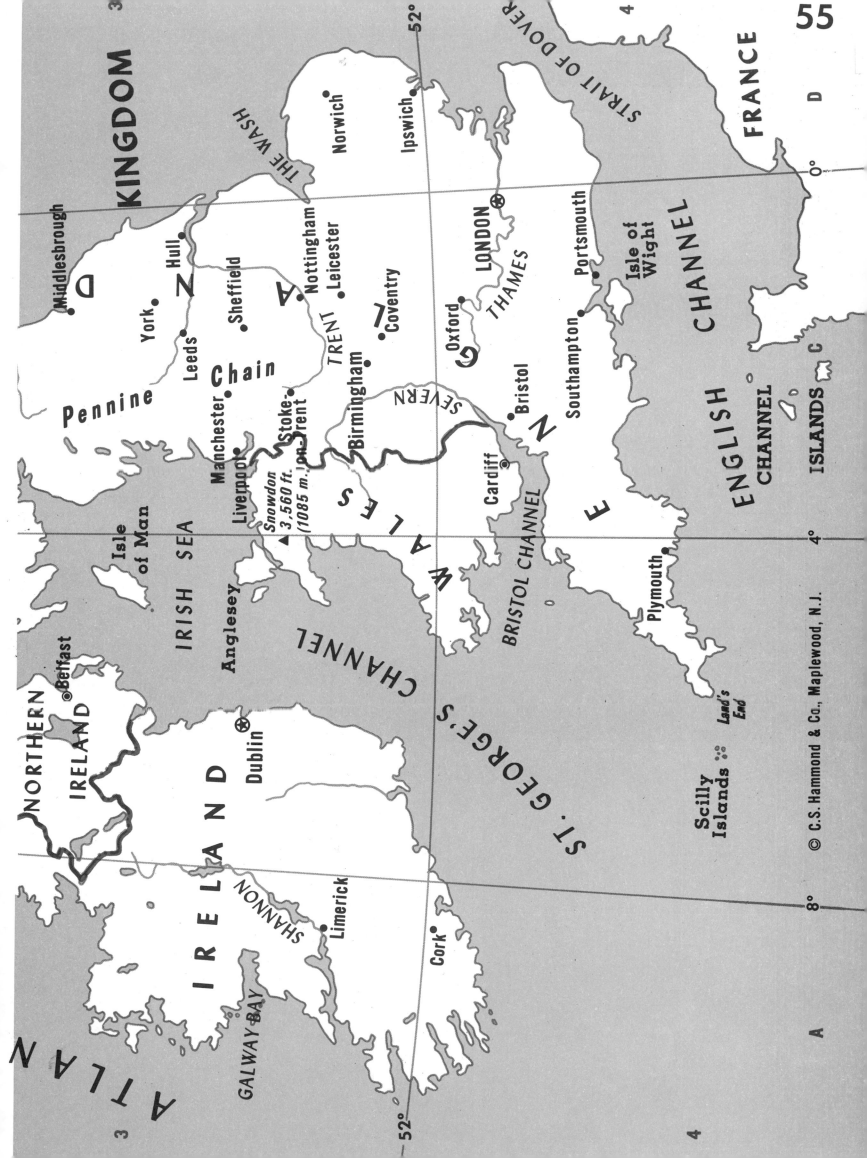

UNITED KINGDOM

FRANCE

Middlesbrough

York

Hull

Leeds

Sheffield

Pennine Chain

Manchester

Liverpool

Stoke-on-Trent

Snowdon
3,560 ft.
(1085 m.)

Nottingham

Leicester

TRENT

Birmingham

Coventry

SEVERN

Oxford

LONDON

THAMES

Cardiff

Bristol

Southampton

Portsmouth

Isle of Wight

Norwich

Ipswich

STRAIT OF DOVER

ENGLAND

WALES

BRISTOL CHANNEL

ENGLISH CHANNEL

CHANNEL

ISLANDS

Isle
of Man

IRISH SEA

Anglesey

NORTHERN
IRELAND

Belfast

IRELAND

Dublin

ST. GEORGE'S CHANNEL

GALWAY BAY

SHANNON

Limerick

Cork

Plymouth

Land's
End

Scilly
Islands

ATLAN

THE WASH

52°

0°

4°

52°

8°

4°

© C.S. Hammond & Co., Maplewood, N.J.

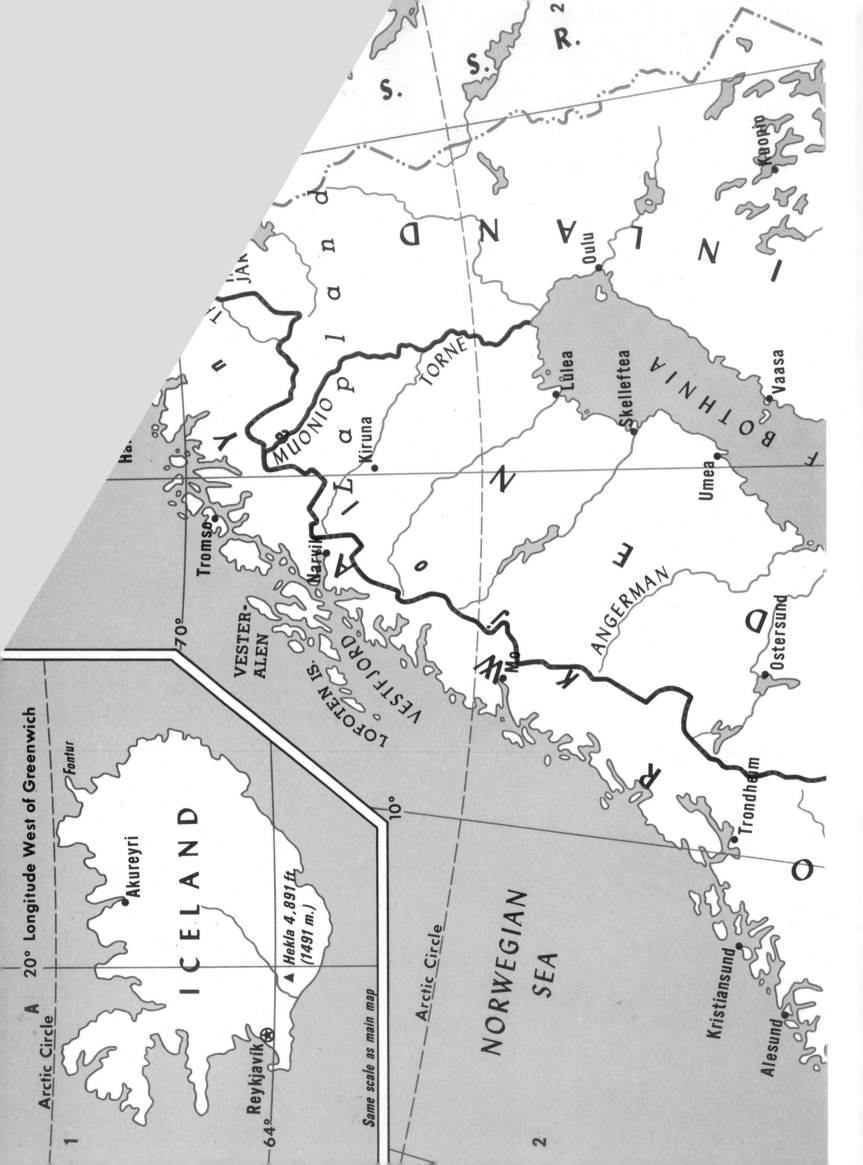

S. S. R.

Kuopio

Oulu

F I N L A N D

Lūlea

Skelleftea

Vaasa

B O T H N I A

Umea

Kiruna

TORNE

MUONIO

L a p l a n d

N

E

D

ANGERMAN

Ostersund

Tromso

Narvik

VESTER-
ALEN

VESTFJORD

LOFOTEN IS.

K

R

Trondheim

70°

10°

Arctic Circle

Kristiansund

NORWEGIAN
SEA

Alesund

O

A   20° Longitude West of Greenwich

1

Fontur

Akureyri

I C E L A N D

▲ Hekla 4,891 ft.
(1491 m.)

⊛ Reykjavik

64°

Same scale as main map

Arctic Circle

2

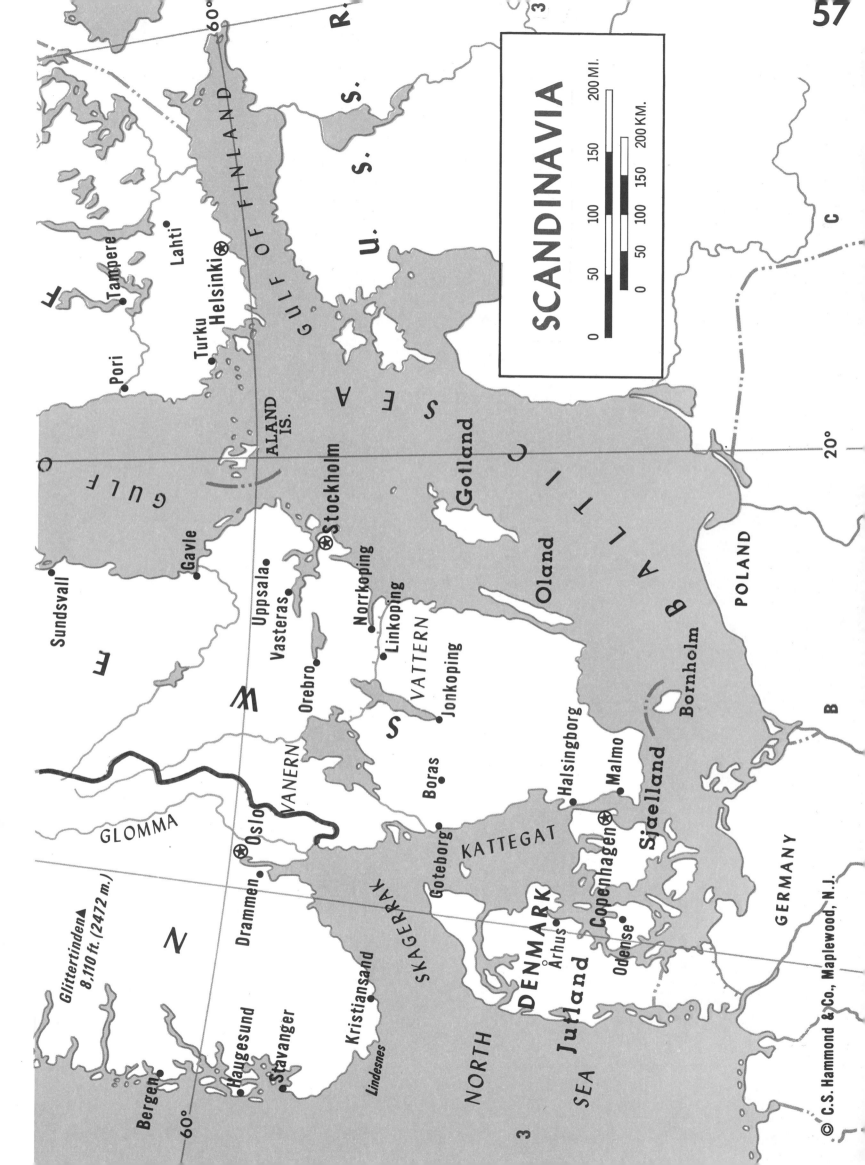

SCANDINAVIA

0 50 100 150 200 MI.

0 50 100 150 200 KM.

R.

S.

S.

U.

GULF OF FINLAND

Tampere

Lahti

Helsinki

Turku

Pori

F

GULF

Sundsvall

Gavle

Uppsala

Vasteras

Orebro

VANERN

Oslo

GLOMMA

Glittertinden▲
8,110 ft. (2472 m.)

N

Drammen

Kristiansand

Lindesnes

Haugesund

Stavanger

Bergen

60°

ALAND IS.

Stockholm

Norrkoping

Linkoping

VATTERN

Jonkoping

Boras

Goteborg

SKAGERRAK

W

S

E

BALTIC

SEA

Gotland

Oland

Bornholm

Halsingborg

Malmo

Copenhagen

Sjælland

KATTEGAT

DENMARK

Arhus

Jutland

Odense

NORTH
SEA

POLAND

GERMANY

20°

60°

3

3

B

C

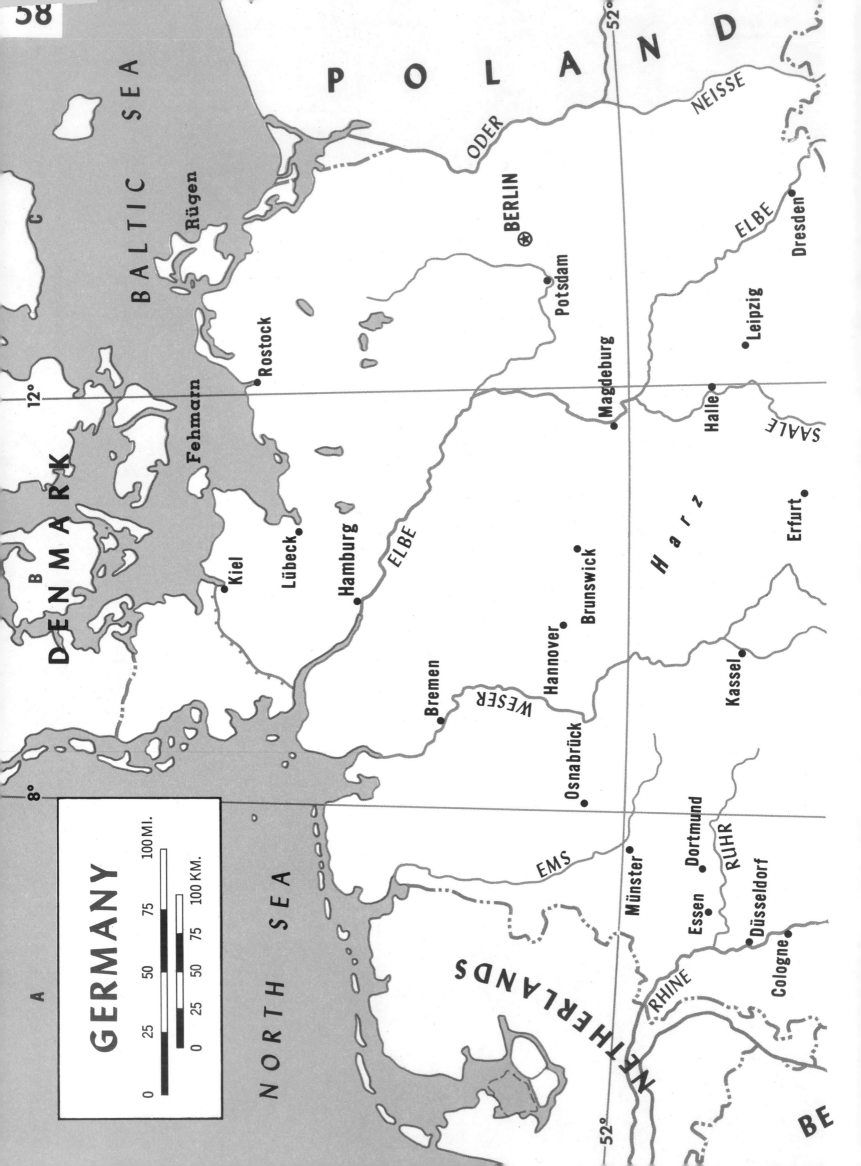

A

POLAND

ODER

NEISSE

BERLIN

BALTIC SEA

Rügen

DENMARK

B

Fehman

Rostock

12°

Potsdam

ELBE

Dresden

Magdeburg

Leipzig

Halle

SAALE

Kiel

Lübeck

Hamburg

ELBE

Harz

Erfurt

Brunswick

Bremen

Hannover

Kassel

WESER

Osnabrück

8°

EMS

Münster

Dortmund

RUHR

Essen

Düsseldorf

Cologne

NORTH SEA

NETHERLANDS

RHINE

BE

52°

52°

GERMANY

100 MI.

0   25   50   75

100 KM.

0   25   50   75

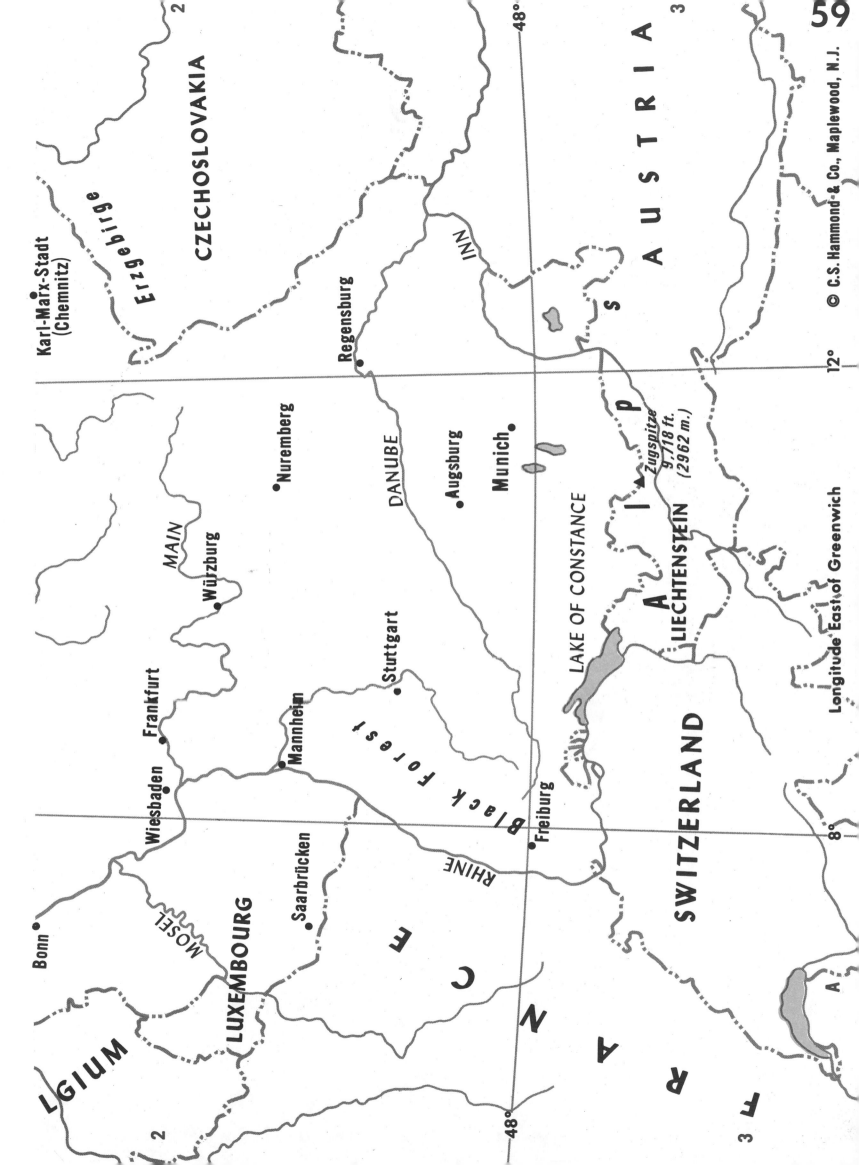

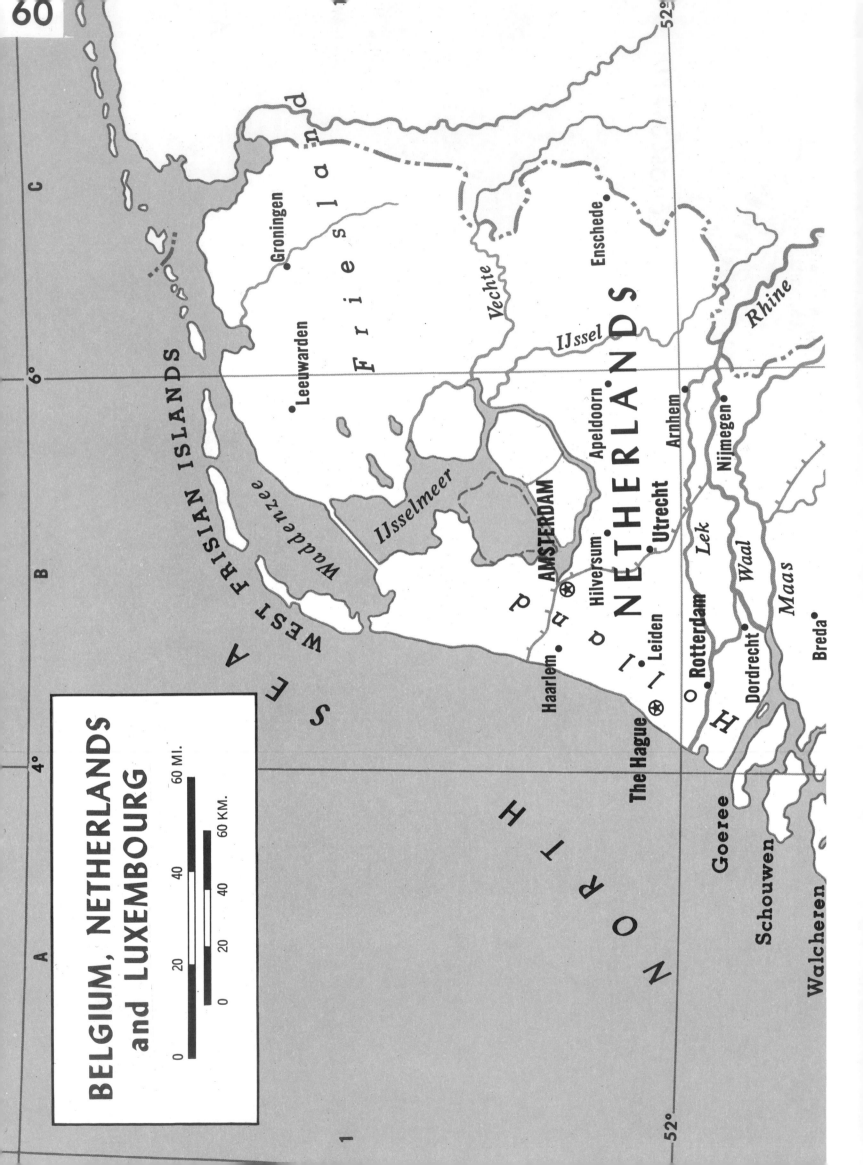

BELGIUM, NETHERLANDS and LUXEMBOURG

60 MI.

0   20   40

0   20   40   60 KM.

NETHERLANDS

Groningen

Leeuwarden

Friesland

Enschede

Vechte

IJssel

Rhine

Apeldoorn

Arnhem

Nijmegen

AMSTERDAM

Hilversum

Utrecht

Lek

Waal

Maas

Haarlem

Leiden

Rotterdam

Dordrecht

Breda

The Hague

IJsselmeer

Waddenzee

WEST FRISIAN ISLANDS

NORTH SEA

Goeree

Schouwen

Walcheren

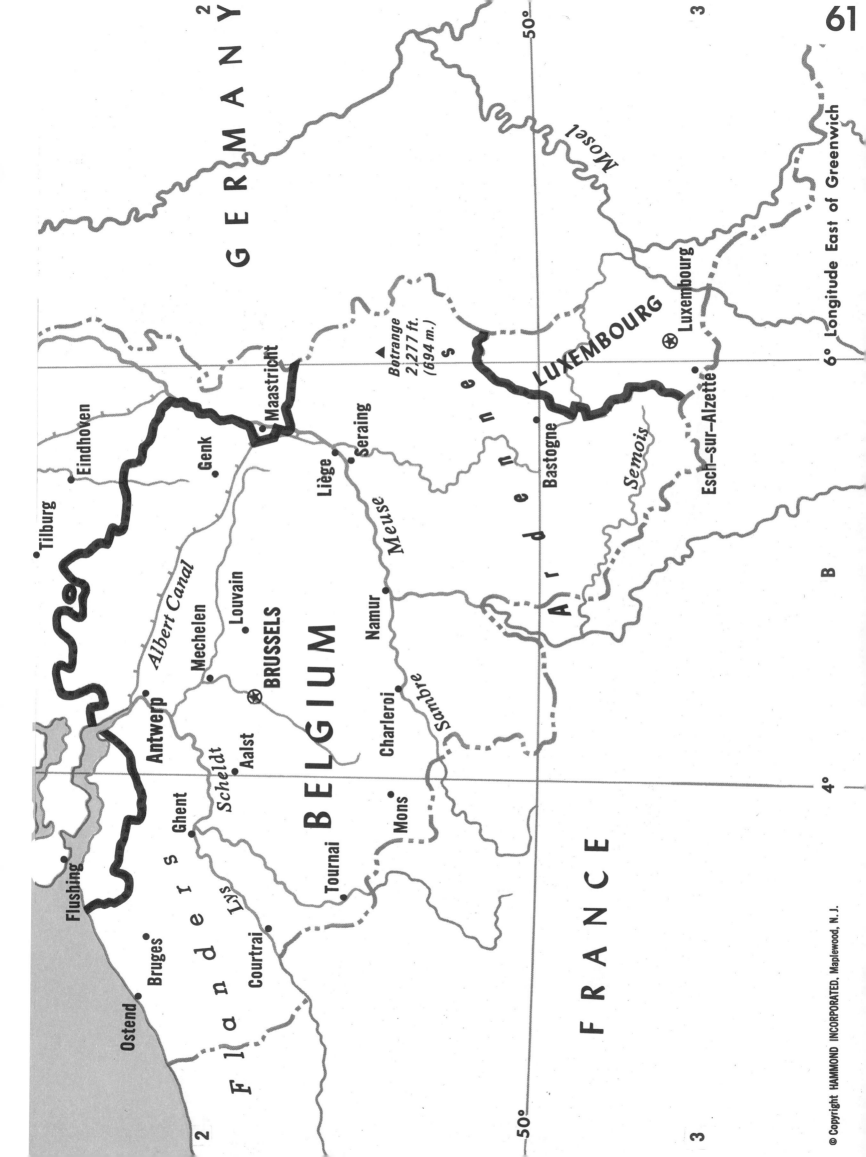

GERMANY

2

50°

3

Mosel

6° Longitude East of Greenwich

LUXEMBOURG

Luxembourg

⊛ Luxembourg

Esch-sur-Alzette

Botrange
2,277 ft.
(694 m.)
▲
S

Maastricht

Eindhoven

Genk

Seraing

Liège

Bastogne

Semois

Ardenne

Tilburg

Meuse

Albert Canal

Louvain

Mechelen

Namur

BRUSSELS
⊛ BRUSSELS

B

Antwerp

Charleroi

Sambre

Aalst

BELGIUM

Ghent

Scheldt

Mons

Flanders

Tournai

Lys

FRANCE

Bruges

Courtrai

Ostend

Flushing

50°

4°

3

2

B

3

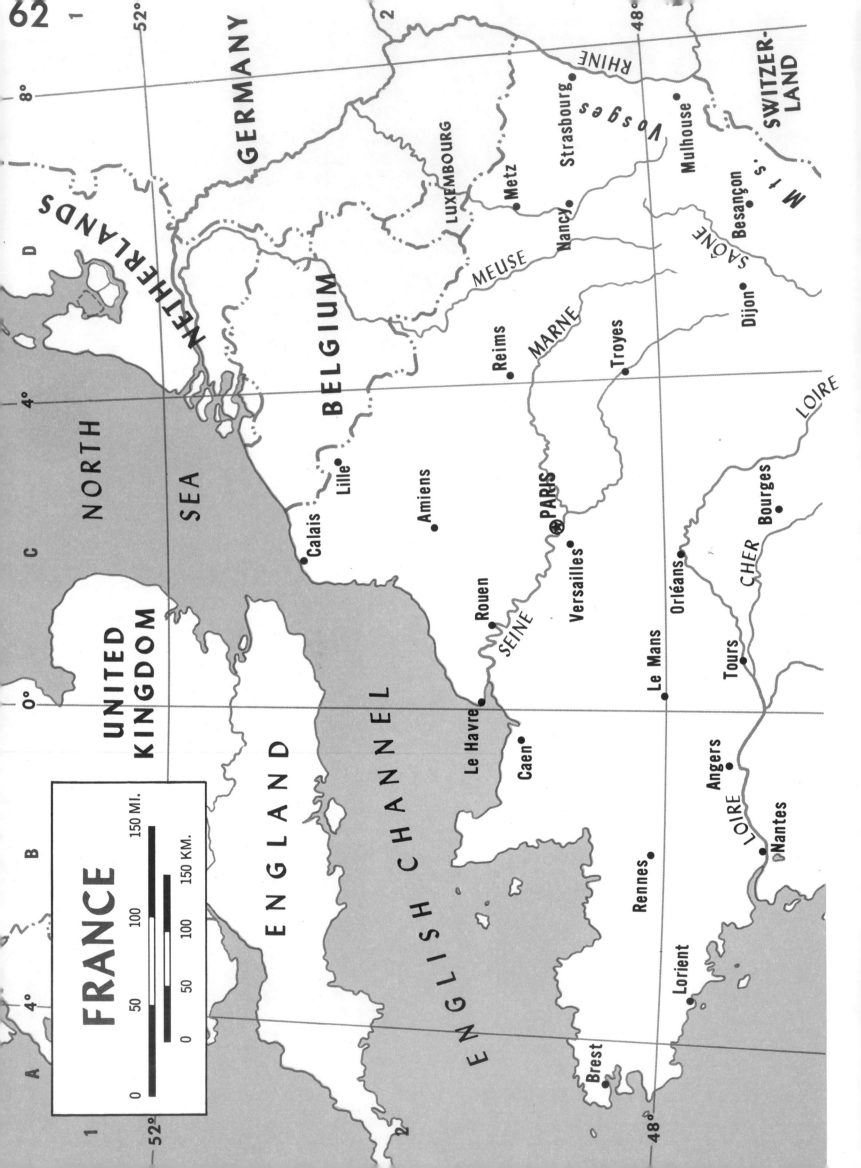

FRANCE

150 MI.

150 KM.

0   50   100   150 MI.

0   50   100   150 KM.

NETHERLANDS

GERMANY

NORTH

SEA

UNITED

KINGDOM

ENGLAND

ENGLISH CHANNEL

BELGIUM

LUXEMBOURG

SWITZER-
LAND

RHINE

Vosges

Mts.

SAÔNE

MEUSE

MARNE

LOIRE

SEINE

CHER

LOIRE

Metz

Strasbourg

Nancy

Mulhouse

Besançon

Dijon

Reims

Troyes

Calais

Lille

Amiens

PARIS

Versailles

Rouen

Bourges

Orléans

Le Mans

Tours

Le Havre

Caen

Angers

Rennes

Nantes

Lorient

Brest

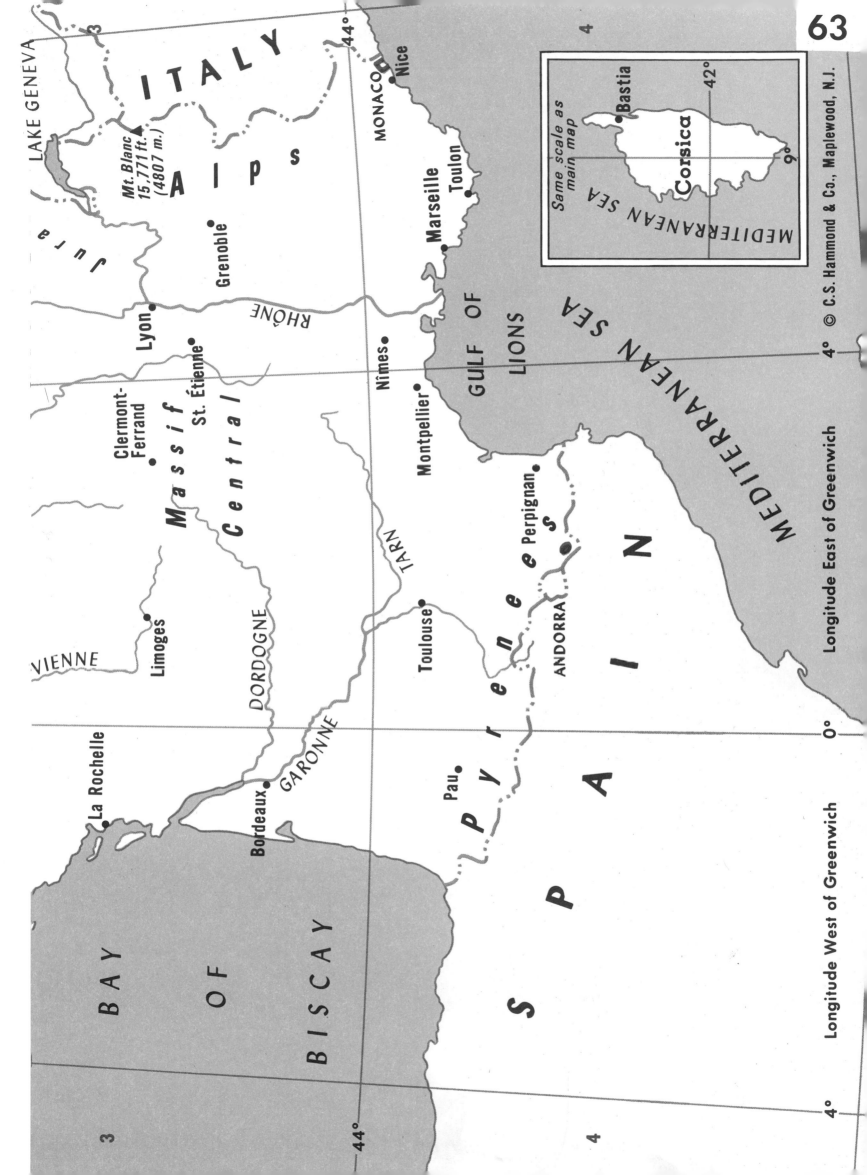

LAKE GENEVA

ITALY

Jura

Alps

Mt. Blanc
15,771 ft.
(4807 m.)

Grenoble

Lyon

RHÔNE

Clermont-
Ferrand

St. Étienne

Massif

Central

Nîmes

Montpellier

TARN

Limoges

VIENNE

DORDOGNE

Toulouse

Perpignan

ANDORRA

Pyrenees

La Rochelle

GARONNE

Bordeaux

Pau

SPAIN

BAY

OF

BISCAY

MONACO

Nice

Marseille

Toulon

GULF

OF

LIONS

MEDITERRANEAN SEA

Corsica

Bastia

Same scale as
main map

MEDITERRANEAN SEA

42°

9°

4

© C.S. Hammond & Co., Maplewood, N.J.

Longitude East of Greenwich

Longitude West of Greenwich

0°

4°

4

44°

44°

3

4

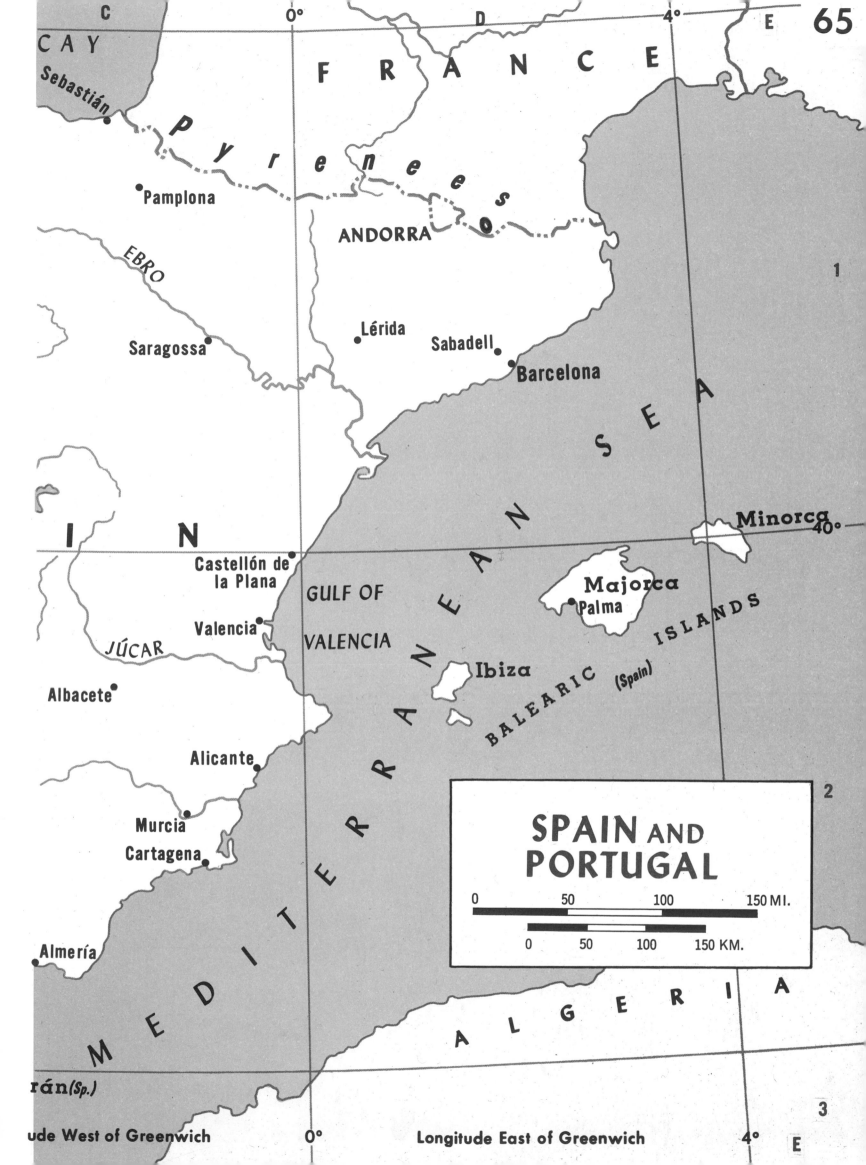

FRANCE

CAY

Sebastián

Pyrenees

Pamplona

EBRO

ANDORRA

Lérida

Saragossa

Sabadell

Barcelona

I N

Castellón de
la Plana

GULF OF

Valencia

JÚCAR

VALENCIA

Albacete

Alicante

Murcia

Cartagena

Almería

rán(Sp.)

M E D I T E R R A N E A N   S E A

40°

Minorca

Majorca

Palma

Ibiza

BALEARIC ISLANDS

(Spain)

1

2

SPAIN AND PORTUGAL

| 0 | 50 | 100 | 150 MI. |

| 0 | 50 | 100 | 150 KM. |

A L G E R I A

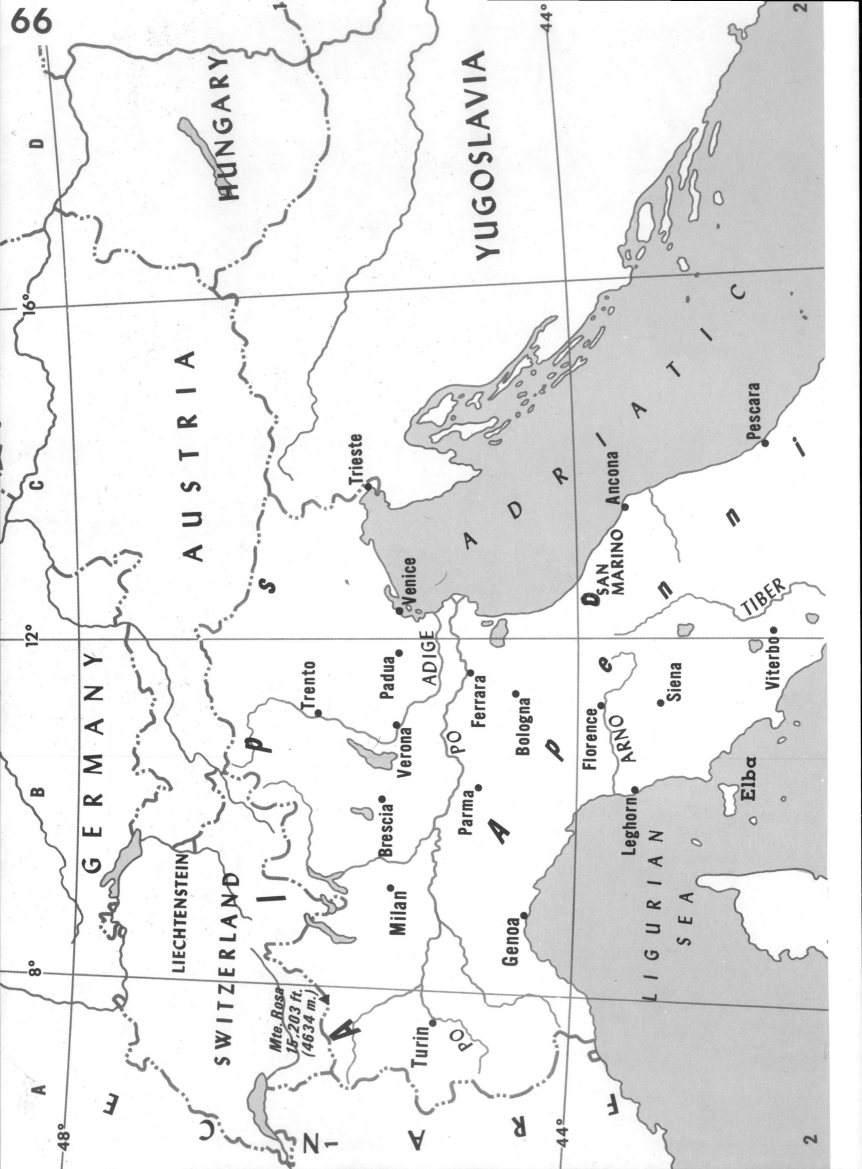

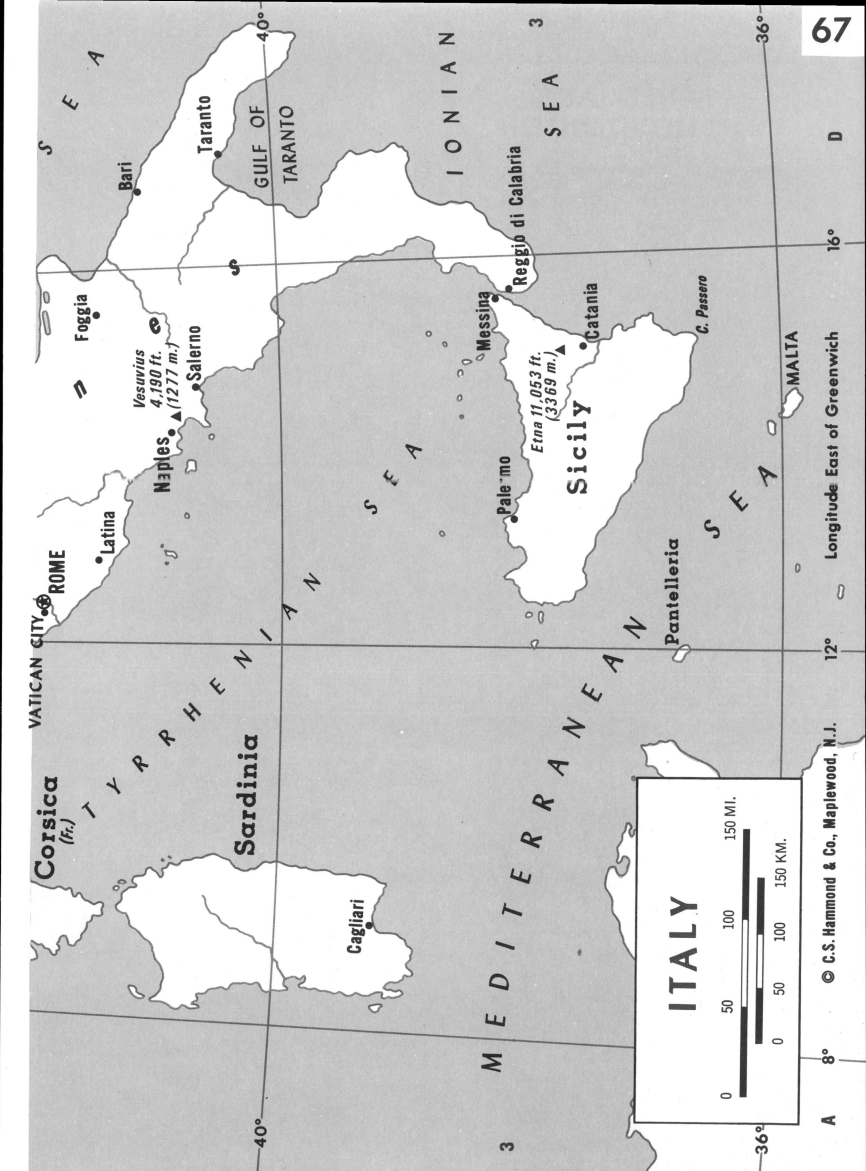

ITALY

| 0 | 50 | 100 | 150 MI. |

| 0 | 50 | 100 | 150 KM. |

© C.S. Hammond & Co., Maplewood, N.J.

Corsica (Fr.)

Sardinia

Cagliari

ROME
VATICAN CITY
Latina

Foggia

Naples
Vesuvius
4,190 ft.
(1277 m.)
Salerno

Bari

Taranto

GULF OF
TARANTO

TYRRHENIAN SEA

MEDITERRANEAN SEA

Pantelleria

MALTA

Palermo

Messina

Etna 11,053 ft.
(3369 m.)

Sicily

Catania

C. Passero

Reggio di Calabria

IONIAN SEA

Longitude East of Greenwich

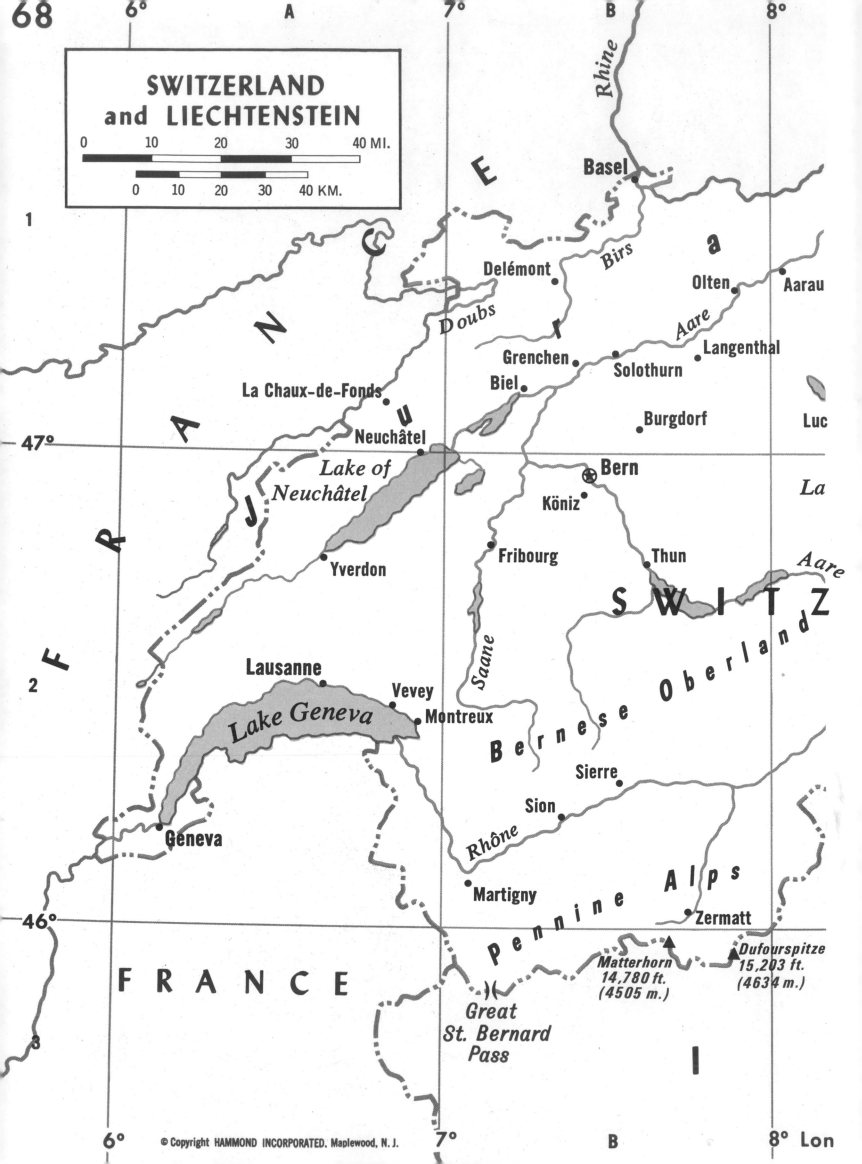

SWITZERLAND and LIECHTENSTEIN

0 10 20 30 40 MI.

0 10 20 30 40 KM.

FRANCE

JURA

Rhine

Basel

Doubs

Birs

Delémont

Olten

Aarau

Aare

Langenthal

Grenchen

Solothurn

Biel

Burgdorf

Luc

La Chaux-de-Fonds

Neuchâtel

Bern

Lake of Neuchâtel

Köniz

La

Yverdon

Fribourg

Thun

Aare

SWITZ

Saane

Bernese Oberland

Lausanne

Vevey

Montreux

Lake Geneva

Sierre

Sion

Geneva

Rhône

Pennine Alps

Martigny

Zermatt

Great St. Bernard Pass

Matterhorn 14,780 ft. (4505 m.)

Dufourspitze 15,203 ft. (4634 m.)

FRANCE

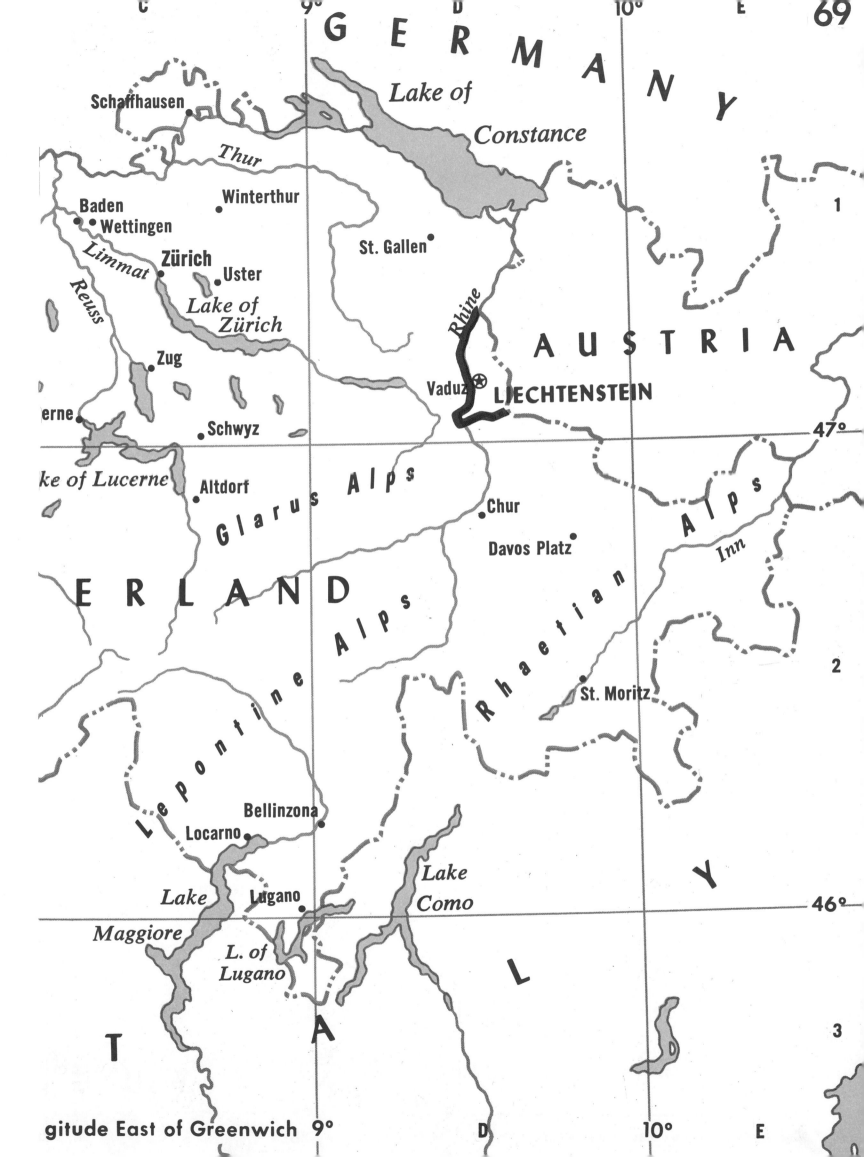

GERMANY

Schaffhausen

Thur

Winterthur

Baden
Wettingen

Limmat

Reuss

Zürich

Uster

Lake of
Zürich

Zug

erne

Schwyz

ke of Lucerne

Altdorf

Glarus Alps

Lepontine Alps

E R L A N D

Lake

Maggiore

Locarno

Bellinzona

Lugano

L. of
Lugano

Lake of

Constance

St. Gallen

Rhine

Vaduz ⊛ LIECHTENSTEIN

AUSTRIA

47°

Chur

Davos Platz

Rhaetian Alps

Inn

St. Moritz

Lake
Como

Y

L

A

46°

1

2

3

A · 12° · B · 16°

Erzgebirge

Sude

Liberec

Usti nad Labem

Hradec Kralove

PRAGUE ⊛

Plzen

VLTAVA

C Z E C H

1

GERMANY

Bohemian Forest

DANUBE

Ceske Budejovice

INN

Linz

48° · **VIEN**

LAKE OF CONSTANCE

Salzburg

Wiener-Neustadt

A U S T R I A

S

Leoben

LIECHTENSTEIN

A

Innsbruck

I

P

▲ Grossglockner
12,457 ft. (3797 m.)

Graz

ITALY

DRAU

Klagenfurt

2

AUSTRIA, CZECHOSLOVAKIA AND HUNGARY

0   25   50   75   100 MI.

0   25   50   75   100 KM.

Y U G

12°

B · 16°

C

20°

D

POLAND

ten

Mts.

Ostrava

B *e* *s* *k* *i* *d* *s*

Olomouc

OSLOVAKIA

C *a* *r* *p* *a* *t* *h* *i* *a* *n* *s*

Gerlachovka
8,707 ft. (2654 m.)

Brno

Kosice

U.S.S.R.

MORAVA

HRON

Miskolc

48°

NA

Bratislava

DANUBE

TISZA

Gyor

BUDAPEST

Debrecen

HUNGARY

Szombathely

Kecskemet

Bekescsaba

2

LAKE
BALATON

Szeged

ROMANIA

Pecs

DRAVA

TISZA

OSLAVIA

DANUBE

20°

D

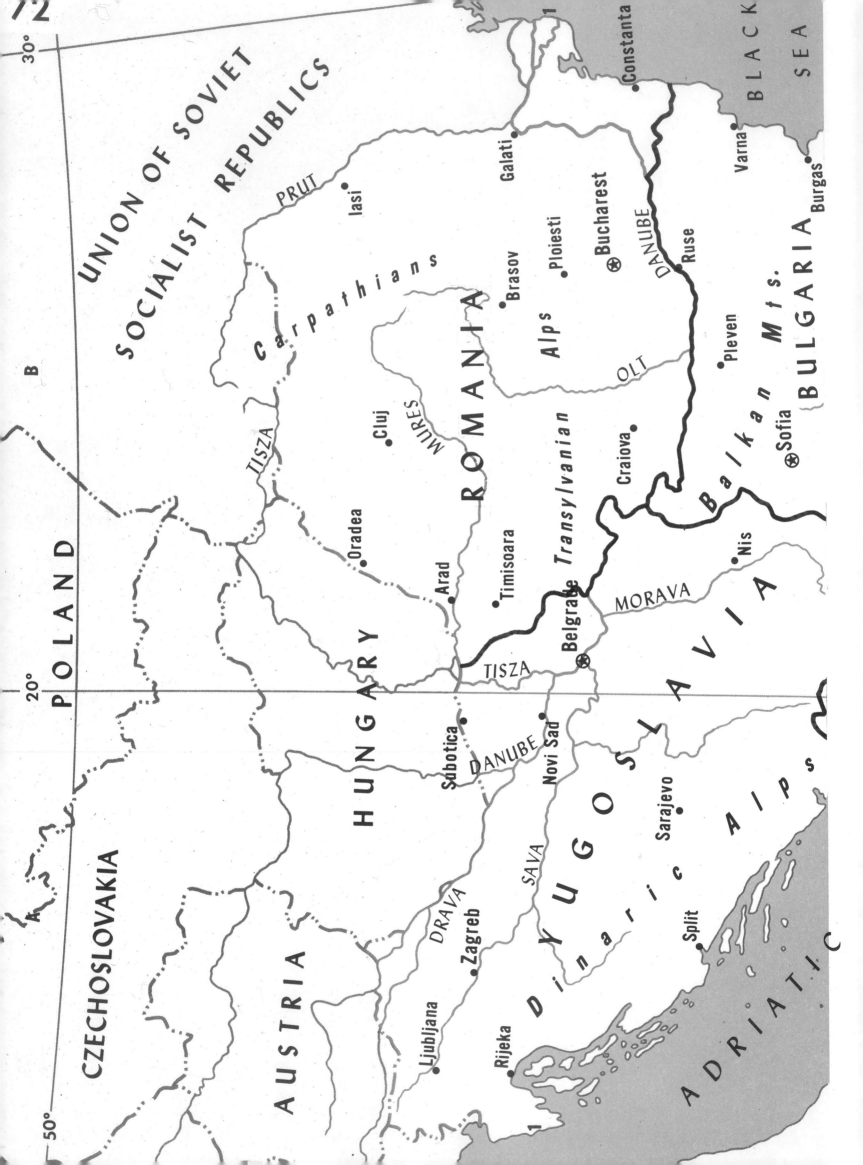

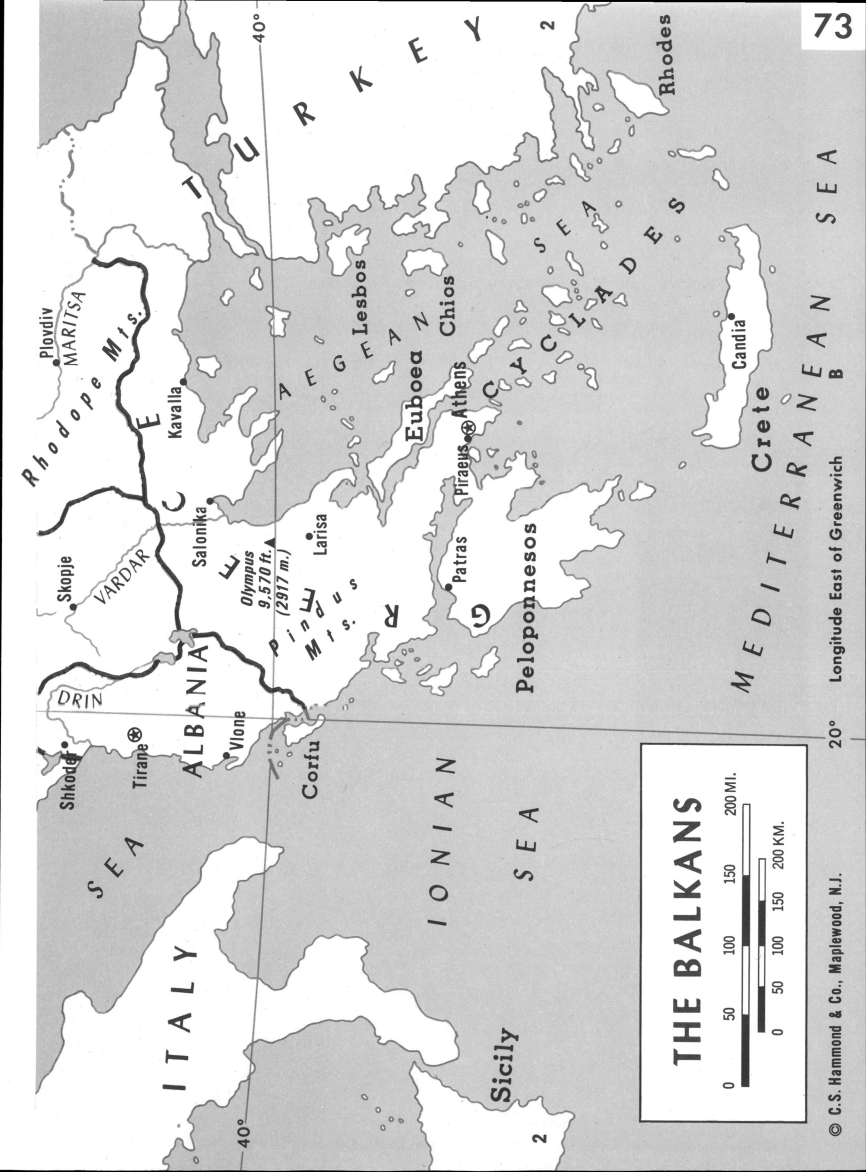

THE BALKANS

TURKEY

Rhodes

Plovdiv
MARITSA
Rhodope Mts.

Skopje
VARDAR

Kavalla

Salonika

Olympus
9,570 ft.
(2917 m.)
Larisa

Pindus Mts.

G R E E C E

Lesbos

A E G E A N S E A

Euboea
Chios

Athens
Piraeus

Patras

Peloponnesos

CYCLADES

Candia

Crete

M E D I T E R R A N E A N   S E A

Longitude East of Greenwich

DRIN

Shkoder

Tirane

ALBANIA

Vlone

Corfu

I O N I A N   S E A

Sicily

ITALY

S E A

40°

20°

40°

2

B

2

0	50	100	150	200 MI.
0	50	100	150	200 KM.

BALTIC SEA

Wolin

Koszalin

Słupsk

Gdynia

Gulf of Gdańsk

Gdańsk (Danzig)

Elbląg

Pomerania

Szczecin

Oder

Vistula

Gorzów Wielkopolski

Bydgoszcz

Toruń

Warta

Włocławek

Poznań

GERMANY

Zielona Góra

Kalisz

Łódź

Silesia

Neisse

Legnica

Warta

Wrocław

Wałbrzych

Oder

Częstochowa

Sudeten

Bytom

Małopols

Zabrze

Katowice

Cra

Mts.

CZECHOSLOVAKIA

Car Bes

Hi

Tatra

C

24°

D

UNION OF SOVIET SOCIALIST REPUBLICS

1

Olsztyn

Masurian

Lakes

Narew

Białystok

Bug

WARSAW

52°

Pilica

Vistula

Radom

Lublin

Lubelska

Hills

Kielce

ka Hills

Vistula

San

2

cow

Rzeszów

Tarnów

Przemyśl

pathian

kids

gh

Rysy

▲ 8,199 ft.(2499 m.)

C

24°

POLAND

0   25   50   75   100 MI.

0   25   50   75   100 KM.

© Copyright HAMMOND INCORPORATED, Maplewood, N.J.

② ①

0° 80° 0°
60° 20°
40°

NORWEGIAN SEA

SVALBARD

A
R
C
T
I
C

B 40°

C 60°

D 80°

FRANZ JOSEF LAND

BARENTS
SEA

NOVAYA ZEMLYA

0° NORTH
SEA

KARA SEA

N
O
R
W
A
Y

S
W
E
D
E
N

FINLAND

Kola
Pen.

BALTIC SEA

WHITE SEA

Archangel

POLAND

EST. S.S.R.
LAT. S.S.R.
LITH. S.S.R.

WHITE
RUSSIAN
S.S.R.
Minsk

Leningrad

MOSCOW ⊗

Yaroslavl

RUSSIAN

Salekhard S

20°
3

UKRAINIAN

Kiev

Gorkiy
VOLGA Kazan

Perm

SOVIET

OB

YENISEY

MOLD.
S.S.R.
Odessa

Kharkov
S.S.R.

DON

Saratov

Ufa

U
r
a
l

M
o
u
n
t
a
i
n
s

Sverdlovsk

Chelyabinsk

FEDE

Crimea

Rostov
Astrakhan

VOLGA
Volgograd

Kuybyshev

OB

BLACK
SEA

Caucasus

GEORGIAN
S.S.R.

URAL

KAZAKH

Omsk

IRTYSH

Barnaul

Novosibirsk

Novo

40°

TURKEY

ARM.
S.S.R.
AZER.
S.S.R.

C
A
S
P
I
A
N

SEA

Baku

ARAL
SEA

Karaganda

S. S. R.

LAKE
BALKHASH

C
H
I
N
A

40°

4

I
R
A
N

UZBEK S.S.R.

TURKMEN S.S.R.

Ashkhabad

Tashkent

Dushanbe

TADZHIK
S.S.R.

Alma-Ata

KIRGIZ
S.S.R.

Tian Shan

C. S. Hammond & Co., Maplewood, N.J.

AFGHANISTAN

D 80° E

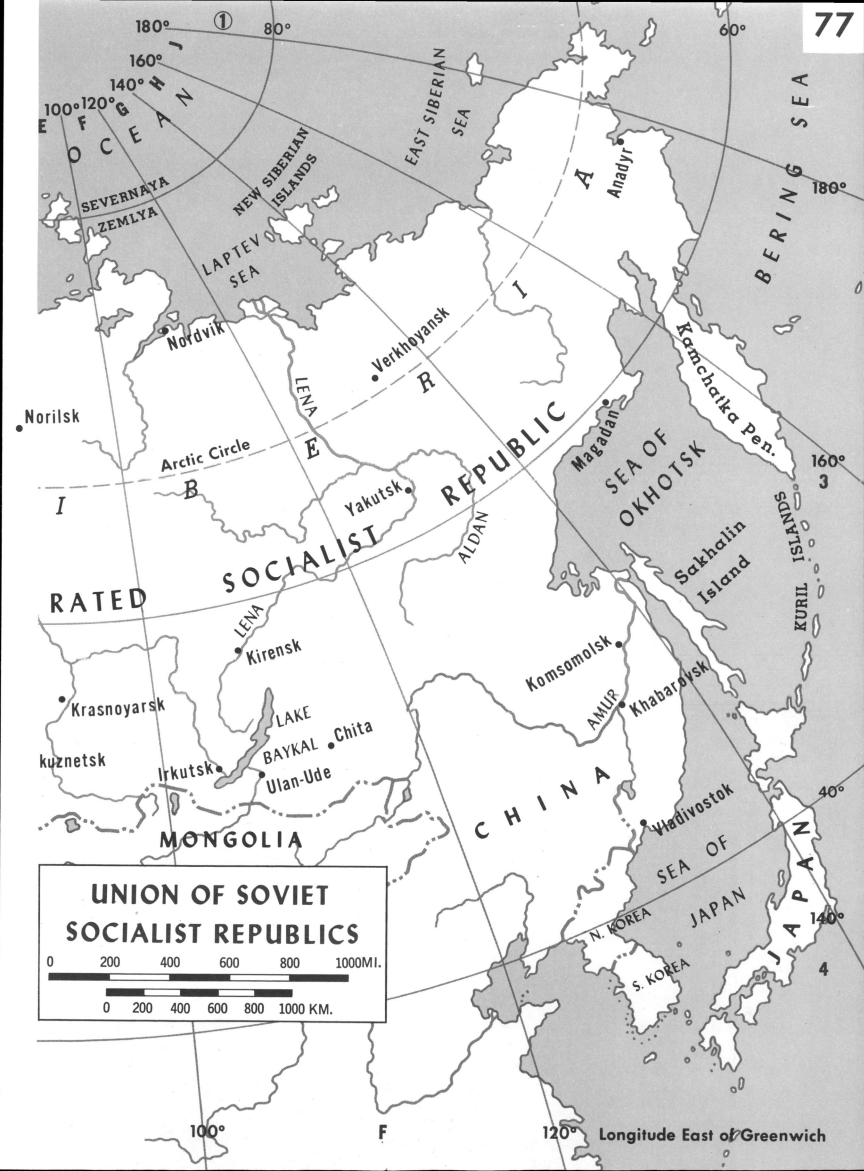

180° ① 80°

160°

140°

100°120° G

E F

OCEAN

60°

BERING SEA

180°

SEVERNAYA
ZEMLYA

NEW SIBERIAN ISLANDS

EAST SIBERIAN SEA

A

• Anadyr

LAPTEV SEA

I

• Nordvik

• Verkhoyansk

R

Kamchatka Pen.

160°

3

• Norilsk

LENA

E

• Magadan

SEA OF
OKHOTSK

Arctic Circle

B

I

SOCIALIST

• Yakutsk

ALDAN

REPUBLIC

Sakhalin
Island

KURIL ISLANDS

RATED

LENA

• Kirensk

Komsomolsk •

AMUR

• Khabarovsk

40°

• Krasnoyarsk

LAKE
BAYKAL • Chita

CHINA

kuznetsk

Irkutsk •

Ulan-Ude

• Vladivostok

MONGOLIA

SEA OF

JAPAN

JAPAN

140°

N. KOREA

S. KOREA

4

UNION OF SOVIET
SOCIALIST REPUBLICS

0   200   400   600   800   1000MI.

0   200   400   600   800   1000 KM.

100°

F

120° Longitude East of Greenwich

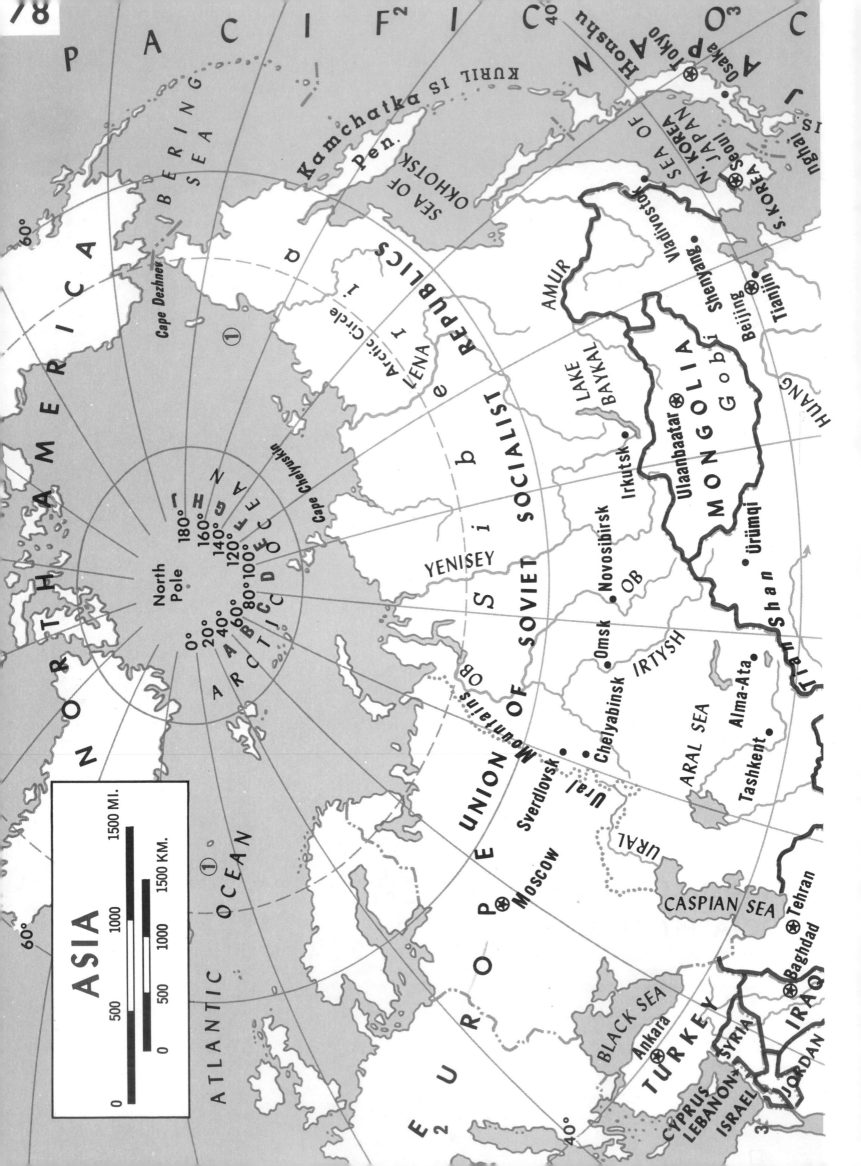

P A C I F I C² O C E A N³ C J

PACIFIC OCEAN

BERING SEA

Kamchatka Pen.

KURIL IS

SEA OF OKHOTSK

Cape Dezhnev

Cape Chelyuskin

Arctic Circle

A R C T I C O C E A N

North Pole

180° 160° 140° 120° 100° 80° 60° 40° 20° 0°

N O R T H   A M E R I C A

ATLANTIC OCEAN

LENA

YENISEY

OB

OB

Ural

URAL

Mountains

S i b e r i a

U N I O N   O F   S O V I E T   S O C I A L I S T   R E P U B L I C S

AMUR

LAKE BAYKAL

Irkutsk

Novosibirsk

Omsk

Chelyabinsk

IRTYSH

Sverdlovsk

Moscow

E U R O P E

CASPIAN SEA

BLACK SEA

Ankara

TURKEY

CYPRUS

LEBANON

ISRAEL

SYRIA

JORDAN

IRAQ

Baghdad

Tehran

Vladivostok

SEA OF JAPAN

N. KOREA

S. KOREA

Seoul

JAPAN

Honshu

Tokyo

Osaka

Shanghai

MONGOLIA

Ulaanbaatar

Gobi

Shenyang

Beijing

Tianjin

HUANG

Ürümqi

Tian Shan

Alma-Ata

Tashkent

ARAL SEA

40°

60°

60°

40°

ASIA

1500 MI.
1000
500
0

1500 KM.
1000
500
0

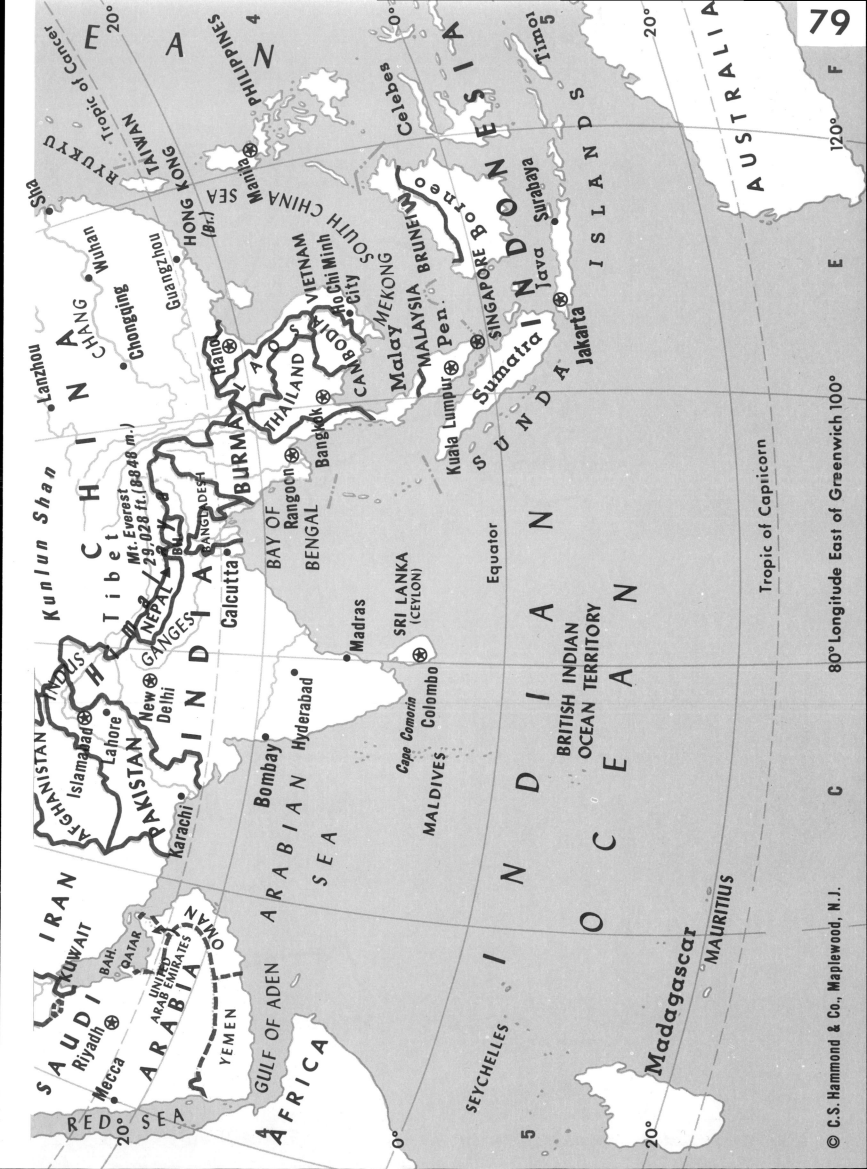

BOSPORUS BLACK SEA

Istanbul

U.S.S.R.

CASPIAN SEA

GREECE

Izmir

Ankara

TURKEY

Ararat 16,946 ft. (5165 m.)

ARAXES

Tabriz

Taurus Mts.

Elburz

Nicosia

Aleppo

Mosul

CYPRUS

SYRIA

TIGRIS

Teh

MEDITERRANEAN

EUPHRATES

SEA

Beirut

LEBANON

Damascus

Baghdad

Zagros Mts.

ISRAEL

Jerusalem

Amman

IRAQ

Is

SUEZ CANAL

JORDAN

Basra

Abadan

Neutral Zone

KUWAIT

PERSIAN

SAUDI

EGYPT

RED

Dhahran

BAHRAIN

QATAR

Medina

Riyadh

20°

Jidda

Mecca

ARABIA

Rub' al Kh

SEA

SUDAN

ETHIOPIA

San'a

YEMEN

Ta'izz

Aden

GULF OF ADEN

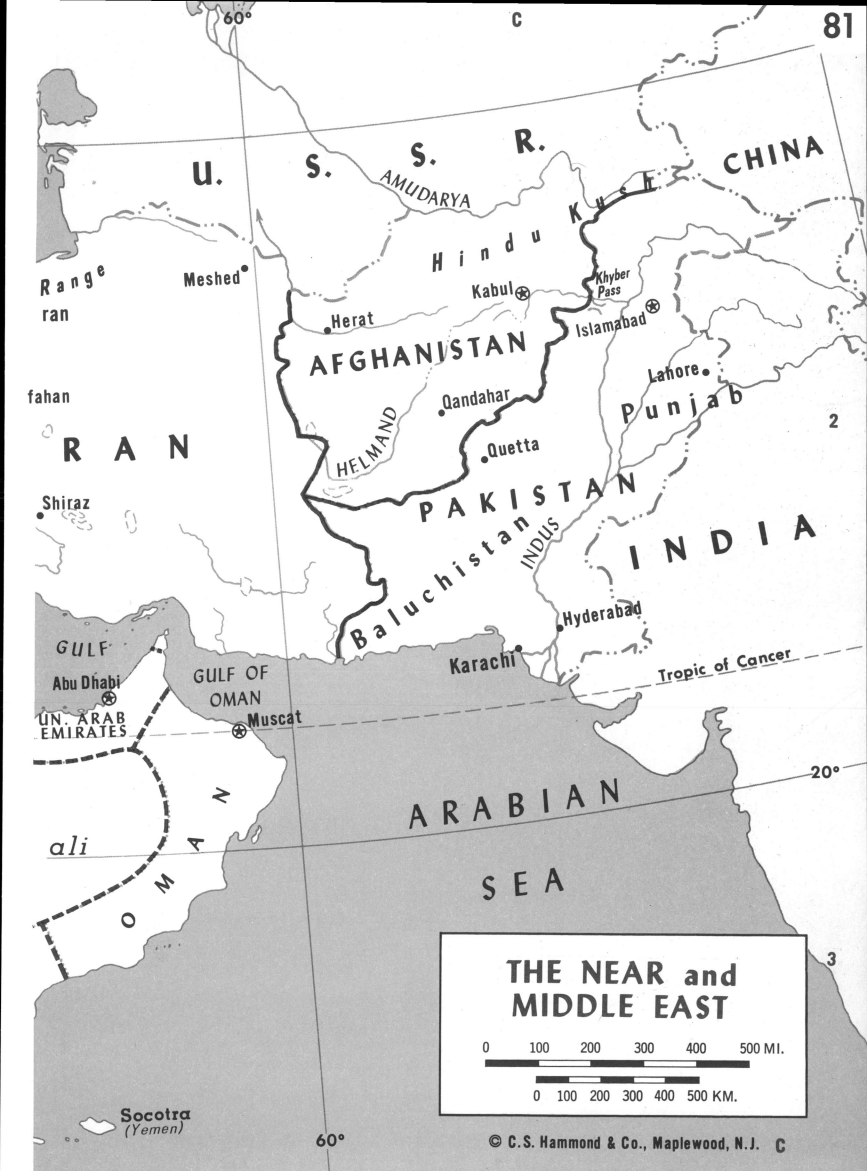

60°

C

U. S. S. R.

CHINA

AMUDARYA

R a n g e

ran

Meshed•

H i n d u   K u s h

Kabul ⊛

Khyber
Pass

fahan

Herat•

Islamabad ⊛

AFGHANISTAN

Lahore•

2

Qandahar•

P u n j a b

R A N

HELMAND

Quetta•

Shiraz•

P A K I S T A N

I N D I A

B a l u c h i s t a n

INDUS

GULF

Hyderabad•

Tropic of Cancer

Abu Dhabi
⊛

GULF OF
OMAN

Muscat

Karachi•

UN. ARAB
EMIRATES

⊛

20°

ali

O
M
A
N

A R A B I A N

S E A

THE NEAR and
MIDDLE EAST

0   100   200   300   400   500 MI.

3

0   100 200 300 400 500 KM.

Socotra
(Yemen)

60°

© C.S. Hammond & Co., Maplewood, N.J.   C

BULGARIA

B L A C K

B

Cape İnce

GREECE

İSTANBUL

Zonguldak

Bosporus

Sea of
Marmara

İzmit

Adapazarı

Koroglu Mts.

40°

Bursa

Sakarya

Kızılırmak

Dardanelles

Balıkesir

Eskişehir

Ankara ⊛

T U R

Gediz

Plateau

İzmir

of

Lake Tuz

A n a t o l i a

Menderes

Lake
Beyşehir

Konya

Seyhan

A E G E A N   S E A

Antalya

Taurus Mountains

Gulf of
Adalia

Mersin

Rhodes
(Greece)

Crete
(Greece)

35°

CYPRUS

Nicosia

Lata

⊛

Famagusta

M E D I T E R R A N E A N

(Br.)

Limassol

Tarabu

(Br.)

Beir

S E A

LEBANON

**TURKEY, SYRIA,
LEBANON and CYPRUS**

ISRAEL

0   50   100   150   200 MI.

0   50   100   150   200 KM.

30°

B

35°

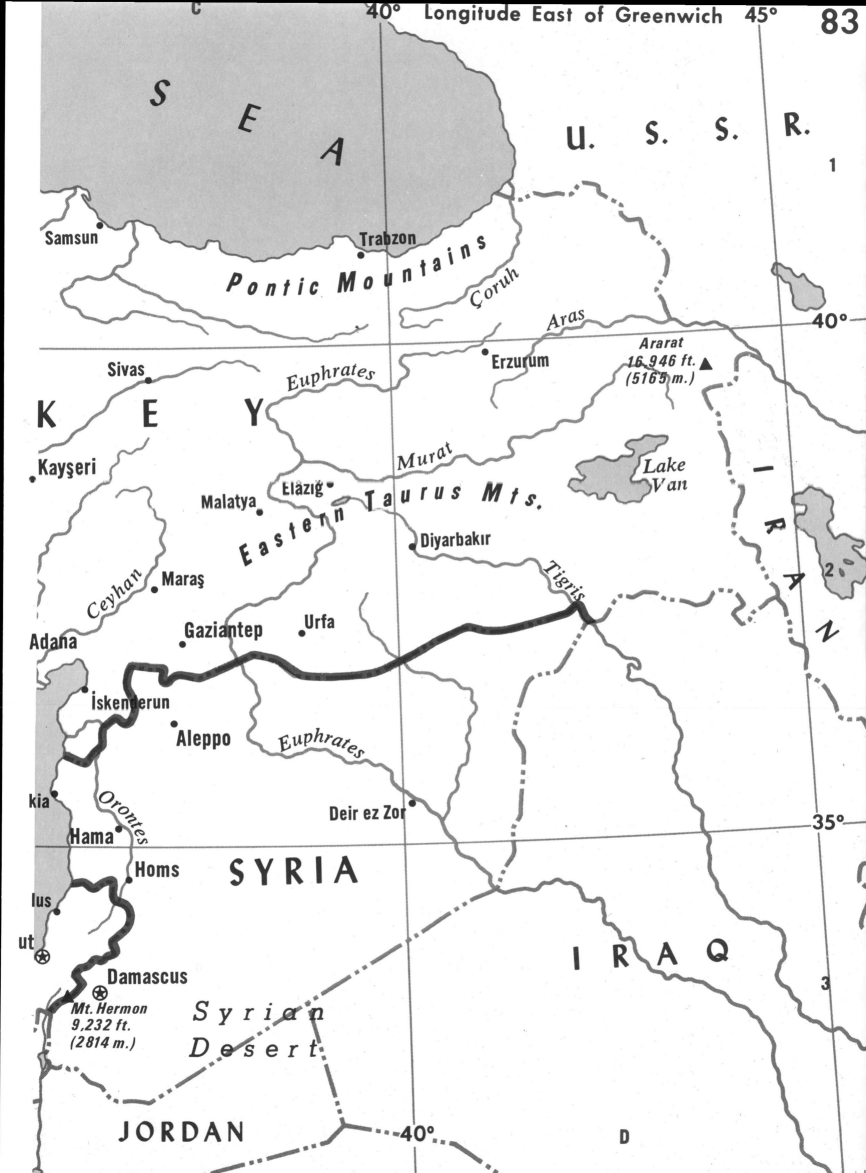

S E A

U. S. S. R.

1

Samsun

Trabzon

Pontic Mountains

Çoruh

Aras

40°

Sivas

Euphrates

Erzurum

Ararat
16,946 ft. ▲
(5165 m.)

K E Y

Kayşeri

Murat

Elâzığ

Lake
Van

I R A N

Malatya

Eastern Taurus Mts.

Diyarbakır

2

Ceyhan

Maraş

Tigris

Adana

Gaziantep

Urfa

İskenderun

Aleppo

Euphrates

kia

Oronte s

Deir ez Zor

35°

Hama

I R A Q

lus

Homs

SYRIA

ut ⊛

Damascus ⊛

3

▲ Mt. Hermon
9,232 ft.
(2814 m.)

Syrian
Desert

JORDAN

40°

D

MEDITERRANEAN SEA

LEBANON

S Y

Acre

Cape Carmel
Haifa

Tiberias

LAKE TIBERIAS
(SEA OF GALILEE)

Nazareth

YARMUK

Irbid

1

Netanya

Nablus

West
Bank

ZARQA

Es Salt

Ez Zarqa

JORDAN

Tel Aviv-Jaffa

32°

ISRAEL

Jericho

Amman ⊛

Jerusalem ⊛

Madaba

Ashqelon

Bethlehem

GAZA
STRIP

Hebron

DEAD

S Y r

R D

SEA

HABESOR

Beersheba

El Karak

HASA

J O

2

N
e
g
e
v

ARABA

PETRA

El
Jafr

EGYPT

Maan

30°

3

Elath

Aqaba

GULF OF
AQABA

A

34°

36°

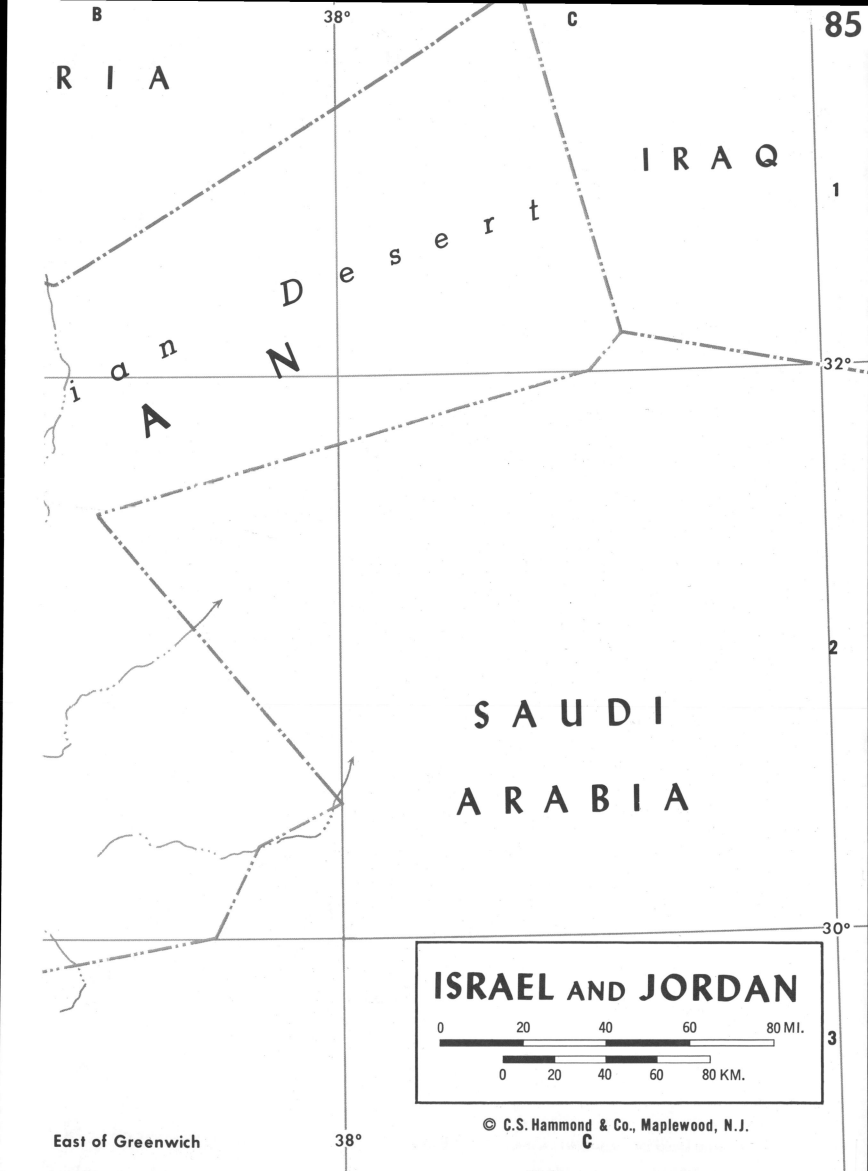

B 38° C **85**

R I A

I R A Q

i a n D e s e r t

A N

32°

1

2

S A U D I

A R A B I A

30°

ISRAEL AND JORDAN

| 0 | 20 | 40 | 60 | 80 MI. |

| 0 | 20 | 40 | 60 | 80 KM. |

3

© C.S. Hammond & Co., Maplewood, N.J.

C

East of Greenwich 38°

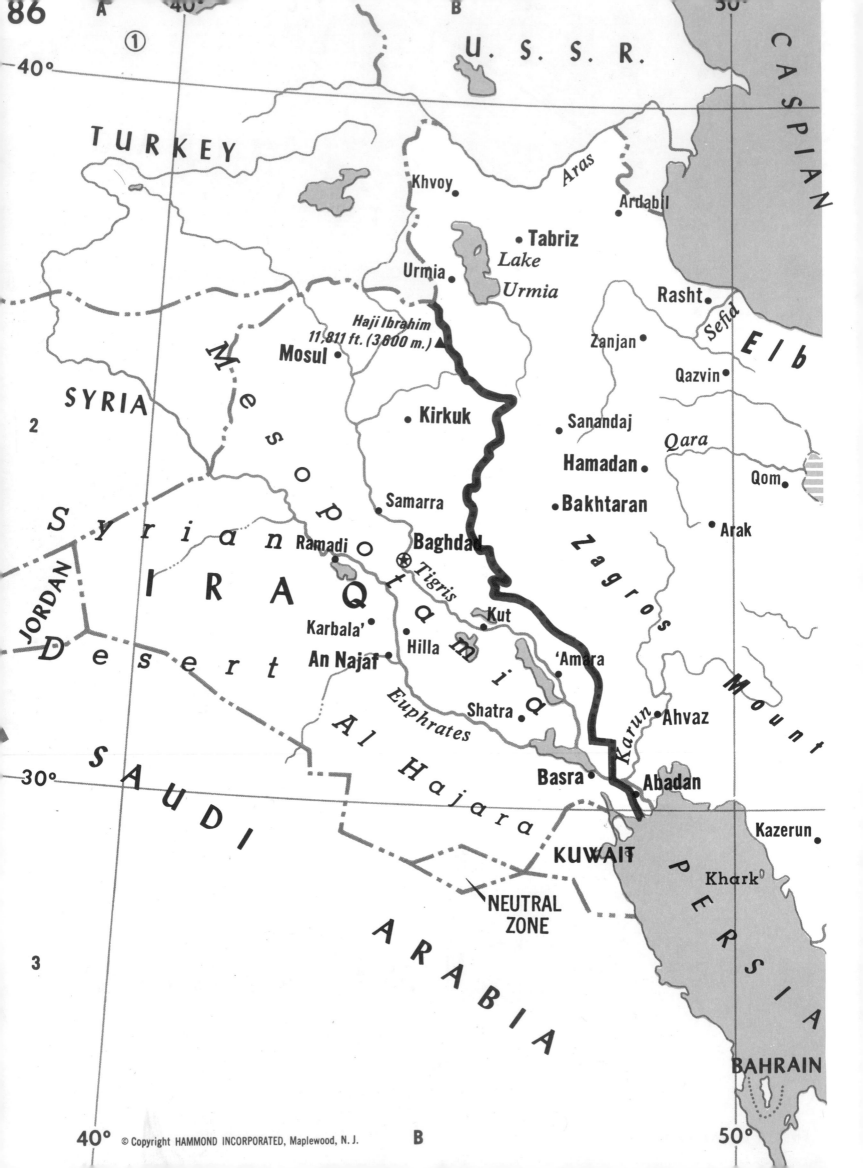

①

U. S. S. R.

CASPIAN

TURKEY

Khvoy

Aras

Ardabil

Tabriz

Urmia

Lake
Urmia

Rasht

Elb

SYRIA

Mosul

Haji Ibrahim
11,811 ft. (3,600 m.) ▲

Zanjan

Qazvin

Sefid

2

Mesopotamia

Kirkuk

Sanandaj

Hamadan

Qara

Qom

Bakhtaran

Arak

Samarra

Syrian

Ramadi

Baghdad

⊛ Tigris

Zagros

S

I R A Q

Karbala'

Hilla

Kut

Mount

JORDAN

Desert

An Najaf

i q

'Amara

Al Hajara

Shatra

Euphrates

Karun

Ahvaz

Basra

Abadan

SAUDI

30°

Kazerun

KUWAIT

P E R S I A

NEUTRAL
ZONE

Khark

3

A R A B I A

BAHRAIN

40°

B

50°

Longitude East of Greenwich 60° D 87

IRAN and IRAQ

0 100 200 300 MI.

0 100 200 300 KM.

U. S. S. R.

Atrek

SEA

Babol

urz Range

Damavand 18,376 ft. (5601 m.)

Sabzevar

Meshed

2

⊗ TEHRAN

Daryacheh-ye Namak

Dasht-e Kavir

Torbat-e Heydariyeh

Hari

Kashan

AFGHANISTAN

IRAN

Isfahan

Yazd

Birjand

Dasht-e Lut

Seistan

ains

Namakzar-e Shahdad

Kerman

30°

Shiraz

Mand

Zahedan

PAKISTAN

N

GULF

Bandar 'Abbas

3

Qishm I.

Str. of Hormuz (To Oman)

Baluchistan

QATAR

U.A.E.

GULF OF OMAN

D

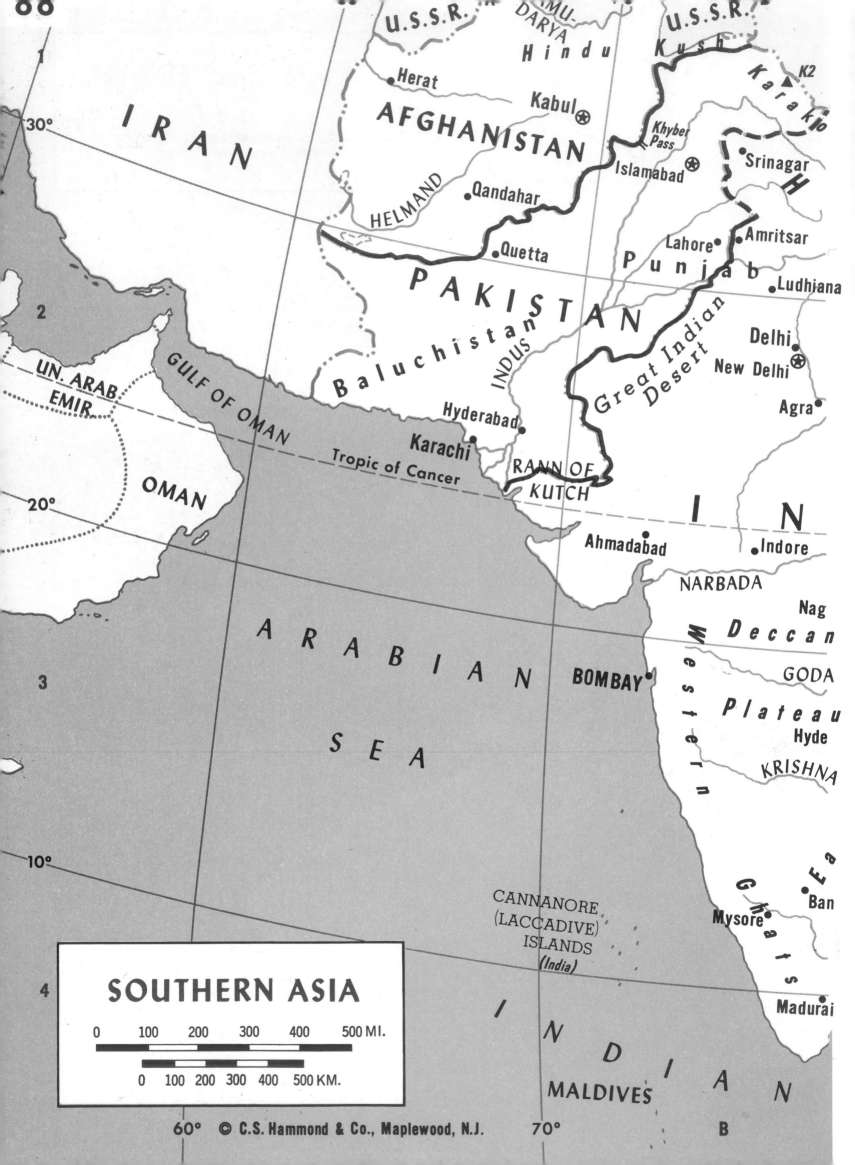

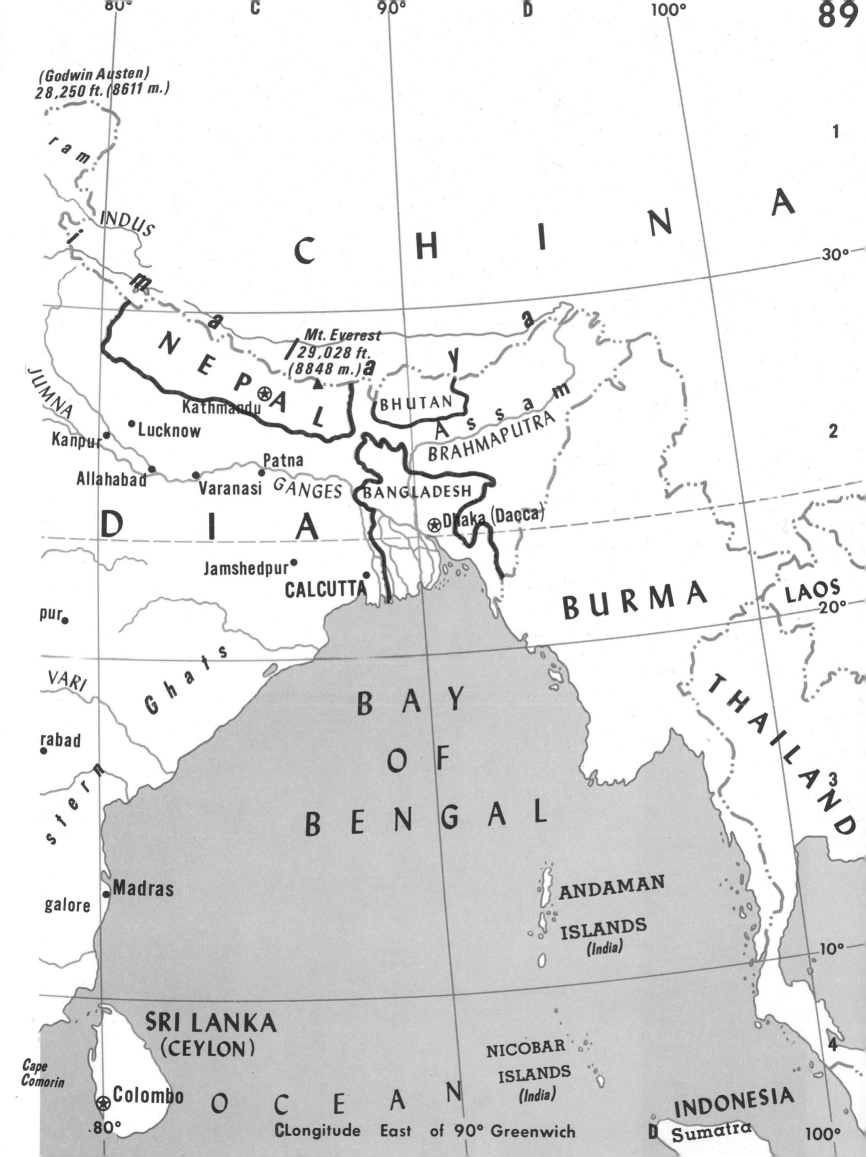

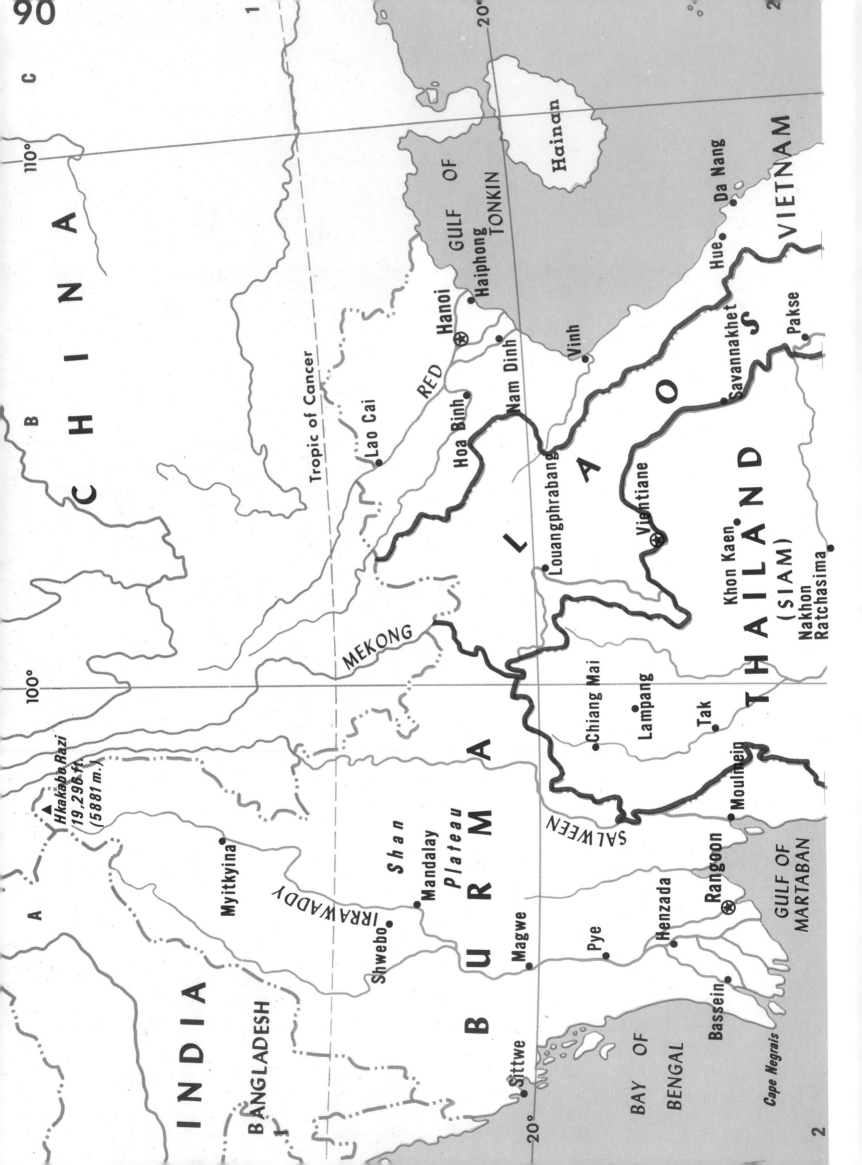

INDIA

BANGLADESH

CHINA

A

B

C

110°

100°

Tropic of Cancer

Hkakabo Razi
19,296 ft.
(5,881 m.)

Myitkyina

Shwebo

Mandalay

IRRAWADDY

Shan

Plateau

Magwe

Pye

Henzada

BURMA

Sittwe

Bassein

Cape Negrais

BAY OF
BENGAL

Rangoon

Moulmein

GULF OF
MARTABAN

SALWEEN

Lao Cai

Hoa Binh

RED

Hanoi

Haiphong

GULF OF
TONKIN

Nam Dinh

Vinh

Hainan

MEKONG

Louangphrabang

Vientiane

L A O S

Da Nang

Hue

VIETNAM

Pakse

Savannakhet

Chiang Mai

Lampang

Tak

Khon Kaen

Nakhon
Ratchasima

THAILAND

(SIAM)

Moulmein

20°

100°

20°

1

2

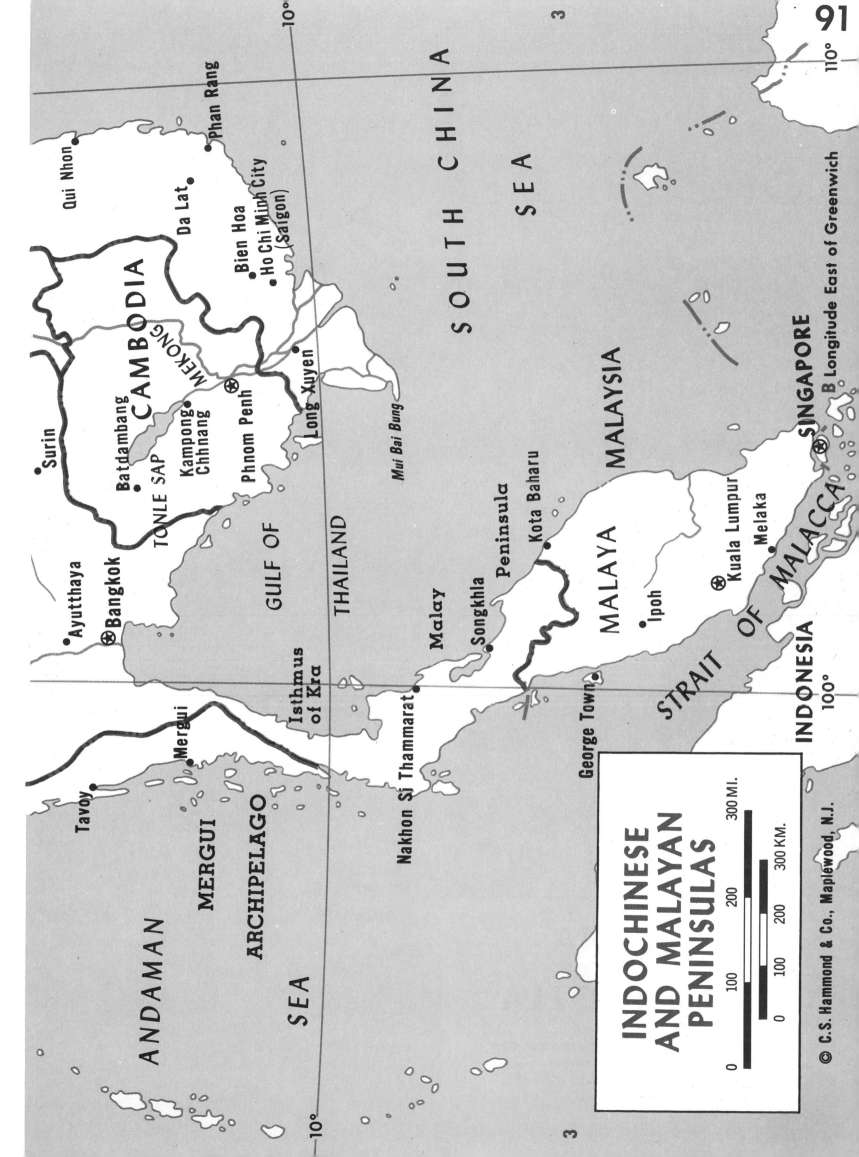

INDOCHINESE AND MALAYAN PENINSULAS

© C.S. Hammond & Co., Maplewood, N.J.

0   100   200   300 MI.

0   100   200   300 KM.

SOUTH CHINA SEA

ANDAMAN SEA

MERGUI ARCHIPELAGO

GULF OF THAILAND

STRAIT OF MALACCA

Qui Nhon

Phan Rang

Da Lat

Bien Hoa
Ho Chi Minh City
(Saigon)

CAMBODIA

MEKONG

Surin

Batdambang

TONLE SAP

Kampong
Chhnang

Phnom Penh

Long Xuyen

Ayutthaya

Bangkok

THAILAND

Isthmus
of Kra

Tavoy

Merqui

Nakhon Si Thammarat

Mui Bai Bung

Malay

Songkhla

Peninsula

Kota Baharu

George Town

MALAYSIA

MALAYA

Ipoh

Kuala Lumpur

Melaka

SINGAPORE

INDONESIA

100°

110°

B Longitude East of Greenwich

10°

10°

3

3

1

LAKE
BALKHASH

UNION

OF

SOVIET

A l t a i

SO

• Uliastay

Ulaa

MONGO

M t s.

G

Yining

Ürümqi

T i a n   S h a n

40°

X i n j i a n g

Kashi

Taklimakan Shamo

Yumen •

HUANG

Hotan •

K u n l u n   S h a n

H

I

2

I

N

D

I

A

m

a

T

i

C

b

e

t

H

CHANG

t

Qamdo

Gongga
24,79
(7556

N

E

P

A

L

a

y

Lhasa

Mt. Everest
29,028 ft (8848 m.)

BH.

a

BRAHMAPUTRA

BANG.

Kunming

MEKONG

Tropi

CHINA
AND
MONGOLIA

0   200   400   600 MI.

0   200   400   600 KM.

BURMA

LAOS

3

C

LAKE BAYKAL

CIALIST

120°

Da Hingan Ling

D

REPUBLICS

AMUR

SONGHUA

1

Choybalsan

Qiqihar

nbaatar

Harbin

LIA

Jilin

o b i

Changchun

Fushun

40°

Inner Mongolia

Shenyang

SEA OF

JAPAN

Anshan

NORTH

KOREA

Baotou

BEIJING

Dalian

SOUTH

KOREA

Tianjin

Taiyuan

Zibo

Jinan

Qingdao

YELLOW

SEA

Lanzhou

(YELLOW)

HUANG

Zhengzhou

Xuzhou

Xi'an

Luoyang

N

A

Nanjing

SHANGHAI

EAST

CHINA

Wuhan

CHANG

Hangzhou

SEA

Chengdu

Shan

0 ft.

Chongqing

Nanchang

Wenzhou

RYUKYU ISLANDS

m.)

Changsha

PACIFIC

Fuzhou

Guiyang

Taipei

OCEAN

TAIWAN STRAIT

Xiamen

TAIWAN

(Formosa)

20°

c of Cancer

Guangzhou
(Canton)

Shantou

Nanning

HONG KONG
(Br.)

Macau
(Port.)

SOUTH

CHINA

SEA

PHILIPPINES

VIETNAM

Hainan

C

120° Longitude East of Greenwich

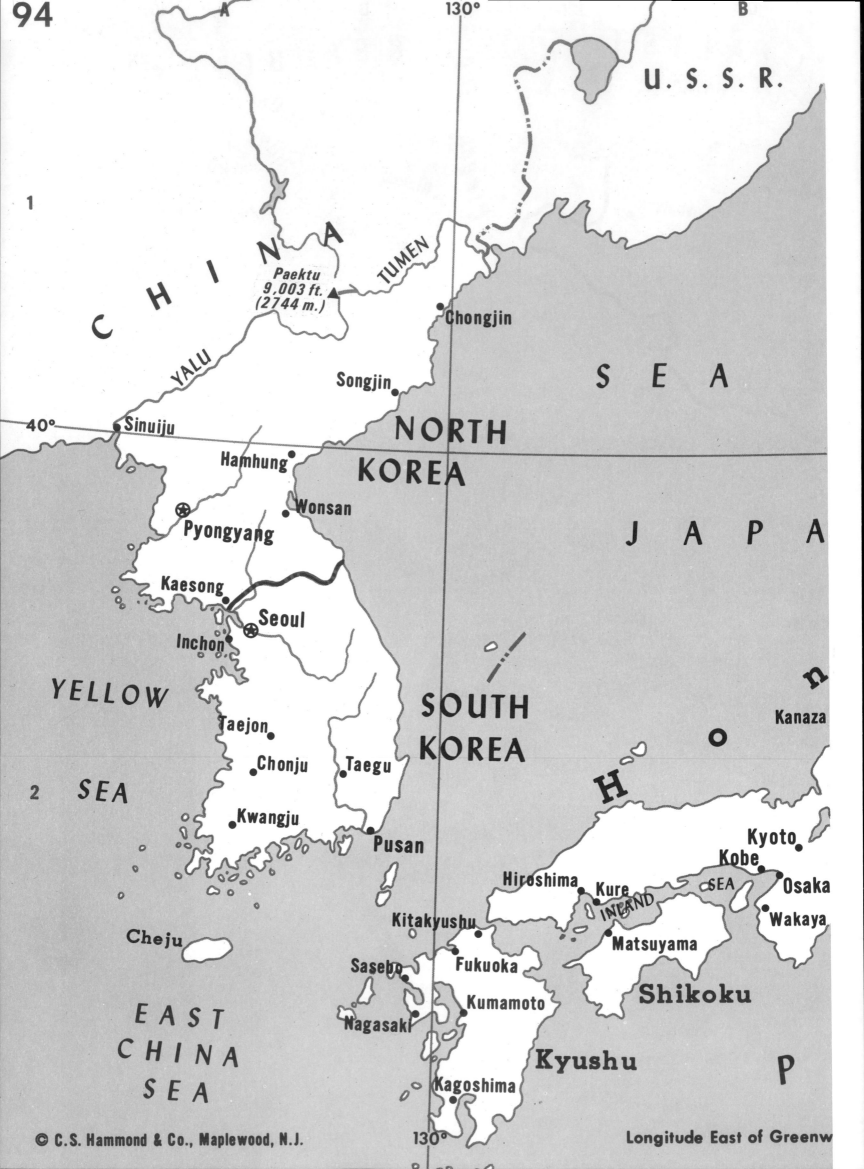

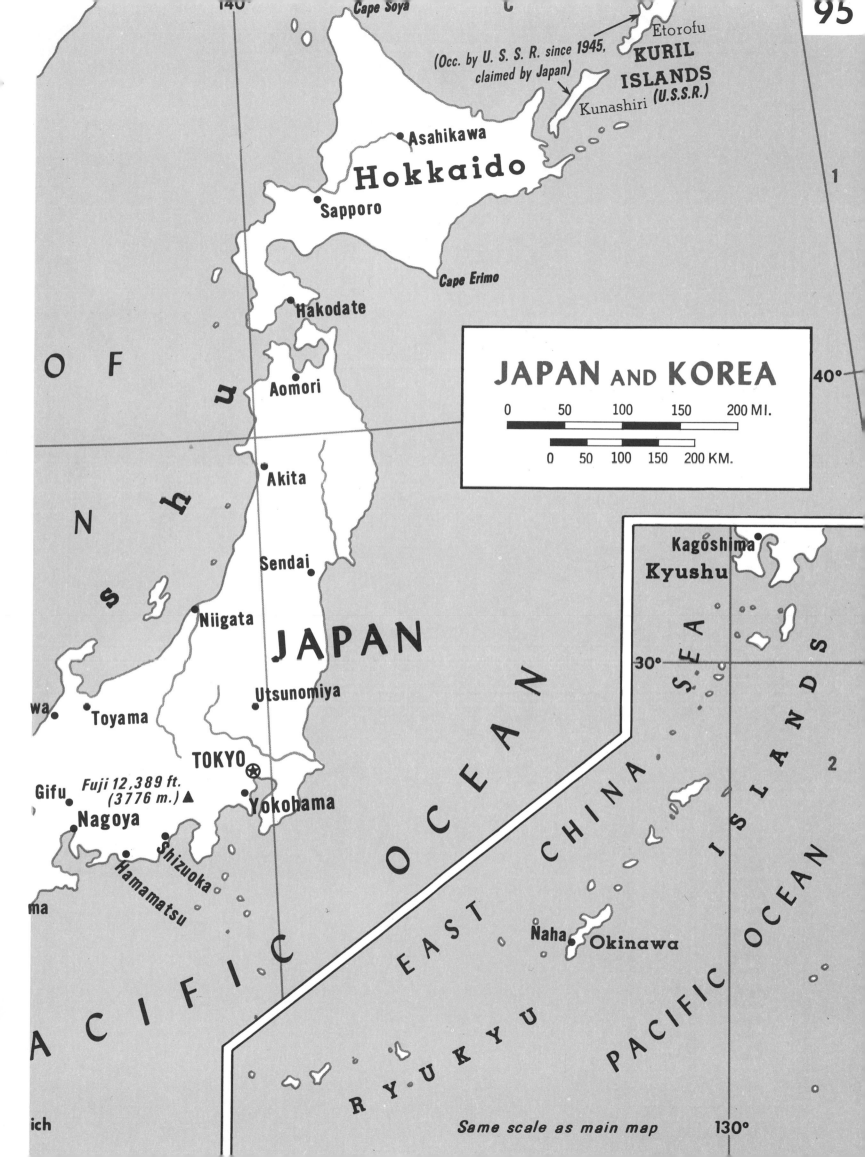

Cape Soya

Etorofu
**KURIL
ISLANDS**
(U.S.S.R.)

*(Occ. by U.S.S.R. since 1945,
claimed by Japan)*

Kunashiri *(U.S.S.R.)*

1

• Asahikawa

Hokkaido

• Sapporo

Cape Erimo

• Hakodate

• Aomori

40°

```
JAPAN AND KOREA

0      50     100    150    200 MI.

0    50    100   150   200 KM.
```

Kagoshima
Kyushu

• Akita

• Sendai

• Niigata

JAPAN

• Utsunomiya

30°

wa • • Toyama

TOKYO ⊗

*Fuji 12,389 ft.
(3776 m.)* ▲

Gifu •   • Yokohama

Nagoya

Shizuoka

Hamamatsu

ma

Naha • Okinawa

P A C I F I C   O C E A N

E A S T   C H I N A   S E A

I S L A N D S

2

R Y U K Y U

P A C I F I C   O C E A N

Same scale as main map

130°

140

O F

N

s

h

u

ich

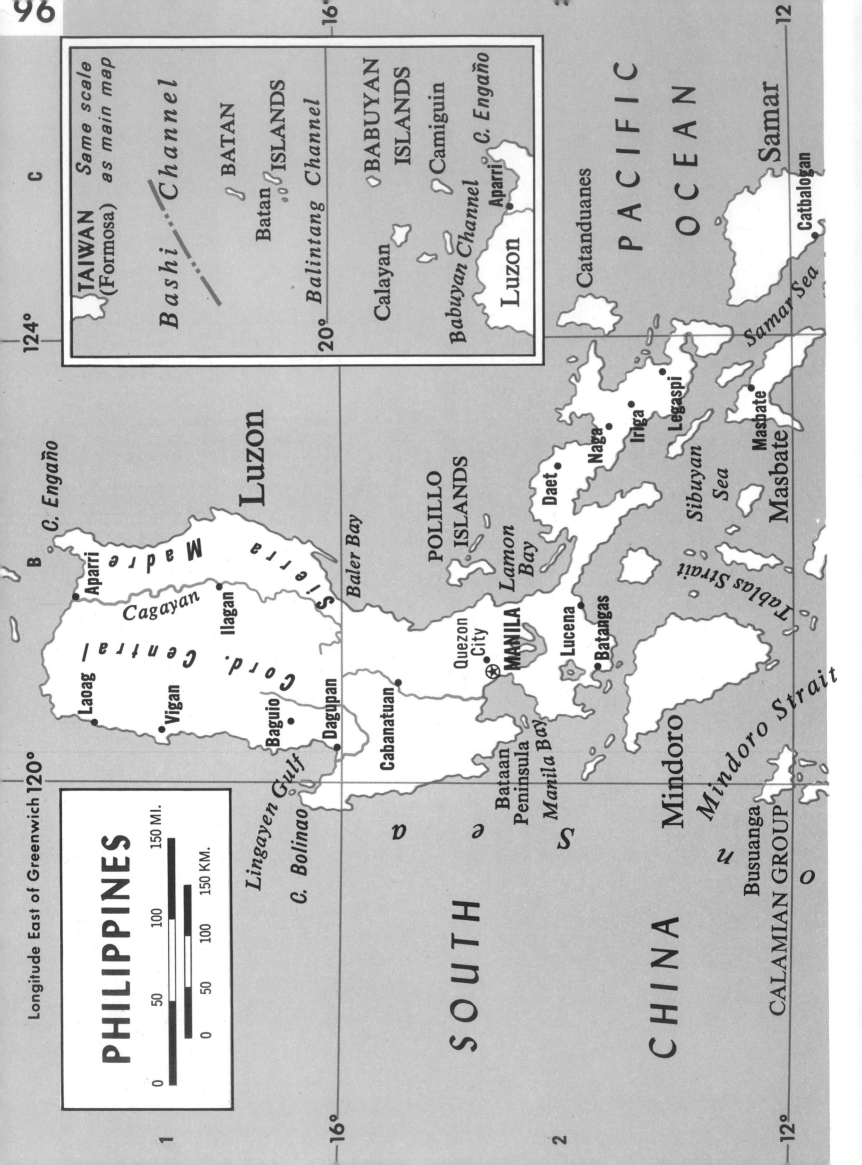

PHILIPPINES

Longitude East of Greenwich

0   50   100   150 MI.

0   50   100   150 KM.

TAIWAN (Formosa)   *Same scale as main map*

Bashi Channel

BATAN ISLANDS
Batan

Balintang Channel

BABUYAN ISLANDS
Camiguin
Calayan
Babuyan Channel
Aparri   C. Engaño

Luzon

C. Engaño
Aparri

Cagayan
Ilagan
Sierra Madre
Central Cord.
Laoag
Vigan
Baguio
Dagupan
Cabanatuan
Lingayen Gulf
C. Bolinao

Luzon

Baler Bay

POLILLO ISLANDS

Lamon Bay

Quezon City
MANILA
Lucena
Batangas
Bataan Peninsula
Manila Bay

Daet
Naga
Iriga
Legaspi

Catanduanes

PACIFIC OCEAN

Samar
Catbalogan

Samar Sea

Sibuyan Sea
Masbate
Masbate

Tablas Strait

SOUTH CHINA SEA

Mindoro

Mindoro Strait

Busuanga
CALAMIAN GROUP

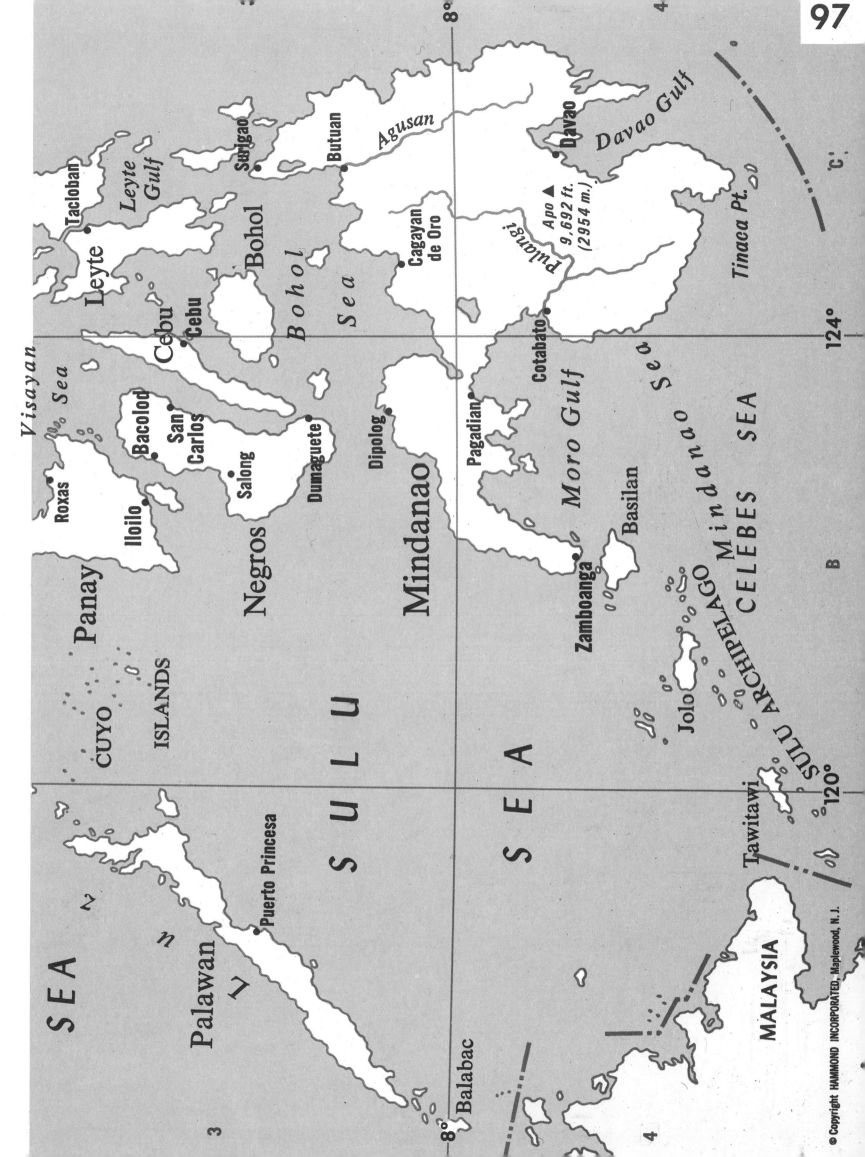

INDIA

BANG.

IRRAWADDY

CHINA

Mandalay

BURMA

20°

SALWEEN

Chiang Mai

RED

Hanoi ⊛ • Haiphong
GULF OF
TONKIN

HONG KONG
(Br.)

Rangoon ⊛

Moulmein •

Vientiane ⊛

Vinh

L A O S

MEKONG

Hainan

THAILAND
(SIAM)

Bangkok •

ANDAMAN

2

Isthmus
of Kra
SEA

Hue •

• Da Nang

VIETNAM

• Qui Nhon

CAMBODIA

Phnom Penh ⊛

GULF OF
THAILAND

Ho Chi Minh
City

Manila ⊛

S O U T H   C H I N A   S E A

Palawan

SULU
SEA

Malay

George Town •

MALAYA

Medan •

STRAIT OF MALACCA

Kuala
Lumpur ⊛

Sumatra

Peninsula

M A L A Y S I A

Bandar Seri Begawan

BRUNEI

⊙Kota Kinabalu

SABAH

Basilan •

CELE

SEA

Kuching

0°

Pontianak

⊛ SINGAPORE

SUNDA

Palembang •

Bangka

Banjarmasin •

SARAWAK

Borneo

Kalimantan

MAKASSAR STRAIT

Celebes

3

INDIAN

Jakarta ⊛

J A V A   S E A

Bandung •

J a v a

• Surabaya

Ujung Pandang •

FLORES

Sumbawa

Flores

OCEAN

I S L A N D S

• Bali

Sumba

100°

120°

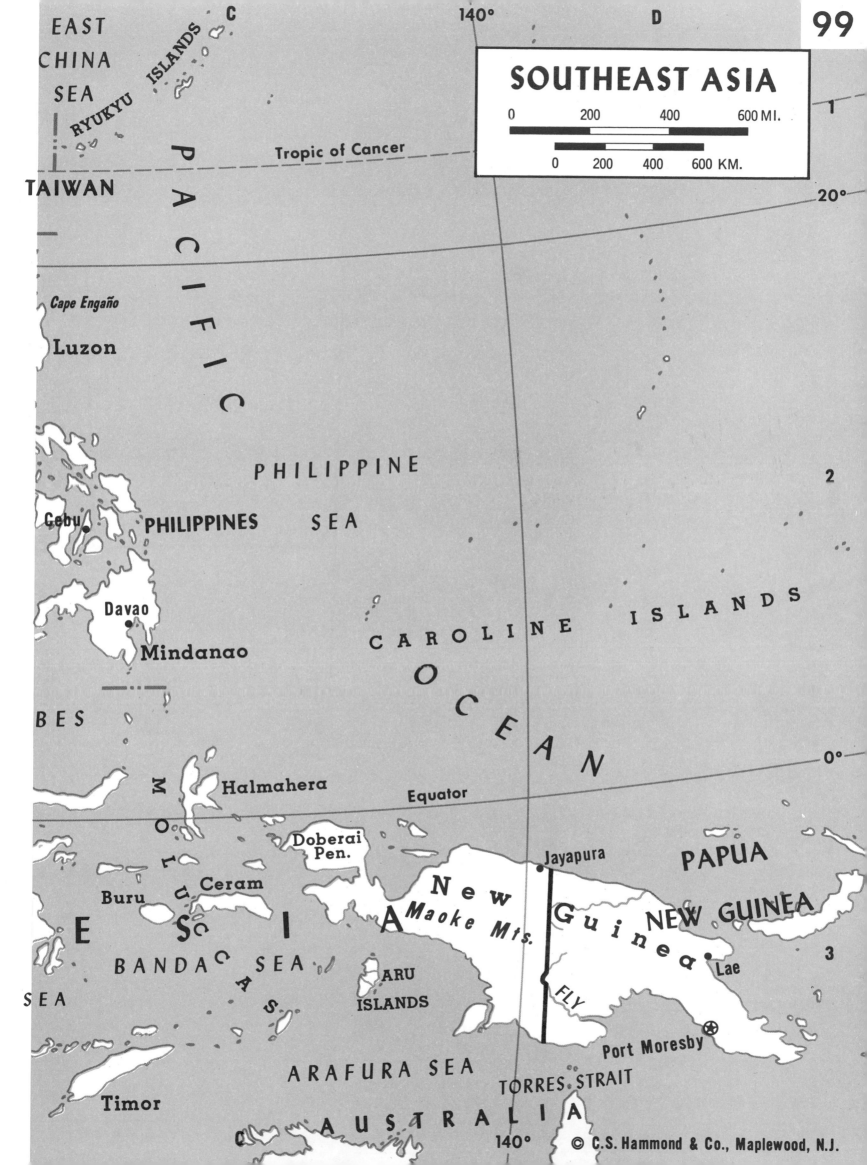

EAST
CHINA
SEA

RYUKYU ISLANDS

C

140°

D

1

Tropic of Cancer

TAIWAN

20°

PACIFIC

Cape Engaño

Luzon

PHILIPPINE

2

Cebu

PHILIPPINES

SEA

Davao

C A R O L I N E   I S L A N D S

Mindanao

O C E A N

BES

0°

Halmahera

Equator

Doberai
Pen.

Jayapura

PAPUA

Ceram

M
O
L
U
C
C
A
S

A

N e w

G u i n e a

NEW GUINEA

Buru

Maoke Mts.

E S I A

Lae

3

BANDA   SEA

ARU
ISLANDS

FLY

SEA

Port Moresby

ARAFURA SEA

TORRES STRAIT

Timor

A U S T R A L I A

140°

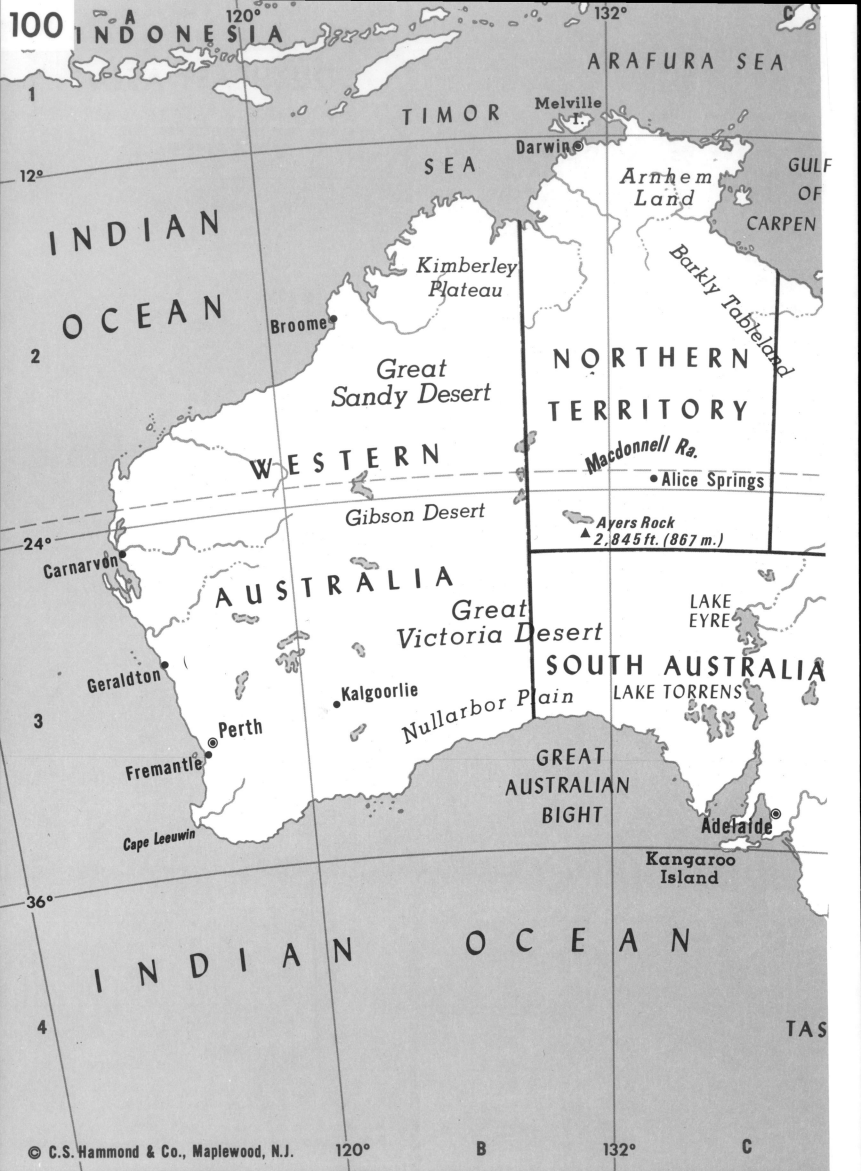

INDONESIA

A 120°

132° C

ARAFURA SEA

TIMOR

Melville I.

12°

SEA

Darwin⊙

GULF OF CARPEN

Arnhem Land

INDIAN

Kimberley Plateau

NORTHERN

OCEAN

Broome

Barkly Tableland

2

Great Sandy Desert

TERRITORY

WESTERN

Macdonnell Ra.

• Alice Springs

Gibson Desert

Ayers Rock
▲ 2,845 ft. (867 m.)

24°

Carnarvon

AUSTRALIA

LAKE EYRE

Great
Victoria Desert

SOUTH AUSTRALIA

Geraldton

LAKE TORRENS

3

• Kalgoorlie

Nullarbor Plain

⊚ Perth

Fremantle

GREAT
AUSTRALIAN
BIGHT

Adelaide ⊚

Cape Leeuwin

Kangaroo Island

36°

INDIAN OCEAN

4

TAS

120° B 132° C

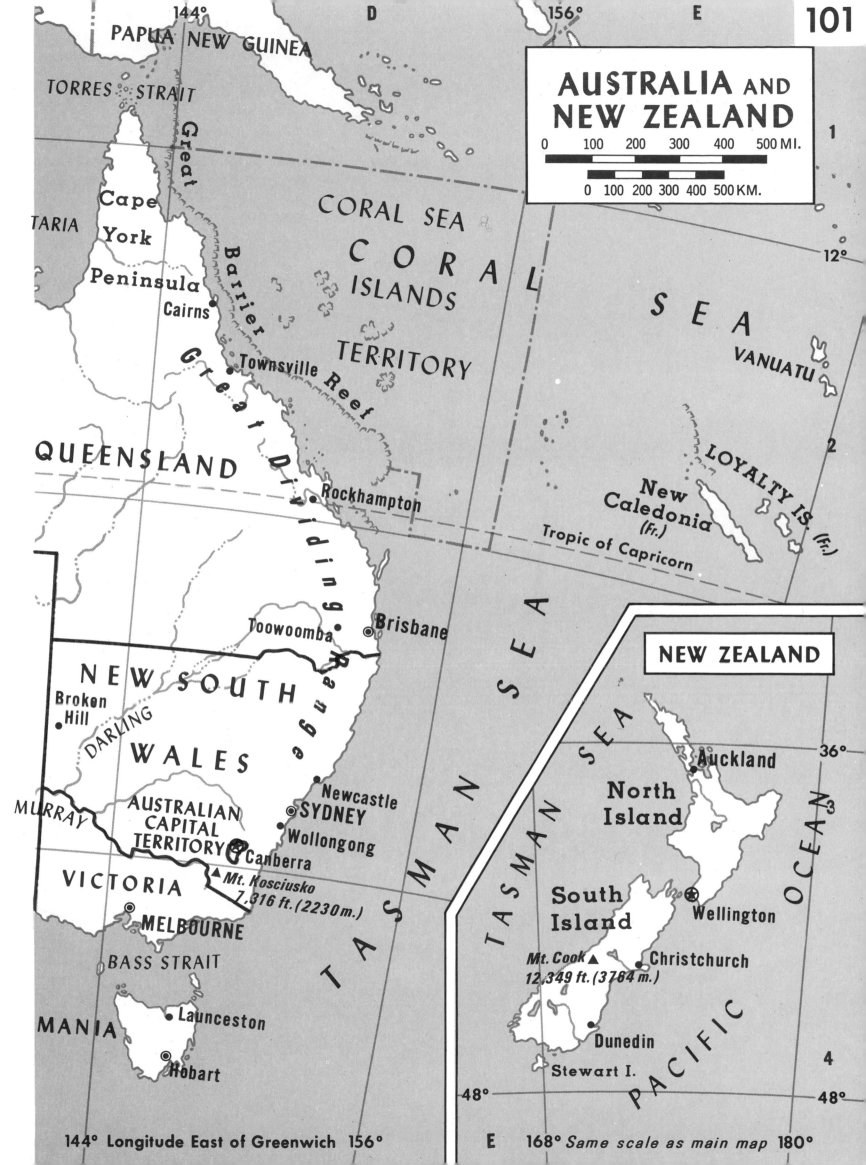

144°

PAPUA NEW GUINEA

TORRES STRAIT

TARIA

Cape
York
Peninsula

Cairns

Great

Barrier

Reef

Townsville

QUEENSLAND

Great Dividing Range

Rockhampton

CORAL SEA

CORAL
ISLANDS

TERRITORY

D

156° E

AUSTRALIA AND
NEW ZEALAND

0   100   200   300   400   500 MI.

0 100 200 300 400 500 KM.

1

12°

SEA

VANUATU

2

LOYALTY IS. (Fr.)

New
Caledonia
(Fr.)

Tropic of Capricorn

Toowoomba

Brisbane

NEW SOUTH

Broken
Hill

DARLING

WALES

MURRAY

AUSTRALIAN
CAPITAL
TERRITORY

Newcastle

SYDNEY

Wollongong

Canberra

Mt. Kosciusko
7,316 ft. (2230 m.)

VICTORIA

MELBOURNE

BASS STRAIT

MANIA

Launceston

Hobart

TASMAN SEA

NEW ZEALAND

TASMAN SEA

Auckland

North
Island

36°

South
Island

Mt. Cook ▲
12,349 ft. (3764 m.)

Wellington

Christchurch

PACIFIC OCEAN

3

Dunedin

Stewart I.

48°

48°

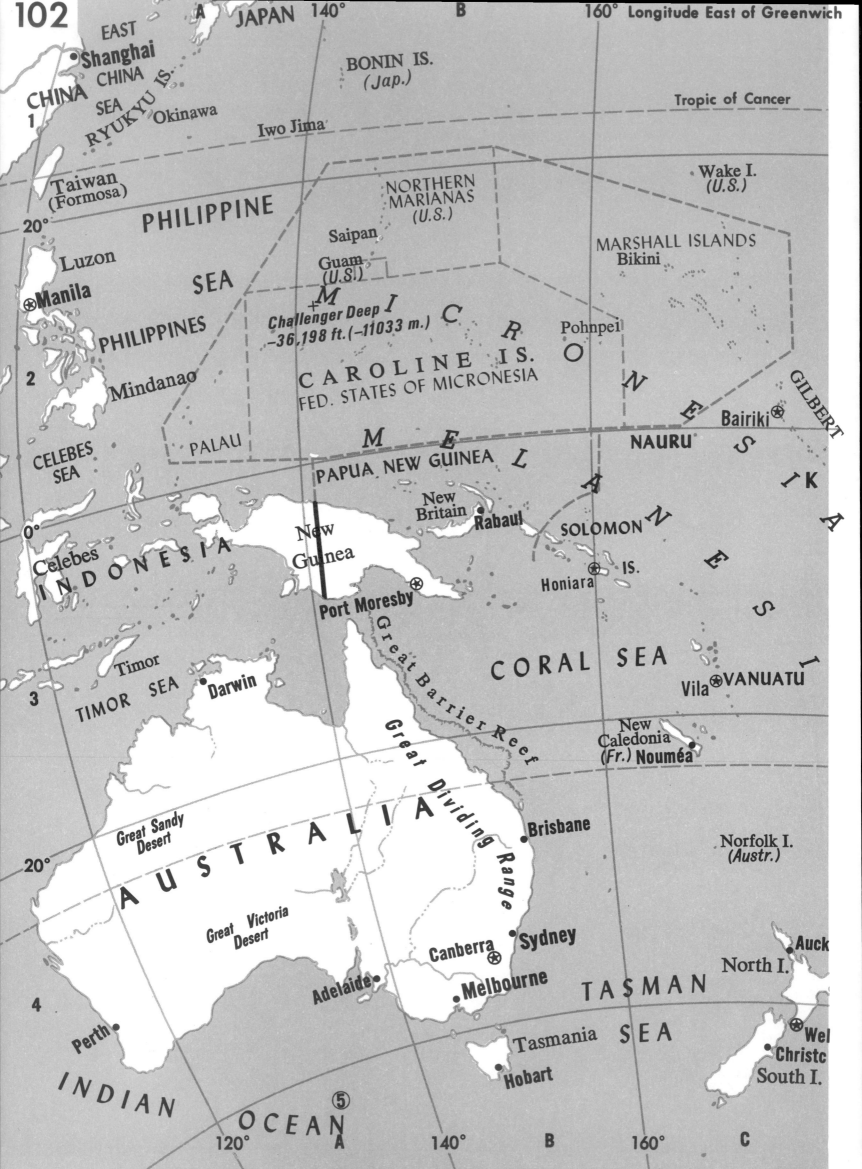

EAST
Shanghai JAPAN 140° 160° Longitude East of Greenwich
CHINA CHINA
CHINA SEA BONIN IS.
(Jap.)
1 RYUKYU IS. Okinawa
Iwo Jima Tropic of Cancer

Taiwan Wake I.
(Formosa) NORTHERN (U.S.)
20° PHILIPPINE MARIANAS
(U.S.)
Luzon Saipan MARSHALL ISLANDS
SEA Guam Bikini
⊗**Manila** (U.S.)
M
PHILIPPINES +*Challenger Deep* I C R O
2 *—36,198 ft. (—11033 m.)* Pohnpei
CAROLINE IS. N
Mindanao FED. STATES OF MICRONESIA E
S
CELEBES Bairiki⊗ GILBERT
SEA PALAU M E L A NAURU I A
PAPUA NEW GUINEA A K
New N
0° Britain E
Celebes New Rabaul SOLOMON S
Guinea ⊗ Honiara IS. I
INDONESIA A
⊗
Port Moresby
Timor CORAL SEA
TIMOR SEA •Darwin Great Barrier Reef Vila⊗VANUATU
3
New
Caledonia
(Fr.)**Nouméa**

Great Dividing Range
Great Sandy •Brisbane
Desert Norfolk I.
20° A U S T R A L I A (Austr.)
Great Victoria
Desert •Sydney Auck
Canberra⊗ North I.
Adelaide• •Melbourne T A S M A N
4
SEA
Perth• Tasmania Wel
Hobart Christc
INDIAN ⑤ South I.
OCEAN A B C
120° 140° 160°

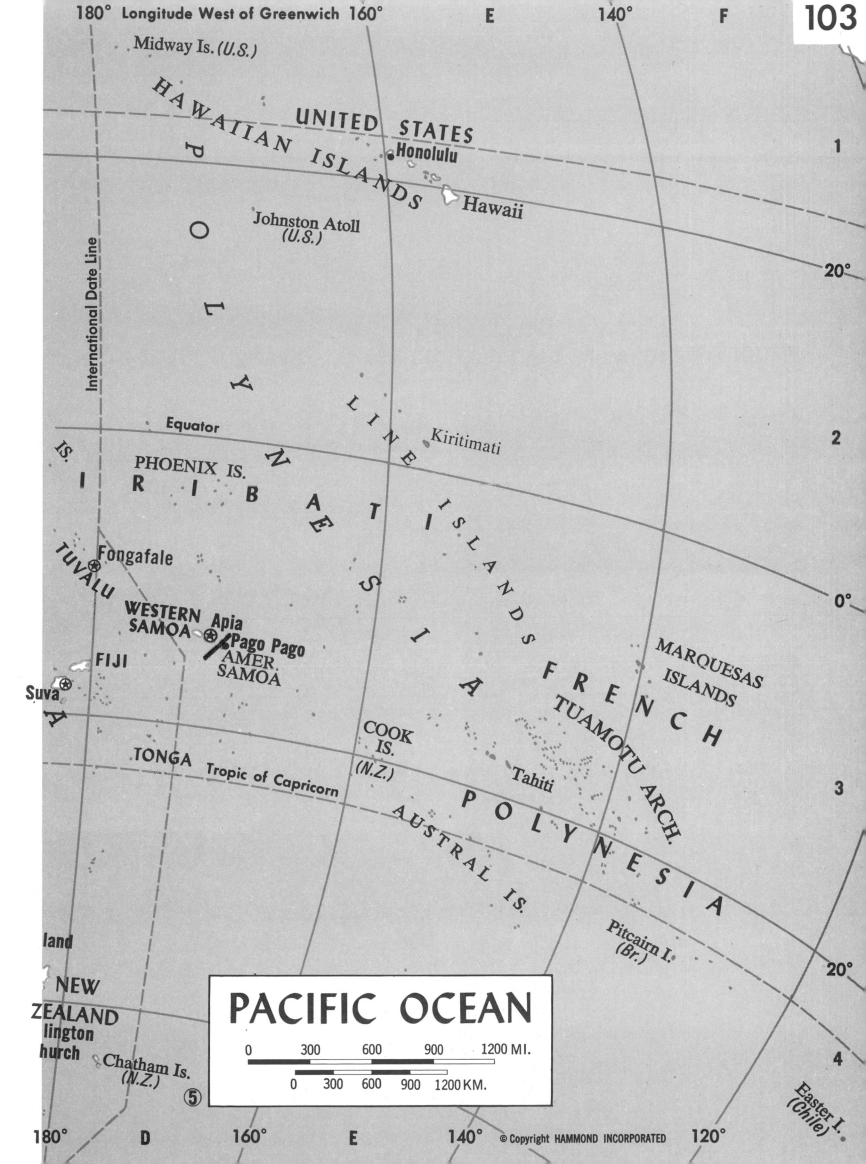

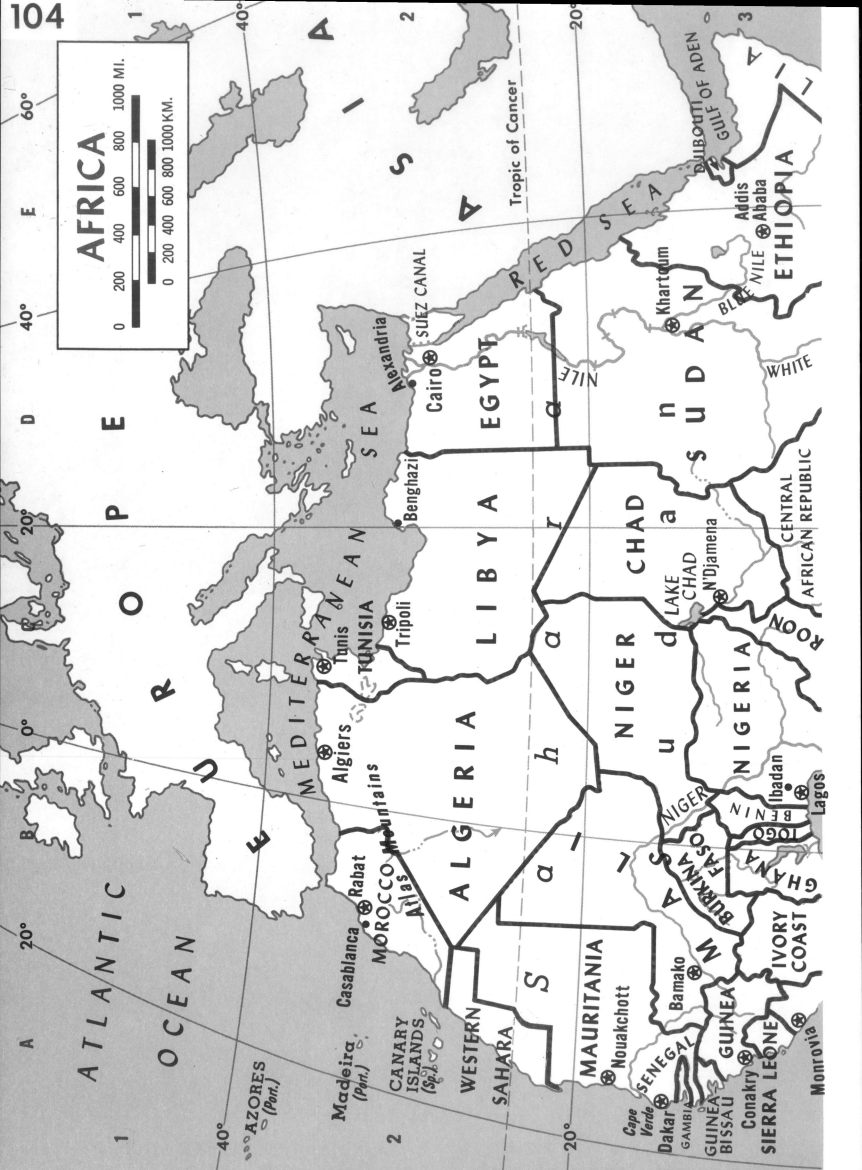

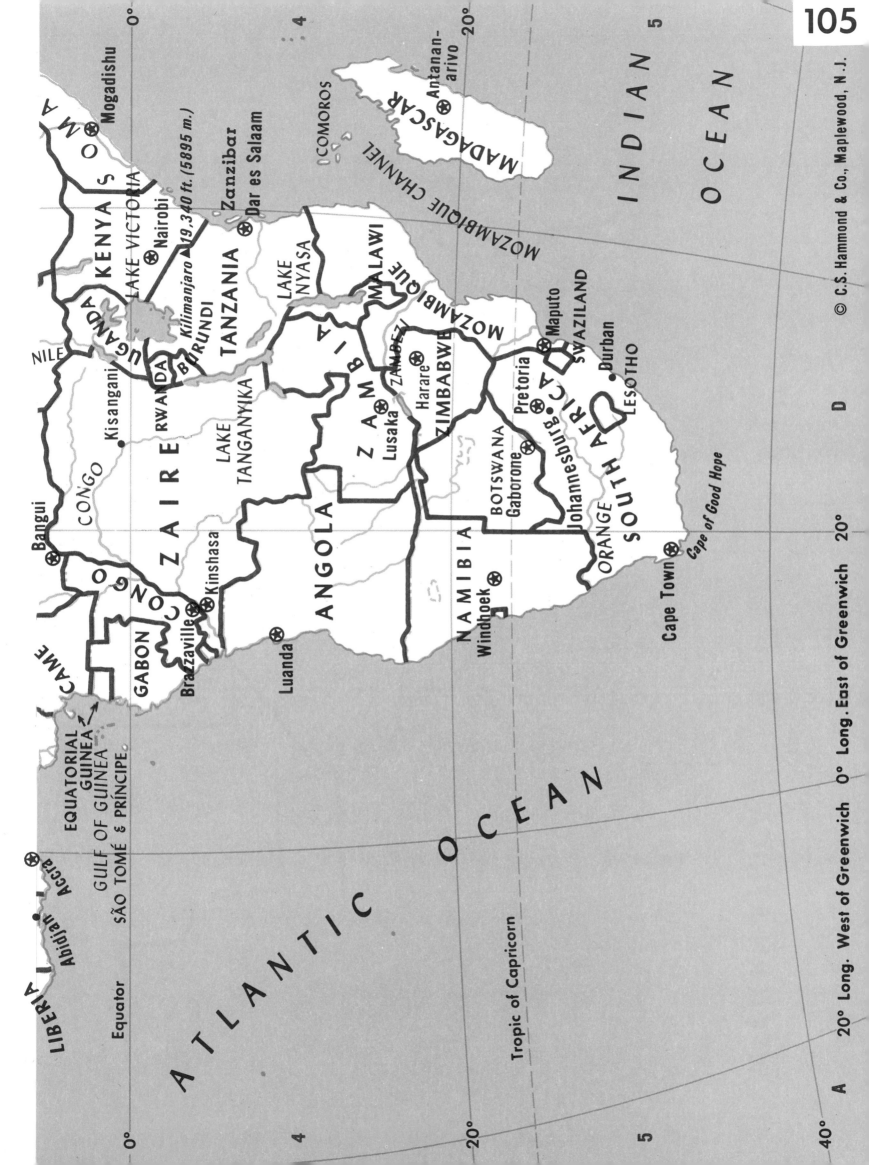

INDIAN OCEAN

MADAGASCAR

⊛ Antanan-arivo

COMOROS

MOZAMBIQUE CHANNEL

© C.S. Hammond & Co., Maplewood, N.J.

SOMA

⊛ Mogadishu

Zanzibar

⊛ Dar es Salaam

KENYA

LAKE VICTORIA

⊛ Nairobi

Kilimanjaro ▲ 19,340 ft. (5895 m.)

BURUNDI

UGANDA

NILE

RWANDA

TANZANIA

LAKE NYASA

MALAWI

MOZAMBIQUE

SWAZILAND

⊛ Maputo

Durban

ZAIRE

Kisangani

CONGO

LAKE TANGANYIKA

ZAMBIA

ZAMBEZI

Harare ⊛

ZIMBABWE

Lusaka ⊛

Pretoria ⊛

Johannesburg ⊛

LESOTHO

Bangui ⊛

ANGOLA

BOTSWANA

Gaborone ⊛

ORANGE

SOUTH AFRICA

CONGO

Kinshasa ⊛

Brazzaville ⊛

NAMIBIA

Windhoek ⊛

Cape of Good Hope

GABON

Luanda ⊛

Cape Town ⊛

CAME

EQUATORIAL GUINEA

GULF OF GUINEA

SÃO TOMÉ & PRÍNCIPE

LIBERIA

⊛ Accra

Abidjan

ATLANTIC OCEAN

Equator

Tropic of Capricorn

20° Long. West of Greenwich 0° Long. East of Greenwich 20°

0° 4 20° 5

A 20° 4 20° 5 40°

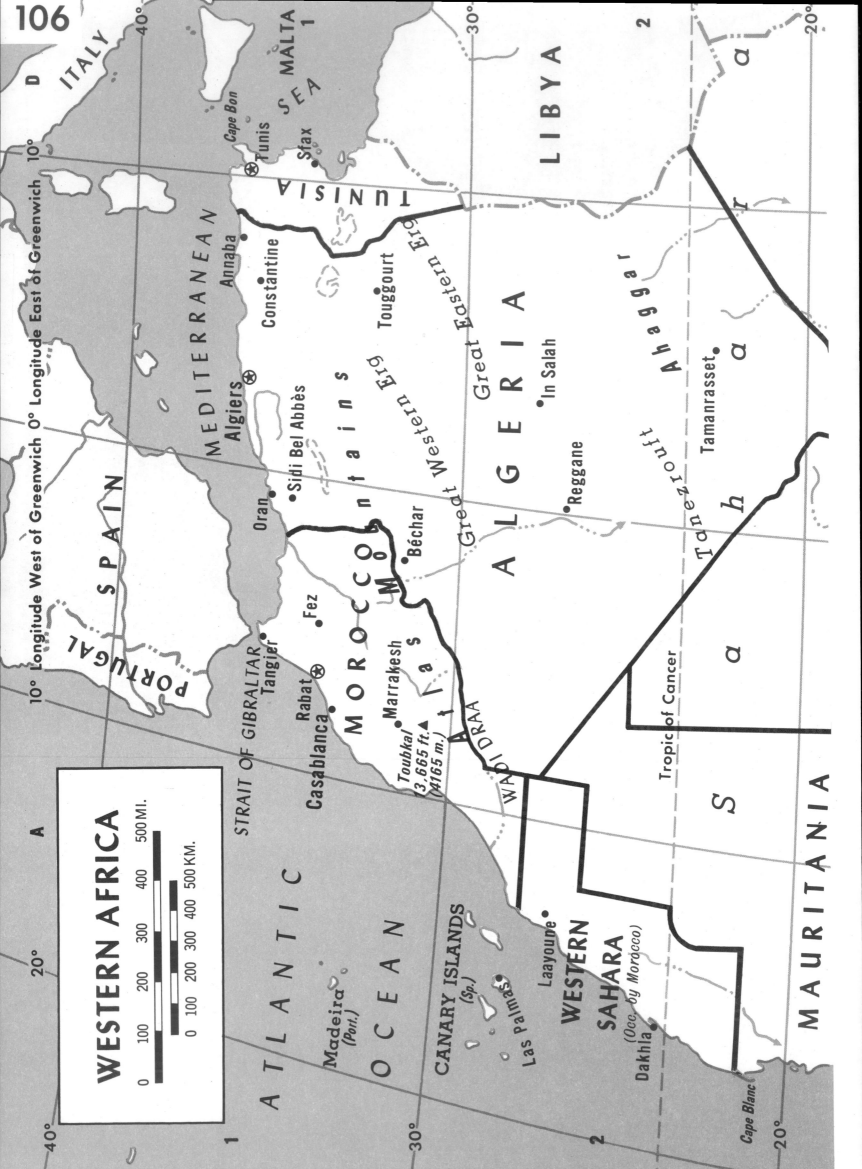

WESTERN AFRICA

500 MI.
400
300
200
100
0

500 KM.
400
300
200
100
0

ITALY

D

MALTA

Cape Bon

Tunis

Sfax

MEDITERRANEAN SEA

TUNISIA

LIBYA

Longitude West of Greenwich 0° Longitude East of Greenwich

SPAIN

PORTUGAL

MEDITERRANEAN

Annaba

Constantine

Touggourt

Great Eastern Erg

ALGERIA

Ahaggar

In Salah

Tamanrasset

Algiers

Sidi Bel Abbès

Oran

Great Western Erg

Béchar

Reggane

Tanezrouft

STRAIT OF GIBRALTAR

Tangier

Fez

MOROCCO

Mountains

A t l a s

Rabat

Casablanca

Marrakesh

Toubkal
3,665 ft.▲
(4165 m.)

WADI DRAA

Tropic of Cancer

S a h a r a

MAURITANIA

ATLANTIC

OCEAN

Madeira
(Port.)

CANARY ISLANDS
(Sp.)

Las Palmas

Laayoune

WESTERN
SAHARA
(Occ. by Morocco)

Dakhla

Cape Blanc

A

1

2

40°

30°

20°

10°

20°

30°

40°

10°

20°

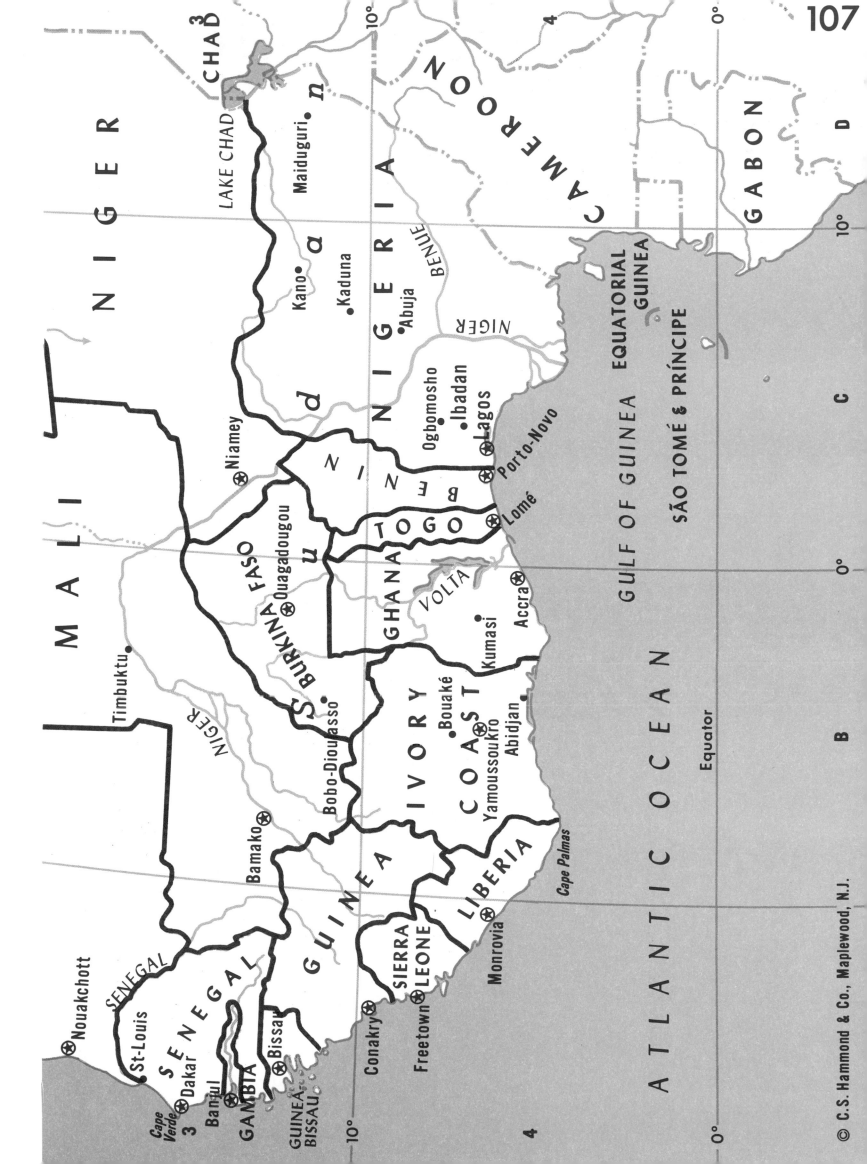

NIGER

CHAD

LAKE CHAD

MALI

Maiduguri•

Kano•

•Kaduna

N I G E R I A

•Abuja

BENUE

CAMEROON

GABON

Ogbomosho•
•Ibadan
Lagos
⊛ Porto-Novo

NIGER

EQUATORIAL GUINEA

SÃO TOMÉ & PRÍNCIPE

Niamey
⊛

BENIN

⊛ Lomé

TOGO

GULF OF GUINEA

BURKINA FASO

Ouagadougou
⊛

GHANA

VOLTA

Accra
⊛

Kumasi
•

Timbuktu•

NIGER

Bobo-Dioulasso•

I V O R Y

C O A S T

•Bouaké

Yamoussoukro
⊛ Abidjan

ATLANTIC OCEAN

Equator

Bamako
⊛

G U I N E A

LIBERIA

Cape Palmas

Nouakchott
⊛

SENEGAL

St-Louis

S E N E G A L

Dakar•
⊛

Banjul
⊛

GAMBIA

Bissau
⊛

GUINEA-
BISSAU

Conakry
⊛

SIERRA
LEONE

Freetown
⊛

Monrovia
⊛

Cape Verde

3

4

10°

0°

10°

0°

10°

0°

D

C

B

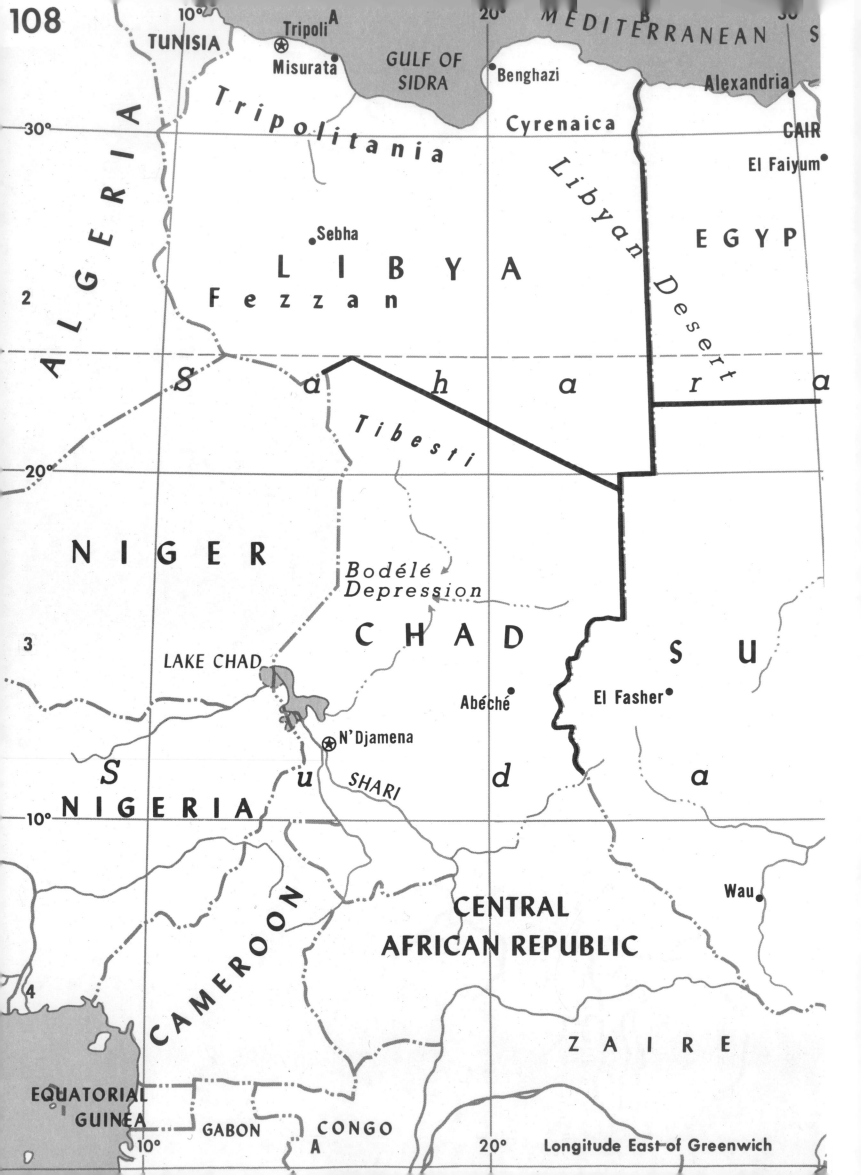

EA ISRAEL

Port Said

SUEZ CANAL

JORDAN

40°

IRAQ

D

50°

30°

NORTHEASTERN AFRICA

0   100   200   300   400   500 MI.

0   100 200 300 400 500 KM.

Sinai Pen.

El Minya

Asyut

T

ASWAN HIGH DAM

Aswan

LAKE NASSER

Nubian Desert

Tropic of Cancer

SAUDI

ARABIA

BAHRAIN

QATAR

U. A. E.

20°

Port Sudan

ATBARA

Eritrea

RED SEA

YEMEN

3

Omdurman

Khartoum

Kassala

D   A   N

Asmara

Wad Medani

BLUE NILE

Ras Dashan
15,157 ft. ▲
(4620 m.)

LAKE TANA

GULF OF ADEN

El Obeid

n

Ethiopian

DJIBOUTI

Djibouti

Dessye

Malakal

ETHIOPIA

Dire Dawa

10°

Addis Ababa ⊗

Harar

Highlands

WHITE NILE

Jimma

WEBI SHABELLE

S   O   M   A   L   I   A

INDIAN

4

Juba

UGANDA

KENYA

OCEAN

© C.S. Hammond & Co., Maplewood, N.J.

30°   D   40°   E   50°

YEMEN

GULF OF ADEN

Ras Asér

1

DJIBOUTI

• Berbera   10°

ETHIOPIA   • Harghessa

WEBI SHABELLE

2

WHITE NILE

LAKE
TURKANA
(RUDOLF)

SOMALIA

UGANDA   KENYA

SE SEKO
LBERT)

Kampala ⊛   Kisumu •   Mt. Kenya
17,058 ft.
(5199 m.)
▲   Mogadishu ⊛

Equator   0°

• Kigali   Nairobi ⊛
LAKE VICTORIA   TANA

BURUNDI   Killmanjaro ▲
19,340 ft.
(5895 m.)

INDIAN

• Tabora   • Mombasa
Tanga •   OCEAN   3

TANZANIA   Zanzibar •
• Dodoma   Zanzibar
LAKE   Dar es Salaam ⊛
TANGANYIKA

RUFIJI

ALDABRA
ISLANDS
(Seychelles)

LAKE
NYASA   Mtwara •   10°

BIA   RUVUMA   COMOROS

MALAWI   4

MOZAMBIQUE   MOZAMBIQUE
CHANNEL

30°   Longitude East of Greenwich   40°   MADAGASCAR   50°

Cabinda
(Angola)

CONGO

A

20°

B

Z A I R E

KASAI

LUAPULA

Luanda

10°

A N G O L A

Benguela

Huambo

Ndola

Z A M B

Namibe

CUBANGO

Kabwe

Lusaka

ZAMBEZI

CUNENE

Capriwi Strip

LAKE KARIBA

Livingstone

VICTORIA FALLS

Cape Fria

ETOSHA
PAN

ZIMBAB

Namib

N A M I B I A

20°

Bulawayo

MAKGADIKGADI SA

B O T S W A N A

LIMP

Desert

Walvis Bay
(S. Africa)

Windhoek

K a l a h a r i
D e s e r t

Transva

Gaborone

3

Pretoria

A T L A N T I C

Lüderitz

JOHANNESBURG

VAAL

S O U T H

Drakensb

ORANGE

Kimberley

Bloemfontein

Pie

O C E A N

Maseru

30°

LESOTHO

A F R I C A

Great Karoo

4

Port Elizabeth

East London

Cape Town
Cape of Good Hope

Cape Agulhas

C.S. Hammond & Co., Maplewood, N.J.

20°

B

30°

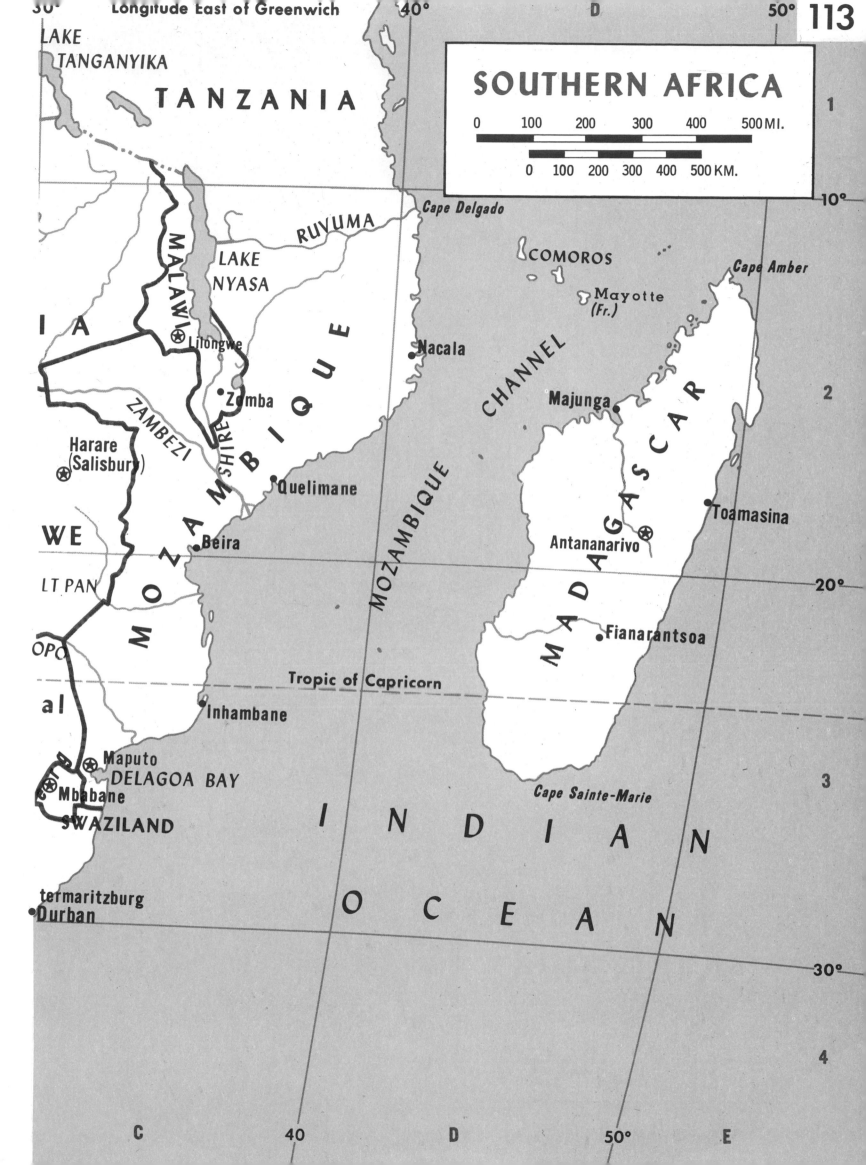

LAKE
TANGANYIKA

Longitude East of Greenwich

TANZANIA

RUVUMA

MALAWI

LAKE
NYASA

Lilongwe

Zomba

Cape Delgado

COMOROS

Mayotte
(Fr.)

Cape Amber

Nacala

MOZAMBIQUE CHANNEL

Majunga

ZAMBEZI

Harare
(Salisbury)

SHIRE

Quelimane

MADAGASCAR

Toamasina

WE

Beira

Antananarivo

LT PAN

20°

OPO

Fianarantsoa

al

Inhambane

Tropic of Capricorn

Maputo
DELAGOA BAY

Mbabane

Cape Sainte-Marie

SWAZILAND

INDIAN

termaritzburg
Durban

OCEAN

30°

SOUTHERN AFRICA

| 0 | 100 | 200 | 300 | 400 | 500 MI. |

| 0 | 100 | 200 | 300 | 400 | 500 KM. |

MOZAMBIQUE

IA

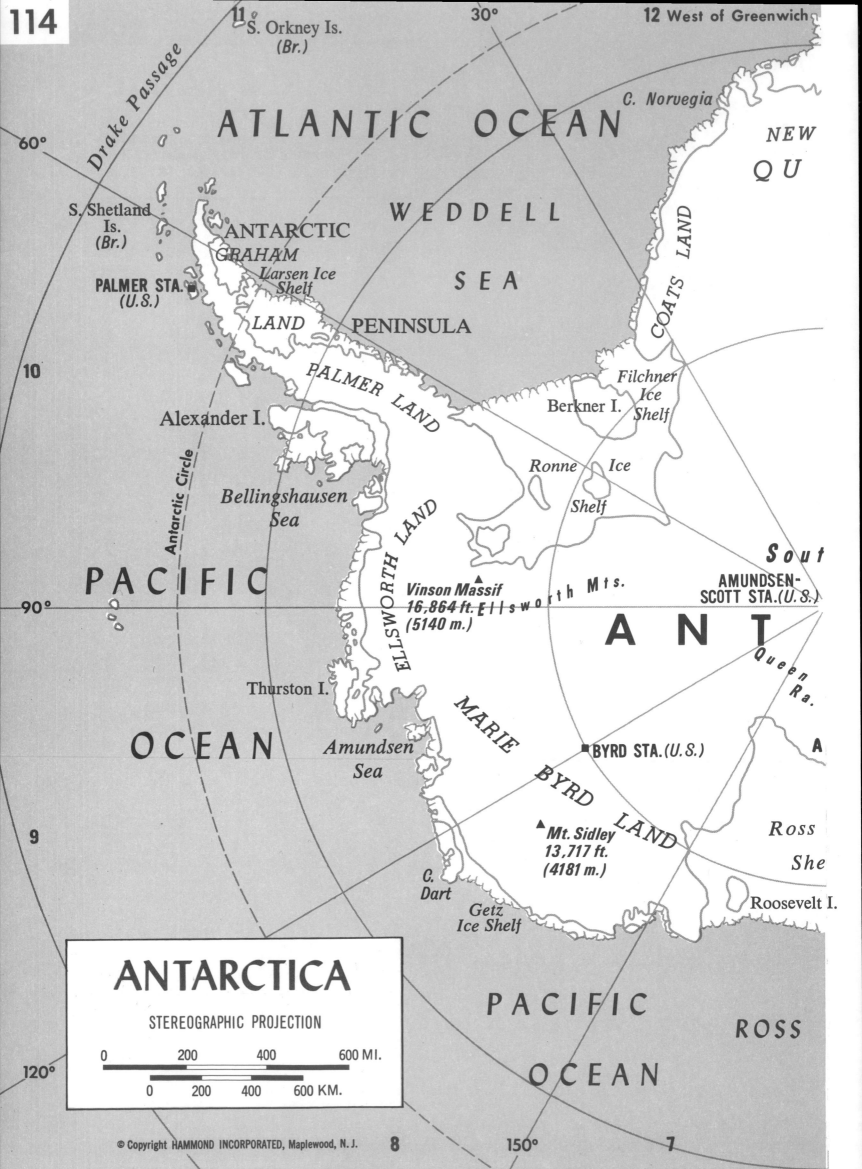

ATLANTIC OCEAN

11 S. Orkney Is.
(Br.)

30°

12 West of Greenwich

Drake Passage

C. Norvegia

NEW
QU

60°

WEDDELL

S. Shetland
Is.
(Br.)

ANTARCTIC
GRAHAM
Larsen Ice
Shelf
LAND

SEA

COATS LAND

PALMER STA.
(U.S.)

PENINSULA

10

PALMER LAND

Filchner
Ice
Shelf

Berkner I.

Alexander I.

Ronne   Ice

Antarctic Circle

Bellingshausen
Sea

Shelf

ELLSWORTH LAND

Sout
AMUNDSEN-
SCOTT STA.(U.S.)

PACIFIC

90°

Vinson Massif
16,864 ft. Ellsworth Mts.
(5140 m.)

ANT

Queen Ra.

Thurston I.

OCEAN

Amundsen
Sea

MARIE

BYRD STA.(U.S.)

A

Ross

9

Mt. Sidley
13,717 ft.
(4181 m.)

BYRD LAND

She

C.
Dart

Roosevelt I.

Getz
Ice Shelf

ANTARCTICA

STEREOGRAPHIC PROJECTION

| 0 | 200 | 400 | 600 MI. |

| 0 | 200 | 400 | 600 KM. |

PACIFIC

ROSS

120°

OCEAN

8

150°

7

0° East of Greenwich 1
30°
2

C
70°
NOVOLAZAREVSKAYA
(U.S.S.R.)

SCHWABENLAND

Riiser-Larsen
Peninsula

Lützow-Holm Bay

INDIAN

B

EEN MAUD LAND

MOLODEZHNAYA
(U.S.S.R.)

OCEAN

C. Batterbee

60°

ENDERBY
LAND

80°

PLATEAU STA.
(U.S.)

MAWSON (Austr.)

3

A

American

Highland

Amery
Ice Shelf

West
Ice Shelf

h Polar

SOUTH POLE

Davis
Sea

90°

ARCTICA

MIRNYY
(U.S.S.R.)

Plateau

Maud

VOSTOK
(U.S.S.R.)

Shackleton

Ice Shelf

▲ Mt. Markham
14,272 ft.(4350 m.)

WILKES LAND

Antarctic Circle

Vincennes
Bay

4

Ice

lf

C. Poinsett

MC MURDO (U.S.)
SCOTT (N.Z.)

VICTORIA LAND

INDIAN

Ross I.

McMurdo Sd.

SEA

C. Goodenough

OCEAN

SOUTH MAGNETIC
POLAR AREA

120°

C. Adare

180°
6

150°

DUMONT d'URVILLE (Fr.)

5

INDEX OF THE WORLD

A

Aalst, Belgium 61/B2
Aarau, Switzerland 68/C1
Aare (riv.), Switz. 68/C2
Abadan, Iran 86/B2
Abéché, Chad 108/A3
Aberdeen, Scotland 54/C2
Aberdeen, S. Dak. 28/B2
Abidjan (cap.),
    Ivory Coast 107/B4
Abilene, Texas 30/C2
Abu Dhabi (cap.), United
    Arab Emirates 81/B2
Abuja, Nigeria 107/C4
Acapulco, Mexico 37/B3
Accra (cap.), Ghana .. 107/B4
Acklins (isl.),
    Bahamas 40/B2
Aconcagua (mt.),
    Argentina 50/B3
Acre, Israel 84/A1
Adalia (gulf), Turkey ... 82/B2
Adana, Turkey 83/C2
Adapazarı, Turkey 82/B1
Adare (cape),
    Antarctica 115/B6
Addis Ababa (cap.),
    Ethiopia 109/C4
Adelaide (cap.),
    South Australia 100/C3
Aden,
    Yemen 80/B3
Aden (gulf) 79/B4
Adige (riv.), Italy 66/B1
Adirondack (mts.),
    New York 24/D1
Adriatic (sea), Europe .. 52/C3
Aegean (sea) 73/B2

Agra, India 88/B2
Aguascalientes, Mex. 36/B2
Aguja (pt.), Peru 46/A3
Agulhas (cape),
    S. Africa 112/B4
Agusan (riv.), Phil. 97/C3
Ahaggar (mts.),
    Algeria 106/C2
Ahmadabad, India 88/B2
Ahvaz, Iran 86/B2
Akita, Japan 95/C2
Akron, Ohio 29/F3
Akureyri, Iceland 56/B1
Alabama (riv.), Ala. 27/B4
Aland (isls.), Finland 57/C3
Albacete, Spain 65/C2
Albany, Georgia 27/B4
Albany (cap.), N.Y. 24/D2
Albert (canal), Belg. 61/B2
Alborán (isl.), Spain 64/C3
Albuquerque, N.M. 35/F3
Aldabra (isls.),
    Seychelles 111/E3
Aldan (riv.), U.S.S.R ... 77/G3
Aleppo, Syria 83/C2
Alesund, Norway 56/A2
Aleutian (isls.),
    Alaska 20/B3
Alexander (isl.),
    Antarctica 114/C10
Alexandria, Louisiana 31/D3
Alexandria, Egypt 108/B1
Alexandria, Virginia 26/D2
Algiers (cap.),
    Algeria 106/C1
Al Hajara (plain),
    Iraq 86/B2
Alicante, Spain 65/C2
Alice Springs, N. Terr.,
    Australia 100/C2
Allahabad, India 89/C2

Allegheny (mts.), U.S. .. 25/B4
Allegheny (plateau),
    U.S. 25/A4
Allegheny (riv.), U.S. 24/B3
Allentown, Pa. 25/D3
Alma-Ata, U.S.S.R. 76/D3
Almería, Spain 65/C2
Alps (mts.), Europe 52/C3
Altay (mts.), Asia 92/B1
Altdorf, Switzerland 69/C2
Altiplano (plat.),
    S. America 48/B3
Alton, Illinois 29/D4
Altoona, Pa. 25/B3
'Amara, Iraq 86/B2
Amarillo, Texas 30/B2
Amazon (riv.),
    S. America 42/B2
Ambato, Ecuador 46/B2
Amber (cape),
    Madagascar 113/D2
American (highland),
    Antarctica 115/B3
Amery (ice shelf),
    Antarctica 115/C3
Amiens, France 62/C2
Amistad (res.),
    N. America 30/B3
Amman (cap.),
    Jordan 84/A2
Amritsar, India 88/B1
Amsterdam (cap.),
    Netherlands 60/B1
Amudarya (riv.),
    Asia 81/C2
Amundsen (sea),
    Antarctica 114/B9
Amundsen-Scott (station),
    Antarctica 114/A10
Amur (riv.), Asia 77/G3
Anadyr, U.S.S.R. 77/J2

Anatolia (plat.),
    Turkey 82/B2
Anchorage, Alaska 20/B3
Ancohuma (mt.),
    Bolivia 48/B3
Ancona, Italy 66/C2
Andaman (isls.),
    India 89/D3
Andaman (sea), Asia 98/A2
Andes (mts.), S. Amer. .. 42/B2
Andros (isl.),
    Bahamas 40/B1
Angel (fall), Venez. 45/C2
Angerman (riv.),
    Sweden 56/B2
Angers, France 62/B3
Anglesey (isl.), Wales 55/B3
Angostura (falls),
    Colombia 44/B2
Ankara (cap.),
    Turkey 82/B2
Ann (cape), Mass. 23/B3
Annaba, Algeria 106/C1
An Najaf, Iraq 86/B2
Annapolis (cap.), Md. ... 25/C4
Ann Arbor, Michigan 29/D3
Anshan, China 93/D1
Antalya, Turkey 82/B2
Antananarivo (cap.),
    Madagascar 105/E4
Antarctic (pen.),
    Antarctica 114/C11
Antofagasta, Chile 50/A2
Antwerp, Belgium 61/B2
Aomori, Japan 95/C1
Aparri, Phil. 96/B1
Apeldoorn, Neth. 60/B1
Apennines (mts.),
    Italy 66/B1
Apia (cap.),
    Western Samoa 103/D3

Apo (volcano), Phil. 97/C4
Appalachian (mts.),
    North America 21/E2
Appleton, Wisconsin 29/D2
Apurímac (riv.), Peru .. 47/C5
Aqaba, Jordan 84/A3
Aqaba (gulf), Asia 84/A3
Araba (dry river),
    Asia 84/A2
Arabian (sea) 79/C4
Aracaju, Brazil 49/E3
Arad, Romania 72/B1
Arafura (sea) 99/C3
Arak, Iran 86/B2
Aral (sea), U.S.S.R. 76/C3
Ararat (mt.), Turkey 83/D2
Aras (Araxes) (riv.),
    Asia 83/D1
Arauca (riv.),
    S. America 44/B2
Araxes (riv.), Asia 80/B2
Archangel, U.S.S.R. 76/C2
Arctic Ocean 14-15
Ardabil, Iran 86/B2
Ardennes (forest),
    Europe 61/B2-3
Arequipa, Peru 47/D6
Arguello (pt.), Calif. 34/B3
Århus, Denmark 57/A3
Arica, Chile 50/A1
Arkansas (riv.), U.S. 20/C2
Arnhem, Neth. 60/B1
Arnhem Land (region),
    N. Terr., Australia 100/C2
Arno (riv.), Italy 66/B2
Aroostook (riv.),
    N. America 22/C1
Aru (isls.), Indonesia 99/C3
Aruba (isl.),
    Neth. Antilles 41/C3
Asahikawa, Japan 95/C1

Asheville, N. Carolina 26/C3
Ashkhabad, U.S.S.R. 76/C4
Ashqelon, Israel 84/A2
Asmara, Ethiopia 109/C3
Assam (reg.), India 89/D2
Astrakhan, U.S.S.R. 76/C3
Asunción (cap.),
    Paraguay 50/C2
Aswan, Egypt 109/C2
Aswan High (dam),
    Egypt 109/C2
Asyut, Egypt 109/C2
Atbara (riv.),
    Africa 109/C3
Athabasca (riv.),
    Alberta 18/C2
Athens, Georgia 26/C3
Athens (cap.),
    Greece 73/B2
Atlanta (cap.),
    Georgia 26/B3
Atlantic City,
    New Jersey 25/D4
Atlas (mts.), Africa 104/B2
Atrek (riv.), Asia 87/C2
Auburn, Maine 23/B2
Auburn, New York 24/C2
Auckland,
    New Zealand 101/E3
Augsburg,
    Germany 59/B2
Augusta, Georgia 26/C3
Augusta (cap.),
    Maine 22/C2
Austin (cap.), Texas 31/C3
Austral (isls.),
    Fr. Polynesia 103/E4
Ayacucho, Peru 47/C5
Ayers Rock (mt.),
    N. Terr., Australia .. 100/C3
Ayutthaya, Thailand 91/B2

Azuero (pen.),
Panama 39/D4

B

Babol, Iran 87/C2
Babuyan (chan.),
Phil. 96/C2
Babuyan (isls.),
Phil. 96/C2
Bacolod, Phil. 97/B3
Badajoz, Spain 64/B2
Baden, Switzerland 69/C1
Baffin (bay),
N. America 16/F1
Baffin (isl.),
Canada 19/E1
Baghdad (cap.),
Iraq 86/B2
Baguio, Phil. 96/B1
Bahía (isls.),
Honduras 38/C1
Bahía Blanca,
Argentina 51/B3
Bairiki (cap.), Kiribati 102/C2
Bakersfield, Calif. 34/C3
Bakhtaran, Iran 86/B2
Baku, U.S.S.R. 76/C3
Balabac (isl.), Phil. 97/A4
Balaton (lake),
Hungary 71/C2
Balearic (isls.),
Spain 65/D2
Baler (bay), Phil. 96/B2
Bali (isl.), Indonesia 98/B3
Balıkesir, Turkey 82/A2
Balintang (chan.),
Phil. 96/C1
Balkan (mts.), Europe .. 72/B1
Balkhash (lake),
U.S.S.R. 76/D3

Balsas (riv.), Mexico 37/B3
Baltic (sea), Europe 52/C3
Baltimore, Maryland 25/C4
Baluchistan (reg.),
Asia 88/A2
Bamako (cap.), Mali.... 107/B3
Banda (sea),
Indonesia 99/C3
Bandar 'Abbas, Iran 87/C3
Bandar Seri Begawan (cap.),
Brunei 98/B2
Bandeira (mt.), Brazil.... 49/D4
Bandung, Indonesia 98/B3
Bangalore, India 88/B3
Bangka (isl.), Indonesia 98/B3
Bangkok (cap.),
Thailand 91/B2
Bangor, Maine 22/C2
Bangui (cap.), Central
African Republic 110/B2
Banjarmasin, Indonesia .. 98/B3
Banjul (cap.), Gambia   107/A3
Banks (isl.), N.W.T.,
Canada 18/B1
Baotou, China 93/C1
Barahona,
Dominican Rep. 41/C2
Barcelona, Spain 65/D1
Barcelona, Venezuela 45/C1
Barents (sea) 53/E1
Bari, Italy 67/D2
Barkley (lake),
Kentucky 26/B2
Barkly Tableland (plat.),
Australia 100/C2
Barnaul, U.S.S.R. 76/E3
Barquisimeto, Venez. 44/B1
Barranquilla, Colombia .. 44/B1
Barre, Vermont 22/A2
Barrow (pt.), Alaska 20/B3
Basel, Switzerland 68/B1

Bashi (chan.), Asia 96/C1
Basilan, Phil. 98/C2
Basilan (isl.), Phil. 97/B4
Basra, Iraq 86/B2
Bass (strait),
Australia 101/D4
Bassein, Burma 90/A2
Basseterre (cap.),
St. Kitts & Nevis 41/D2
Bastia, France 63/D4
Bastogne, Belgium 61/B3
Bataan (pen.),
Phil. 96/A2
Batan (isl.), Phil. 96/C1
Batan (isls.), Phil. 96/C1
Batangas, Phil. 96/B2
Batdambang, Cambodia 91/B2
Bathurst (cape), N.W.T.,
Canada 18/B1
Baton Rouge (cap.),
Louisiana 31/E3
Batterbee (cape),
Antarctica 115/C2
Bauru, Brazil 49/D4
Baykal (lake),
U.S.S.R. 77/F3
Beaufort (sea) 18/A1
Beaumont, Texas 31/D3
Béchar, Algeria 106/B1
Beersheba, Israel 84/A2
Beijing (cap.), China 93/C1
Beira, Mozambique 113/C2
Beirut (cap.),
Lebanon 82/C3
Bekescsaba,
Hungary 71/D2
Belém, Brazil 49/D2
Belfast (cap.),
N. Ireland, U.K. 55/B3
Belgrade (cap.),
Yugoslavia 72/B1

Bellingham,
Washington 32/B1
Bellingshausen (sea),
Antarctica 114/C10
Bellinzona, Switz. 69/C2
Belmopan (cap.),
Belize 38/B1
Belo Horizonte, Brazil ... 49/D3
Bend, Oregon 32/B2
Bengal (bay), Asia 79/D4
Benghazi,
Libya 108/B1
Benguela, Angola 112/A2
Benjamin Constant,
Brazil 48/B2
Ben Nevis (mt.),
Scotland 54/B2
Benue (riv.), Africa 107/C4
Berbera, Somalia 111/E1
Bergen, Norway 57/A2
Bering (sea) 78/J2
Bering (strait) 16/A1
Berkner (isl.),
Antarctica 114/B11
Berlin (cap.),
Germany 58/C1
Berlin,
New Hampshire 22/B2
Bermejo (riv.),
Argentina 50/B2
Bern (cap.),
Switzerland 68/B2
Bernese Oberland (reg.),
Switzerland 68/B2
Besançon, France 62/D3
Beskids (mts.),
Europe 74/B2
Bethlehem, Jordan 84/A2
Bethlehem, Pa. 25/D3
Beyşehir (lake),
Turkey 82/B2

Białystok, Poland 75/C1
Biddeford, Maine 23/B3
Biel, Switzerland 68/B1
Bien Hoa, Vietnam 91/B2
Bikini (isl.),
Pacific Is. 102/C2
Bilbao, Spain 64/C1
Billings, Montana 33/E2
Biloxi, Mississippi 27/A4
Binghamton,
New York 24/D2
Bioko (prov.),
Eq. Guin. 110/B2
Birjand, Iran 87/C2
Birmingham, Alabama .. 26/B3
Birmingham, England 55/C3
Birs (riv.),
Switzerland 68/B1
Biscay (bay), Europe 52/B3
Bismarck (cap.),
N. Dakota 28/A2
Bissau (cap.),
Guinea-Bissau 107/A3
Bitterroot (range),
U.S. 32/D2
Black (forest),
Germany 59/B2
Black (sea) 53/D3
Black Hills (mts.),
U.S. 20/C1
Blanc (cape), Africa .. 106/A2
Blanc (mt.), France 63/D3
Blanco (cape),
Oregon 32/A3
Block (isl.),
Mass. 23/B4
Bloemfontein,
S. Africa 112/B3
Bluefields, Nicaragua 39/D3
Blue Nile (riv.),
Africa 104/D3

Blue Ridge (mts.),
U.S. 26/C3
Blytheville, Arkansas 31/E2
Boa Vista, Brazil 48/B1
Bobo-Dioulasso,
Upper Volta 107/B3
Bodélé (depression),
Chad 108/A3
Bogotá (cap.),
Colombia 44/B2
Bohemian (forest),
Europe 70/B1
Bohol (isl.), Phil. 97/C3
Bohol (sea), Phil. 97/C3
Boise (cap.), Idaho 32/D3
Bolinao (cape), Phil. 96/A1
Bolívar (mt.),
Venezuela 44/B1
Bologna, Italy 66/B1
Bombay, India 88/B3
Bomu (riv.), Africa 110/C2
Bonaire (isl.),
Neth. Antilles 41/C3
Bonin (isls.), Japan 102/B1
Bonn,
Germany 59/A2
Boras, Sweden 57/B3
Bordeaux, France 63/B3
Borneo (isl.), Asia 98/B2
Bornholm (isl.),
Denmark 57/B3
Bosporus (str.),
Turkey 82/A1
Boston (cap.), Mass. 23/B3
Bothnia (gulf), Europe .. 56/C2
Botrange (mt.),
Belgium 61/C2
Bouaké, Ivory Coast ... 107/B4
Boulder, Colorado 35/F2
Bourges, France 62/C3
Bowling Green, Ky. 26/B2

Bozeman, Montana 33/E2
Braga, Portugal 64/A1
Brahmaputra (riv.),
    Asia 89/D2
Brasília (cap.), Brazil ... 49/D3
Brasov, Romania 72/B1
Bratislava,
    Czechoslovakia 71/C1
Brattleboro, Vermont 23/A3
Brazilian (highlands),
    Brazil 49/D3
Brazos (riv.), U.S. 21/D2
Brazzaville (cap.),
    Congo 110/B3
Breda, Netherlands 60/B2
Bremen, Germany 58/B1
Brescia, Italy 66/B1
Brest, France 62/A2
Bridgeport, Conn. 23/A4
Bridgetown (cap.),
    Barbados 41/D3
Brisbane (cap.), Queensland,
    Australia 101/D3
Bristol, England 55/C4
Bristol (chan.), U.K. 55/B4
Brno, Czechoslovakia 71/C1
Brockton, Mass. 23/B3
Broken Hill,
    New South Wales 101/C3
Broome, W.
    Australia 100/B2
Brownsville, Texas 30/C4
Bruges, Belgium 61/A2
Brunswick,
    Germany 58/B1
Brussels (cap.),
    Belgium 61/B2
Bucaramanga,
    Colombia 44/B2
Bucharest (cap.),
    Romania 72/B1

Budapest (cap.),
    Hungary 71/C2
Buenaventura,
    Colombia 44/A2
Buenos Aires (cap.),
    Argentina 50/B3
Buffalo, New York 24/B2
Bug (riv.), Europe 75/C1
Bujumbura (cap.),
    Burundi 110/C3
Bukavu, Zaire 110/C3
Bulawayo, Zim. 112/B3
Burgas, Bulgaria 72/B1
Burgdorf, Switzerland 68/B1
Burgos, Spain 64/C1
Burlington, Vermont 22/A2
Bursa, Turkey 82/A1
Buru (isl.),
    Indonesia 99/C3
Busuanga (isl.), Phil. 96/A2
Butte, Montana 33/D2
Butuan, Phil. 97/C3
Bydgoszcz, Poland 74/B1
Byrd (station),
    Antarctica 114/A8
Bytom, Poland 74/B2

C

Caatingas (reg.),
    Brazil 49/D2
Cabanatuan, Phil. 96/B2
Cabimas, Venezuela 44/B1
Cabinda, Angola 112/A1
Cádiz, Spain 64/B2
Cádiz (gulf), Spain 64/B2
Caen, France 62/B2
Cagayan (riv.), Phil. 96/B1
Cagayan de Oro,
    Phil. 97/C3

Cagliari, Italy 67/B3
Cairns, Queensland 101/D2
Cairo (cap.), Egypt 108/B1
Cajamarca, Peru 46/B3
Calais, France 62/C2
Calama, Chile 50/B2
Calamian Group (isls.),
    Phil. 96/A2
Calayan (isl.), Phil. 96/C2
Calcutta, India 89/C2
Calgary, Alberta 18/C2
Cali, Colombia 44/A2
California (gulf),
    Mexico 36/A2
Callao, Peru 47/B5
Camagüey, Cuba 40/B2
Ca Mau (pt.), Viet. 91/B3
Cambridge, Mass. 23/B3
Camden, New Jersey 25/D4
Cameroon (mt.),
    Cameroon 110/A2
Camiguin (isl.), Phil. 96/C2
Campeche, Mexico 37/C3
Campeche (bay),
    Mexico 37/C2
Campina Grande,
    Brazil 49/E2
Campo Grande, Brazil .. 49/C4
Campos (reg.), Brazil ... 49/C4
Canadian (riv.), U.S. 31/C2
Canaveral (cape), Fla. .. 27/C4
Canberra (cap.),
    Australia 101/D3
Cancún, Mexico 37/D2
Candia, Greece 73/B2
Cannanore (isls.), India 88/A3
Cantabrian (mts.), Spain 64/B1
Canton (Guangzhou),
    China 93/C2
Canton, Ohio 29/F3
Cape Girardeau, Mo. 29/D4

Cape Town (cap.),
S. Africa 112/A4
Cape York (pen.),
Queensland 101/C2
Cap-Haïtien, Haiti 40/B2
Caprivi Strip (reg.),
Namibia 112/B2
Caquetá (riv.),
Colombia 44/B3
Caracas (cap.),
Venezuela 44/C1
Caratasca (lagoon),
Honduras 39/D2
Cardiff, Wales 55/C4
Caribbean (sea) 17/F4
Caribou, Maine 22/C1
Carlsbad, New Mexico.... 35/F3
Carmel (cape), Israel 84/A1
Carnarvon,
W. Australia 100/A3
Caroline (isls.),
Pacific Is. 102/B2
Carpathians (mts.),
Europe 53/D3
Carpentaria (gulf),
Australia 100/C2
Carson City (cap.),
Nevada 34/C2
Cartagena, Colombia 44/A1
Cartagena, Spain 65/C2
Carúpano, Venezuela 45/C1
Casablanca, Morocco .. 106/B1
Cascade (range), U.S. ... 32/B2
Casper, Wyoming 33/F3
Caspian (sea) 78/B2
Castellón de la Plana,
Spain 65/C2
Castries (cap.),
St. Lucia 41/D3
Cat (isl.),
Bahamas 40/B1

Catanduanes (isl.),
Phil. 96/C2
Catania, Italy 67/C3
Catbalogan, Phil 96/C3
Catskill (mts.), N.Y. 24/D2
Cauca (riv.),
Colombia 44/B2
Caucasus (mts.),
U.S.S.R. 76/C3
Cayenne (cap.),
Fr. Guiana 45/D2
Cebu, Phil. 97/C3
Cebu (isl.), Phil. 97/B3
Cedar Rapids, Iowa 28/C3
Celebes (isl.),
Indonesia 98/C3
Celebes (sea), Asia 98/C2
Ceram (isl.), Indonesia.. 99/C3
Cerro de Pasco, Peru 47/C4
Ceske Budejovice,
Czechoslovakia 70/B1
Ceuta, Spain 64/B3
Ceyhan (riv.), Turkey.... 83/C2
Chad (lake), Africa 104/C3
Challenger Deep (trench),
Pacific 102/B2
Champlain (lake),
N. America 22/A2
Chang (riv.), China 93/C2
Changchun, China 93/D1
Changsha, China 93/C2
Charleroi, Belgium 61/B2
Charles (cape), Va. 25/D5
Charleston, S. Car. 26/D3
Charleston (cap.),
W. Virginia 26/C2
Charlotte, N. Carolina .. 26/C3
Charlottetown (cap.), Prince
Edward I., Canada 19/E2
Chattahoochee (riv.),
U.S. 26/B3

Chattanooga,
Tennessee 26/B3
Cheju (isl.), S. Korea ... 94/A2
Chelyabinsk, U.S.S.R. .. 76/D3
Chelyuskin (cape),
U.S.S.R. 78/E1
Chemnitz,
Germany 58/C2
Chengchow, see Zhengzhou
Chengdu, China 93/C2
Cher (riv.), France 62/C3
Chesapeake (bay),
U.S. 25/C5
Chester, Pa. 25/D4
Cheyenne (cap.),
Wyoming 33/F3
Cheyenne (riv.), U.S. ... 28/A3
Chiang Mai, Thailand .. 90/A2
Chicago, Illinois 29/D3
Chiclayo, Peru 46/B3
Chihuahua, Mexico 36/B2
Chiloé (isl.), Chile 51/A4
Chimborazo (mt.),
Ecuador 46/B2
Chimbote, Peru 47/B4
Chinandega, Nicaragua .. 38/C2
Chios (isl.), Greece 73/B2
Chira (riv.),
S. America 46/A3
Chirripó Grande (mt.),
Costa Rica 39/D3
Chita, U.S.S.R. 77/F3
Chongjin, N. Korea 94/B1
Chongqing, China 93/C2
Chonju, S. Korea 94/A2
Chonos (arch.), Chile .. 51/A4
Choybalsan, Mongolia .. 93/C1
Christchurch, New
Zealand 101/E4
Chubut (riv.),
Argentina 51/B4

Chungking, see Chongqing
Chur, Switzerland 69/D2
Churchill, Manitoba 18/D2
Churchill (riv.),
     Canada 18/D2
Cienfuegos, Cuba 40/A2
Cimarron (riv.), U.S. 30/C1
Cincinnati, Ohio 29/E4
Ciudad Bolívar,
     Venezuela 45/C2
Ciudad Juárez,
     Mexico 36/B1
Ciudad Victoria,
     Mexico 37/C2
Claremont,
     New Hampshire 23/A3
Clermont-Ferrand,
     France 63/C3
Cleveland, Ohio 29/F3
Clovis, New Mexico 35/G3
Cluj, Romania 72/B1
Clyde (riv.), Scotland 54/C3
Coari, Brazil 48/B2
Coast (mts.), Canada 18/B2
Coast (ranges), U.S. .. 20/A1-2
Coats Land (reg.),
     Antarctica 114/B12
Cobán, Guatemala 38/B2
Cobija, Bolivia 48/B3
Cochabamba, Bolivia 48/B3
Coco (riv.),
     Central America 38/C2
Cod (cape), Mass. 23/B3
Coiba (isl.), Panama 39/D4
Coimbra, Portugal 64/A1
Cologne, Germany 58/A2
Colombo (cap.),
     Sri Lanka 89/C4
Colón, Panama 39/E3
Colorado (plat.),
     U.S. 35/E2-3

Colorado (riv.),
     Argentina 51/B3
Colorado (riv.),
     Texas 31/C3
Colorado (riv.), U.S. 35/D3
Colorado River Aqueduct,
     California 34/C3
Colorado Springs,
     Colorado 35/F2
Columbia, Missouri 29/D4
Columbia (cap.),
     S. Carolina 26/C3
Columbia (plat.), U.S. .. 32/C2
Columbia (riv.),
     N. America 32/B2
Columbus, Georgia 26/B3
Columbus (cap.),
     Ohio 29/F3
Comodoro Rivadavia,
     Argentina 51/B4
Comorin (cape), India .. 89/B4
Conakry (cap.),
     Guinea 107/A4
Concepción, Chile 51/A3
Concepción, Paraguay .. 50/C2
Conchos (riv.), Mexico .. 36/B2
Concord (cap.),
     New Hampshire 23/B3
Concordia, Argentina 50/C3
Congo (riv.), Africa 105/D3
Connecticut (riv.),
     N. America 23/A4
Constance (lake),
     Europe 69/D1
Constanta, Romania 72/B1
Constantine, Algeria 106/C1
Cook (mt.),
     New Zealand 101/E4
Copenhagen (cap.),
     Denmark 57/B3
Coral (sea) 102/B-C3

Cordillera Central (mts.),
     Phil. 96/B1
Córdoba, Argentina 50/B3
Córdoba, Spain 64/B2
Corfu (isl.), Greece 73/A2
Cork, Ireland 55/A4
Coro, Venezuela 44/B1
Coronel Oviedo,
     Paraguay 50/C2
Corpus Christi, Texas 30/C4
Corrientes, Argentina 50/C2
Corrientes (cape),
     Colombia 44/A2
Corrientes (cape),
     Mexico 36/B2
Çoruh (riv.), Turkey 83/D1
Corvallis, Oregon 32/B2
Cotabato, Phil. 97/B4
Cotopaxi (mt.),
     Ecuador 46/B2
Council Bluffs, Iowa 28/C3
Courantyne (riv.),
     S. America 45/D2
Courtrai, Belgium 61/A2
Coventry, England 55/C3
Covington, Kentucky 26/B2
Cracow, Poland 74/C2
Craiova, Romania 72/B1
Crimea (pen.),
     U.S.S.R. 76/B3
Cristóbal Colón (mt.),
     Colombia 44/B1
Cubango (riv.),
     Africa 112/A2
Cúcuta, Colombia 44/B2
Cuenca, Ecuador 46/B2
Cuiabá, Brazil 49/C3
Culiacán, Mexico 36/B2
Cumaná, Venezuela 45/C1
Cumberland,
     Maryland 25/B4

Cumberland (riv.),
U.S. 26/B2
Cunene (riv.), Africa .. 112/A2
Curitiba, Brazil 49/C4
Cusco, Peru 47/D5
Cuyo (isls.), Phil. 97/B3
Cuyuni (riv.),
S. America 45/C2
Cyclades (isls.),
Greece 73/B2
Cyrenaica (reg.),
Libya 108/B1
Częstochowa, Poland 74/B2

D

Dacca (Dhaka) (cap.),
Bangladesh 89/D2
Daet, Phil. 96/B2
Dagupan, Phil. 96/B1
Da Hingan Ling (range),
China 93/D1
Dakar (cap.), Senegal.. 107/A3
Dakhla, Morocco 106/A2
Da Lat, Vietnam 91/B2
Dallas, Texas 31/C2
Damascus (cap.),
Syria 83/C3
Damavand (mt.), Iran .. 87/C2
Da Nang, Vietnam 90/B2
Danube (riv.), Europe... 53/D3
Danzig (gulf), Europe .. 74/B1
Dardanelles (str.),
Turkey 82/A2
Dar es Salaam (cap.),
Tanzania 111/D3
Darling (riv.),
Australia 101/C3
Dart (cape),
Antarctica 114/B8

Darwin (cap.),
N. Terr., Australia .. 100/B2
Daryacheh-ye Namak (salt
lake), Iran 87/C2
Dashan, Ras (mt.),
Ethiopia 109/C3
Dasht-e Kavir (salt
desert), Iran 87/C2
Dasht-e Lut (desert),
Iran 87/C2
Davao, Phil. 97/C4
Davao (gulf), Phil. 97/C4
Davenport, Iowa 29/D3
David, Panama 39/D3
Davis (mts.), Texas 30/A3
Davis (sea),
Antarctica 115/C3
Davis (str.),
N. America 19/F1
Davos Platz, Switz. 69/D2
Dawson, Yukon 18/B1
Dayton, Ohio 29/E4
Daytona Beach, Fla. 27/C4
Dead (sea), Asia............ 84/A2
Death (valley),
California 34/C2
Debrecen, Hungary 71/D2
Decatur, Illinois 29/D4
Deccan (plat.), India 88/B2
Deir ez Zor, Syria 83/C2
Delagoa (bay),
Mozambique 113/C3
Delaware (bay), U.S. 25/D4
Delaware (riv.), U.S. 24/D3
Delémont, Switzerland .. 68/B1
Delgado (cape),
Mozambique 113/D2
Delhi, India 88/B2
Denver (cap.), Colo. 35/F2
Des Moines (cap.),
Iowa 28/C3

Des Moines (riv.),
U.S. 28/C3
Dessye, Ethiopia 109/C3
Detroit, Michigan 29/F3
Devil's (isl.),
Fr. Guiana 45/D2
Devon (isl.), N.W.T.,
Canada 19/E1
Dezhnev (cape),
U.S.S.R. 78/J1
Dhahran, Saudi
Arabia 80/B2
Dhaka (cap.),
Bangladesh 89/D2
Dijon, France 62/D3
Dinaric Alps (mts.),
Yugoslavia 72/A1
Dipolog, Phil. 97/B3
Dire Dawa, Ethiopia ... 109/D4
Diyarbakır, Turkey 83/D2
Djibouti (cap.),
Djibouti 109/D3
Doberai (pen.),
Papua N.G. 99/C3
Dodge City, Kansas 28/B4
Dodoma, Tanzania 111/D3
Dominica (isl.) 41/D3
Don (riv.), U.S.S.R. 76/C3
Donner (pass), Calif. 34/B2
Dordogne (riv.),
France 63/C3
Dordrecht, Neth. 60/B2
Dortmund,
Germany 58/A2
Dothan, Alabama 27/B4
Douala, Cameroon 110/A2
Doubs (riv.), Europe 68/B1
Douro (riv.), Europe 64/A1
Dover (cap.),
Delaware 25/D4
Dover, New Hampshire .. 23/B3

Dover (strait),
Europe 55/D4
Draa, Wadi (riv.),
Morocco 106/B2
Drake (passage),
Antarctica 114/C11
Drakensberg (range),
Africa 112/B3
Drammen, Norway 57/A3
Drava (Drau) (riv.),
Europe 70-71/B-C2
Dresden,
Germany 58/C2
Drin (riv.), Europe 73/B1
Dublin (cap.),
Ireland 55/B3
Dubuque, Iowa 29/D3
Dufourspitze (mt.),
Europe 68/B3
Duluth, Minnesota 28/C2
Dumaguete, Phil. 97/B3
Dumont d'Urville (sta.),
Antarctica 115/C5
Dundee, Scotland 54/C2
Dunedin,
New Zealand 101/E4
Durango, Colorado 35/F2
Durango, Mexico 36/B2
Durban, S. Africa 113/C3
Durham,
N. Carolina 26/D3
Dushanbe,
U.S.S.R. 76/D4
Düsseldorf,
Germany 58/A2

E

East China (sea),
Asia 93/D2
Easter (isl.), Chile 103/F4

Eastern Ghats (mts.),
India 89/B3
Eastern Taurus (mts.),
Turkey 83/C-D2
East London,
S. Africa 112/B4
Eastport, Maine 22/D2
East Siberian (sea),
U.S.S.R. 77/J2
Eau Claire,
Wisconsin 29/D2
Ebro (riv.), Spain 65/C1
Edinburgh (cap.),
Scotland, U.K. 54/C3
Edmonton (cap.),
Alberta, Canada 18/C2
Edwards (plat.),
Texas 30/B3
Eindhoven, Neth. 61/B2
Elath, Israel 84/A3
Elâziğ, Turkey 83/C2
Elba (isl.), Italy 66/B2
Elbe (riv.), Europe 58/B1
Elbląg, Poland 74/B1
Elbrus (mt.),
U.S.S.R. 53/E3
Elburz (range), Iran 87/C2
El Dorado,
Arkansas 31/D2
Eleuthera (isl.),
Bahamas 40/B1
El Faiyum, Egypt 108/B2
El Fasher, Sudan 108/B3
El Ferrol, Spain 64/A1
Elizabeth, New Jersey 25/D3
El Jafr (plain),
Jordan 84/B2
El Karak, Jordan 84/A2
Elko, Nevada 34/D1
Ellesmere (isl.),
N.W.T., Canada 19/E1

Ellsworth (mts.),
Antarctica 114/B10
Ellsworth Land (reg.),
Antarctica 114/B9
El Minya, Egypt 109/C2
Elmira, New York 24/C2
El Misti (mt.),
Peru 47/D6
El Obeid, Sudan 109/C3
El Paso, Texas 30/A3
El Tigre, Venezuela 45/C1
Ely, Nevada 34/D2
Ems (riv.),
Germany 58/A1
Enderby Land (reg.),
Antarctica 115/C2
Engaño (cape),
Phil. 96/B1
English (chan.),
Europe 52/B3
Enid, Oklahoma 30/C1
Enschede, Neth. 60/C1
Erfurt, Germany 58/B2
Erie, Pa. 24/A2
Erie (lake),
N. America 21/E1
Erimo (cape),
Japan 95/C1
Eritrea (reg.),
Ethiopia 109/C3
Erzgebirge (mts.),
Europe 59/C2
Erzurum, Turkey 83/D2
Esch-sur-Alzette,
Luxembourg 61/B3
Eskişehir, Turkey 82/B2
Esmeraldas, Ecuador 46/A1
Es Salt, Jordan 84/A1
Essen, Germany 58/A2
Essequibo (riv.),
Guyana 45/D2

Estrêla, Serra da (mts.),
    Portugal 64/A1
Ethiopian (highlands),
    Ethiopia 109/C3
Etna (volcano),
    Italy 67/C3
Etosha (salt pan),
    Namibia 112/A2
Euboea (isl.), Greece 73/B2
Eugene, Oregon 32/B2
Euphrates (riv.),
    Asia 80/B2
Eureka, Calif. 34/A1
Evansville, Indiana 29/E4
Everest (mt.), Asia 79/D3
Everett, Washington 32/B1
Éverglades, The (swamp),
    Florida 27/C5
Evora, Portugal 64/B2
Eyre (lake),
    S. Australia 100/C3
Ez Zarqa, Jordan 84/B1

F

Fairbanks, Alaska 20/B3
Falcon (res.),
    N. America 30/C4
Fall River, Mass. 23/B4
Famagusta, Cyprus 82/B2
Fargo, N. Dakota 28/B2
Farmington,
    New Mexico 35/E2
Faro, Portugal 64/B2
Fear (cape),
    N. Carolina 26/D3
Fehmarn (isl.),
        Germany 58/B1
Feira de Santana,
    Brazil 49/E3

Ferrara, Italy 66/B1
Fez, Morocco 106/B1
Fezzan (reg.),
    Libya 108/A2
Fianarantsoa,
    Madagascar 113/D3
Filchner (ice shelf),
    Antarctica 114/B11
Finger (lakes),
    New York 24/C2
Finisterre (cape),
    Spain 64/A1
Finland (gulf),
    Europe 57/C3
Flagstaff, Arizona 35/E3
Flanders (reg.),
    Europe 61/A2
Flattery (cape),
    Washington 32/A1
Flint, Michigan 29/F3
Florence, Italy 66/B2
Flores (isl.), Indonesia .. 98/C3
Flores (sea),
    Indonesia 98/B3
Florianópolis, Brazil 49/D4
Florida (keys),
    Florida 27/C5
Florida (straits),
    N. America 21/E-F3
Flushing, Neth. 61/A2
Fly (river),
    New Guinea 99/D3
Foggia, Italy 67/C2
Fongafale (cap.),
    Tuvalu 103/C3
Fontur (prom.), Ice. 56/B1
Fortaleza, Brazil 49/E2
Fort Collins,
    Colorado 35/F1
Fort Lauderdale,
    Florida 27/D5

Fort Myers, Florida 27/C5
Fort Peck Lake (res.),
    Montana 33/F2
Fort Smith, Arkansas 31/D2
Fort Smith, N.W.T.,
    Canada 18/C1
Fort Wayne, Indiana 29/E3
Fort Worth, Texas 31/C2
Frankfort (cap.),
    Kentucky 26/B2
Frankfurt,
        Germany 59/B2
Franz Josef Land (isls.),
    U.S.S.R. 76/C2
Fraser (riv.),
    Br. Columbia 18/B2
Fredericton (cap.), New
    Brunswick, Canada 19/E2
Freetown (cap.),
    Sierra Leone 107/A4
Freiburg, Germany 59/A3
Fremantle,
    W. Australia 100/A3
Fresno, Calif. 34/B2
Fria (cape), Namibia .. 112/A2
Fribourg, Switzerland 68/B2
Friesland (reg.),
    Europe 60/C1
Frio (cape), Brazil 49/D4
Fuji (mt.), Japan 95/B2
Fukuoka, Japan 94/B2
Fushun, China 93/D1
Fuzhou, China 93/C2

G

Gaborone (cap.),
    Botswana 112/B3
Gadsden, Alabama 26/B3
Gainesville, Florida 27/C4
Galati, Romania 72/B2

Galilee, Sea of (Tiberias) (lake), Israel 84/A1
Galveston, Texas 31/D3
Galway (bay), Ireland 55/A3
Gander, Newfoundland 19/F2
Ganges (riv.), Asia 89/C2
Garonne (riv.), France 63/B3
Gary, Indiana 29/E3
Gavle, Sweden 57/B2
Gaza Strip, Egypt 84/A2
Gaziantep, Turkey 83/C2
Gdańsk, Poland 74/B1
Gdańsk (gulf), Europe .. 74/B1
Gdynia, Poland 74/B1
Gediz (riv.), Turkey 82/A2
Geneva, Switzerland 68/A2
Geneva (lake), Europe 68/A2
Genk, Belgium 61/B2
Genoa, Italy 66/B1
Georgetown (cap.), Guyana 45/D2
George Town, Malaysia 91/A3
Geraldton, W. Australia 100/A3
Gerlachovka (mt.), Czechoslovakia 71/D1
Getz (ice shelf), Antarctica 114/B8
Ghent, Belgium 61/A2
Gibraltar (strait) 64/B3
Gibson (desert), Australia 100/B3
Gifu, Japan 95/B2
Gijón, Spain 64/B1
Gila (riv.), U.S. 35/D3
Gilbert (isls.) 102/C2

Glarus Alps (mts.), Switzerland 69/C2
Glasgow, Scotland 54/B3
Glittertinden (mt.), Norway 57/A2
Glomma (riv.), Norway 57/B2
Gobi (des.), Asia 93/C1
Godavari (riv.), India.... 88/B3
Godwin Austen (K2) (mt.), Asia 89/B2
Goeree (isl.), Neth. 60/A2
Goiânia, Brazil 49/D3
Gongga Shan (mt.), China 92/C2
Goodenough (cape), Antarctica 115/C5
Good Hope (cape), S. Africa 112/A4
Gorkiy, U.S.S.R. 76/C3
Gorzów Wielkopolski, Poland 74/A1
Goteborg, Sweden 57/B3
Gotland (isl.), Sweden 57/B3
Gracias a Dios (cape), Nicaragua 39/D2
Graham Land (reg.), Antarctica 114/C11
Grampian (mts.), Scotland 54/B2
Granada, Nicaragua 38/C3
Granada, Spain 64/C2
Gran Chaco (reg.), S. America 43/B3
Grand (lake), N. America 22/D2
Grand Bahama (isl.), Bahamas 40/B1
Grand Coulee (dam), Washington 32/C1

Grand Forks, N. Dakota 28/B2
Grand Island, Nebr. 28/B3
Grand Junction, Colorado 35/E2
Grand Rapids, Mich. 29/E3
Graz, Austria 70/B2
Great (basin), U.S. 34/C1-2
Great (lakes), N. America 16/E2
Great (plains), N. America 17/D2
Great Abaco (isl.), Bahamas 40/B1
Great Australian (bight), Australia 100/B3
Great Barrier (reef), Australia 101/D2
Great Bear (lake), N.W.T., Canada 18/C1
Great Dividing (range), Australia 101/D2
Great Eastern Erg (des.), Africa 106/C1
Greater Antilles (isls.), W. Indies 40-41/A-C2
Great Falls, Montana 33/E2
Great Inagua (isl.), Bahamas 40/B2
Great Indian (des.), Asia 88/B2
Great Karoo (reg.), S. Africa 112/B4
Great Saint Bernard (pass), Europe 68/B3
Great Salt (lake), Utah 35/D1
Great Sandy (des.), Australia 100/B2
Great Slave (lake), N.W.T., Canada 18/C1

Great Victoria (des.),
    Australia 100/B3
Great Western Erg (des.),
    Africa 106/C1
Greeley, Colorado 35/F1
Green (mts.),
    Vermont 23/A3
Green (riv.), U.S. 35/E1
Green Bay, Wisconsin 29/E2
Greensboro, N. Carolina 26/D2
Greenville, Mississippi ... 26/A3
Greenville, S. Carolina .. 26/C3
Grenchen, Switzerland .. 68/B1
Grenada (isl.) 41/D3
Grenoble, France 63/D3
Groningen, Neth. 60/C1
Grossglockner (mt.),
    Austria 70/B2
Guadalajara, Mexico 36/B2
Guadalquivir (riv.),
    Spain 64/B2
Guadiana (riv.),
    Europe 64/B2
Guajira (pen.),
    S. America 44/B1
Guangzhou, China 93/C2
Guantánamo, Cuba 40/B2
Guantánamo (bay),
    Cuba 40/B2
Guaporé (riv.),
    S. America 48/B3
Guatemala (cap.),
    Guatemala 38/B2
Guaviare (riv.),
    Colombia 44/B2
Guayaquil, Ecuador 46/A2
Guayaquil (gulf),
    S. America 46/A2
Guiana (highlands),
    S. America 42/B1
Guinea (gulf), Africa   105/C3

Guiyang, China 93/C2
Gyor, Hungary 71/C2

H

Haarlem, Neth. 60/B1
Habesor (dry river),
    Israel 84/A2
Hagerstown,
    Maryland 25/C4
Hague, The (cap.),
    Netherlands 60/B1
Haifa, Israel 84/A1
Hainan (isl.), China 93/C3
Haiphong, Vietnam 90/B1
Haji Ibrahim (mt.),
    Iraq 86/B2
Hakodate, Japan 95/C1
Halifax (cap.), Nova
    Scotia, Canada 19/E2
Halle, Germany 58/B2
Halmahera (isl.),
    Indonesia 99/C2
Halsingborg, Sweden 57/B3
Hama, Syria 83/C2
Hamadan, Iran 86/B2
Hamamatsu, Japan 95/B2
Hamburg, Germany 58/B1
Hamhung, N. Korea 94/A2
Hamilton, Ontario 19/D2
Hammerfest, Norway 56/C1
Hangzhou, China 93/C2
Hannover, Germany 58/B1
Hanoi (cap.),
    Vietnam 90/B1
Harar, Ethiopia 109/D4
Harare (cap.),
    Zimbabwe 113/C2
Harbin, China 93/D1
Harghassa, Somalia 111/E2

Harrisburg (cap.),
    Pennsylvania 25/C3
Hartford (cap.),
    Conn. 23/A4
Harz (mts.), Germany .. 58/B2
Hasa (dry riv.),
    Jordan 84/A2
Hastings, Nebraska 28/B3
Hatteras (cape),
    N. Carolina 26/E3
Hattiesburg, Mississippi.. 27/A4
Haugesund, Norway 57/A3
Havana (cap.), Cuba 40/A2
Havre, Montana 33/E1
Hawaii (isl.),
    Hawaii 20/D3
Hawaiian (isls.) 103/D1
Hebrides (isls.),
    Scotland 54/B2
Hebron, Jordan 84/A2
Hekla (mt.), Ice. 56/A2
Helena (cap.), Mont. 33/D2
Helmand (riv.),
    Afghanistan 81/C2
Helsinki (cap.), Fin. 57/C2
Henzada, Burma 90/A2
Herat, Afghanistan 88/A1
Hermon (mt.), Asia 83/C3
Hermosillo, Mexico 36/A2
Hibbing, Minnesota....... 28/C2
High Tatra (range),
    Europe 74/B2
Hilla, Iraq 86/B2
Hilversum, Neth. 60/B1
Himalaya (mts.),
    Asia 79/D3
Hindu Kush (mts.),
    Asia 88/A-B1
Hiroshima, Japan 94/B2
Hkakabo Razi (mt.),
    Burma 90/A1

Hoa Binh, Vietnam 90/B1
Ho Chi Minh City,
   Vietnam 91/B2
Hobart (cap.), Tasmania,
   Australia 101/D4
Hobbs, New Mexico 35/G3
Hokkaido (isl.), Japan .. 95/C1
Holguín, Cuba 40/B2
Holland (reg.), Neth. 60/B1
Homs, Syria 83/C3
Hondo (riv.),
   Central America 38/B1
Honduras (gulf),
   Central America 38/B1
Honiara (cap.),
   Sol. Is. 102/B3
Honolulu (cap.),
   Hawaii 20/C3
Honshu (isl.), Japan 94/B2
Hood (mt.), Oregon 32/B2
Hormuz (strait) 87/C3
Horn (cape), Chile 51/B5
Hotan, China 92/A2
Hot Springs National
   Park, Arkansas 31/D2
Houlton, Maine 22/C1
Houston, Texas 31/D3
Hradec Kralove,
   Czechoslovakia 70/B1
Hron (riv.), Czech. 71/C1
Huacho, Peru 47/B4
Huambo, Angola 112/A2
Huancavelica, Peru 47/B5
Huancayo, Peru 47/C5
Huang (riv.), China 93/C2
Huánuco, Peru 47/C4
Huarás, Peru 47/B4
Huascaran (mt.), Peru .. 47/B4
Hudson (bay), Canada.. 19/D1
Hudson (riv.), U.S. 24/E3
Hudson (str.), Canada .. 19/E1

Hue, Vietnam 90/B2
Huelva, Spain 64/B2
Hull, England 55/C3
Humboldt (riv.), Nev. 34/C1
Huntington,
   W. Virginia 26/C2
Huntsville, Alabama 26/B3
Huron, S. Dakota 28/B2
Huron (lake),
   N. America 21/E1
Hutchinson, Kansas 28/B4
Hyderabad, India 88/B3
Hyderabad, Pakistan 88/A2

I

Iasi, Romania 72/B1
Ibadan, Nigeria 107/C4
Ibagué, Colombia 44/B2
Ibarra, Ecuador 46/B1
Ibiza (isl.), Spain 65/D2
Ica, Peru 47/C5
Idaho Falls, Idaho 33/D3
Iguassu (falls),
   S. America 49/C4
IJssel (riv.), Neth. 60/C1
IJsselmeer (lake),
   Netherlands 60/B1
Ilagan, Phil. 96/B1
Iloilo, Phil. 97/B3
Inari (lake), Finland 56/C2
İnce (cape), Turkey 82/B1
Inchon, S. Korea 94/A2
Indian Ocean 15/N5
Indianapolis (cap.),
   Indiana 29/E4
Indore, India 88/B2
Indus (riv.), Asia 88/A2
Inhambane,
   Mozambique 113/C3
Inland (sea), Japan 94/B2

Inn (riv.), Europe 70/B1
Inner Mongolia (reg.),
   China 93/C1
Innsbruck, Austria 70/A2
In Salah, Algeria 106/C2
Inuvik, N.W.T.,
   Canada 18/B1
Inverness, Scotland 54/C2
Ionian (sea), Europe 73/A2
Ipoh, Malaysia 91/B3
Ipswich, England 55/D3
Iquique, Chile 50/A2
Iquitos, Peru 46/C2
Irbid, Jordan 84/A1
Iriga, Phil. 96/B2
Irish (sea), Europe 55/B3
Irkutsk, U.S.S.R. 77/F3
Irrawaddy (riv.),
   Burma 90/A1
Irtysh (riv.), U.S.S.R. ... 76/D3
Isfahan, Iran 87/C2
İskenderun, Turkey 83/C2
Islamabad (cap.),
   Pakistan 88/B1
Istanbul, Turkey 82/A1
Itabuna, Brazil 49/E3
Ithaca, New York 24/C2
Iwo Jima (isl.),
   Japan 102/A1
Izmir, Turkey 82/A2
Izmit, Turkey 82/A1

J

Jackson (cap.),
   Mississippi 26/A3
Jackson, Tennessee 26/A3
Jacksonville, Florida 27/C4
Jaén, Spain 64/C2
Jakarta (cap.), Indon. .. 98/B3

James (bay), Canada 19/D2

James (riv.), U.S. 28/B2

James (riv.), Virginia.... 26/D2

Jamestown, New York .. 24/B2

Jamestown, N. Dakota .. 28/B2

Jamshedpur, India 89/C2

Japan (sea), Asia 78/F2

Java (isl.), Indonesia 98/B3

Java (sea), Indonesia 98/B3

Jefferson City (cap.),

    Missouri 28/C4

Jérémie, Haiti 40/B2

Jerez de la Frontera,

    Spain 64/B2

Jericho, Jordan 84/A2

Jerusalem (cap.),

    Israel 84/A2

Jerusalem, Jordan 84/A2

Jidda, Saudi Arabia 80/A2

Jilin, China 93/D2

Jimma, Ethiopia 109/C4

Jinan, China 93/C2

João Pessoa, Brazil 49/E2

Johannesburg,

    S. Africa 112/B3

Johnston (atoll) 103/D2

Johnstown, Pa. 25/B3

Joliet, Illinois 29/D3

Jolo (isl.), Phil. 97/B4

Jonkoping, Sweden 57/B3

Joplin, Missouri 28/C4

Jordan (riv.), Asia 84/A1

Juan de Fuca (strait),

    N. America 32/A1

Juan Fernández (isls.),

    Chile 50/A3

Juàzeiro do Norte,

    Brazil 49/D2

Juba, Sudan 109/C4

Júcar (riv.), Spain 65/C2

Juigalpa, Nicaragua 38/C2

Juliaca, Peru 47/D5

Jumna (riv.), India 89/B2

Juneau (cap.),

    Alaska 20/B3

Jura (mts.), Europe 68/B1

Jutland (pen.), Den. 57/A3

Juventud (isl.), Cuba 40/A2

K

K2 (mt.), Asia 88/B1

Kabul (cap.),

    Afghanistan 88/A1

Kabwe, Zambia 112/B2

Kaduna, Nigeria 107/C3

Kaesong, N. Korea 94/A2

Kagoshima, Japan 94/B2

Kalahari (des.),

    Africa 112/B3

Kalamazoo, Michigan 29/E3

Kalemie, Zaire 110/C3

Kalgoorlie,

    W. Australia 100/B3

Kalimantan (reg.),

    Indonesia 98/B2

Kalispell, Montana 33/D1

Kalisz, Poland 74/B2

Kamchatka (pen.),

    U.S.S.R. 77/H3

Kampala (cap.),

    Uganda 111/D2

Kampong Chhnang,

    Cambodia 91/B2

Kananga, Zaire 110/C3

Kanazawa, Japan 94/B2

Kangaroo (isl.),

    S. Australia 100/C4

Kano, Nigeria 107/C3

Kanpur, India 89/B2

Kansas (riv.), Kansas 28/B4

Kansas City, Kansas 28/C4

Kansas City, Missouri 28/C4

Kara (sea), U.S.S.R. 76/D2

Karachi, Pakistan 88/A2

Karaganda, U.S.S.R. 76/D3

Karakoram (mts.),

    Asia 88/B1

Karbala', Iraq 86/B2

Kariba (lake), Africa .. 112/B2

Karun (riv.), Iran 86/B2

Kasai (riv.), Africa 110/B3

Kashan, Iran 87/C2

Kashi, China 92/A2

Kassala, Sudan 109/C3

Kassel,

    Germany 58/B2

Katahdin (mt.),

    Maine 22/C2

Katanga (reg.),

    Zaire 110/C3

Kathmandu (cap.),

    Nepal 89/C2

Katowice, Poland 74/B2

Kattegat (strait),

    Europe 57/B3

Kauai (isl.), Hawaii 20/C3

Kavalla, Greece 73/B1

Kayseri, Turkey 83/C2

Kazan, U.S.S.R. 76/C3

Kazerun, Iran 86/C3

Kecskemet, Hungary 71/C2

Keene, New Hampshire.. 23/A3

Kentucky (lake), U.S. .. 26/A2

Kenya (mt.), Kenya 111/D2

Kerman, Iran 87/C2

Kermanshah, Iran 86/B2

Key West, Florida 27/C5

Khabarovsk, U.S.S.R. 77/G3

Khark (isl.), Iran 86/C3

Kharkov, U.S.S.R. 76/B3

Khartoum (cap.),

    Sudan 109/C3

Khon Kaen, Thailand 90/B2
Khvoy, Iran 86/B2
Khyber (pass), Asia 88/B1
Kiel, Germany 58/B1
Kielce, Poland 75/C2
Kiev, U.S.S.R. 76/B3
Kigali (cap.),
    Rwanda 111/D3
Kilimanjaro (mt.),
    Tanzania 111/D3
Kimberley, S. Africa 112/B3
Kimberley (plat.),
    Australia 100/B2
Kingston (cap.), Jam. ... 40/B2
Kingstown (cap.),
    St. Vin. & Gren. 41/D3
Kinshasa (cap.),
    Zaire 110/B3
Kirensk, U.S.S.R. 77/F3
Kirin, see Jilin
Kiritimati (isl.) 103/E2
Kirkuk, Iraq 86/B2
Kiruna, Sweden 56/C2
Kisangani, Zaire 110/C2
Kisumu, Kenya 111/D2
Kitakyushu, Japan 94/A2
Kızılırmak (riv.),
    Turk. 82/B1
Kjolen (range), Europe.. 56/B2
Klagenfurt, Austria 70/B2
Klamath Falls, Oregon .. 32/B3
Knoxville, Tennessee 26/C2
Kobe, Japan 94/B2
Kola (pen.), U.S.S.R. ... 76/B2
Kolwezi, Zaire 110/C4
Komsomolsk, U.S.S.R. .. 77/G3
Köniz, Switzerland 68/B2
Konya, Turkey 82/B2
Koroglu (mts.), Turk. .. 82/B1
Kosciusko (mt.),
    New South Wales 101/D4

Kosice, Czechoslovakia .. 71/D1
Koszalin, Poland 74/A1
Kota Baharu, Malaysia.... 91/B3
Kota Kinabalu
    (cap.), Sabah 98/B2
Kra (isth.), Thailand 91/A2
Krasnoyarsk, U.S.S.R. ... 77/E3
Krishna (riv.), India 88/B3
Kristiansand, Norway 57/A3
Kristiansund, Norway 56/A2
Kuala Lumpur (cap.),
    Malaysia 91/B3
Kuching (cap.), Sarawak 98/B2
Kumamoto, Japan 94/B2
Kumasi, Ghana 107/B4
Kunlun Shan (mts.),
    China 92/B2
Kunming, China 92/C2
Kuopio, Finland 56/C2
Kure, Japan 94/B2
Kuril (isls.), U.S.S.R. 77/H3
Kut, Iraq 86/B2
Kutch, Rann of (salt
    marsh), Asia 88/A2
Kuybyshev, U.S.S.R. 76/C3
Kwangju, S. Korea 94/A2
Kwango (riv.), Africa .. 110/B3
Kyoto, Japan 94/B2
Kyushu (isl.), Japan 94/B2

L

Laayoune, Morocco 106/A2
Labrador (reg.),
    Newfoundland 19/E2
Labrador (sea),
    N. America 19/F2
Laccadive (isls.), India.. 88/A3
La Ceiba, Honduras 38/C2
La Chaux-de-Fonds,
    Switzerland 68/A1

Laconia, N. H. 23/B3
La Coruña, Spain 64/A1
La Crosse, Wisconsin 29/D3
Lae, Papua New Guinea 99/D3
Lafayette, Louisiana 31/D3
Lagos (cap.), Nigeria .. 107/C4
Lahore, Pakistan 88/B1
Lahti, Finland 57/C2
Lake Charles, La. 31/D3
Lakeland, Florida 27/C4
Lake Oahe (res.) 28/A2
Lake of the Woods (lake),
    N. America 28/C1
Lake Sakakawea (res.),
    N. Dakota 28/A1
Lambaréné, Gabon 110/B3
Lamon (bay), Phil. 96/B2
Lampang, Thailand 90/A2
Lanai (isl.), Hawaii 20/C3
Lancaster, Pa. 25/C3
Land's End (prom.),
    England 55/B4
Langenthal, Switzerland.. 68/B1
Lansing (cap.), Mich. 29/E3
Laoag, Phil. 96/B1
Lao Cai, Vietnam 90/B1
La Oroya, Peru 47/C4
La Paz (cap.), Bolivia .. 48/B3
Lapland (reg.), Europe.. 56/C2
La Plata, Argentina 50/C3
La Plata (est.), S. Amer. 43/C3
Laptev (sea), U.S.S.R. .. 77/G2
Laramie, Wyoming 33/F3
Laredo, Texas 30/C4
La Rioja, Argentina 50/B2
Larisa, Greece 73/B2
La Rochelle, France 63/B3
Larsen (ice shelf),
    Antarctica 114/C11
Las Cruces, N. Mex. 35/F3
La Serena, Chile 50/A2

Las Palmas, Canary Is.,
Spain 106/A2
Las Vegas, Nevada 34/D2
Latakia, Syria 82/C2
Latina, Italy 67/C2
Launceston, Tasmania.. 101/D4
Lausanne, Switz. 68/A2
Lawrence, Mass. 23/B3
Lawton, Oklahoma 30/C2
Leeds, England 55/C3
Leeuwarden, Neth. 60/B1
Leeuwin (cape),
W. Australia 100/A3
Leeward (isls.),
W. Indies 41/D2
Legaspi, Phil. 96/B2
Leghorn, Italy 66/B2
Legnica, Poland 74/A2
Le Havre, France 62/B2
Leicester, England 55/C3
Leiden, Neth. 60/B1
Leipzig, Germany 58/C2
Lek (riv.), Neth. 60/B2
Le Mans, France 62/C2
Lena (riv.), U.S.S.R. 77/G2
Leningrad, U.S.S.R. 76/B3
Leoben, Austria 70/B2
León, Mexico 36/B2
León, Nicaragua 38/C2
León, Spain 64/B1
Lepontine Alps (mts.),
Europe 69/C2
Lérida, Spain 65/D1
Lesbos (isl.), Greece 73/B2
Les Cayes, Haiti 40/B2
Lesser Antilles (isls.),
W. Indies 41/C-D3
Leticia, Colombia 44/B3
Lewiston, Idaho 32/C2
Lewiston, Maine 22/B2
Lexington, Kentucky 26/B2

Leyte (gulf), Phil. 97/C3
Leyte (isl.), Phil. 97/C3
Lhasa, China 92/B2
Liberec, Czech. 70/B1
Libreville (cap.),
Gabon 110/B2
Libyan (des.), Africa .. 108/B2
Liège, Belgium 61/B2
Ligurian (sea), Eur. 66/B2
Likasi, Zaire 110/C4
Lille, France 62/C2
Lilongwe (cap.),
Malawi 113/C2
Lima, Ohio 29/F3
Lima (cap.), Peru 47/B4
Limassol, Cyprus 82/B3
Limerick, Ireland 55/A3
Limmat (riv.), Switz. 69/C1
Limoges, France 63/C3
Limón, Costa Rica 39/D3
Lincoln (cap.), Nebr. 28/B3
Lindesnes (cape), Nor. .. 57/A3
Line (isls.) 103/D2
Lingayen (gulf),
Phil. 96/A1
Linköping, Sweden 57/B3
Linz, Austria 70/B1
Lions (gulf), France 63/D4
Lisbon (cap.), Portugal.. 64/A2
Little Rock (cap.), Ark. 31/D2
Liverpool, England 55/C3
Livingstone, Zambia 112/B2
Ljubljana, Yugoslavia .. 72/A1
Llano Estacado (plain),
U.S. 30/B2
Llanos (plains),
S. America 42/B1
Llullaillaco (vol.),
S. America 50/B2
Locarno, Switzerland 69/C2
Łódź, Poland 74/B2

Lofoten (isls.), Norway.. 56/B2
Logan, Utah 35/E1
Logan (mt.), Yukon 18/B1
Logone (riv.), Cam. 110/B1
Loire (riv.), France 62/B3
Loja, Ecuador 46/B2
Lomé (cap.), Togo 107/C4
London (cap.), U.K. 55/C4
Long (isl.), Bahamas 40/B2
Long (isl.), New York .. 25/E3
Long Beach, Calif. 34/C3
Long Branch, N. J. 25/E3
Longfellow (mts.),
Maine 22/B2
Long Island (sound),
U.S. 23/A4
Long Xuyen,
Vietnam 91/B2
Lorient, France 62/B3
Los Angeles, Calif. 34/C3
Los Angeles Aqueduct,
California 34/C3
Louangphrabang, Laos .. 90/B2
Louisville, Kentucky 26/B2
Louvain, Belgium 61/B2
Lowell, Mass. 23/B3
Lower California (pen.),
Mexico 36/A2
Lualaba (riv.),
Zaire 110/C3
Luanda (cap.), Angola 112/A1
Luapula (riv.), Africa.. 112/B2
Lubbock, Texas 30/B2
Lübeck, Germany 58/B1
Lubelska (hills), Pol. 75/C2
Lublin, Poland 75/C2
Lubumbashi,
Zaire 110/C4
Lucena, Phil. 96/B2
Lucerne, Switzerland 69/C1
Lucerne (lake), Switz. .. 69/C2

Lucknow, India 89/C2
Lüda, China 93/D2
Lüderitz, Namibia 112/A3
Ludhiana, India 88/B1
Lugano, Switzerland 69/C2
Lugano (lake), Europe .. 69/C3
Lulea, Sweden 56/C2
Luoyang, China 93/C2
Lusaka (cap.),
    Zambia 112/B2
Lützow-Holm (bay),
    Antarctica 115/C2
Luxembourg (cap.),
    Luxembourg 61/C3
Luzon (isl.), Phil. 96/B1
Luzon (sea), Phil. 96/A2
Lynchburg, Virginia 26/D2
Lynn, Mass. 23/B3
Lyon, France 63/D3
Lys (riv.), Europe 61/A2

M

Maan, Jordan 84/A2
Maas (riv.), Neth. 60/B2
Maastricht, Neth. 61/B2
Macapá, Brazil 49/C1
Macdonnell (ranges), N. Terr.,
    Australia 100/B-C2
Maceió, Brazil 49/E2
Machala, Ecuador 46/B2
Mackenzie (riv.),
    N.W.T., Canada 18/B1
Macon, Georgia 26/C3
Madaba, Jordan 84/A2
Madagascar (isl.),
    Madagascar 113/D3
Madeira (isl.), Port. 106/A1
Madeira (riv.), Brazil ... 48/B2
Madison (cap.), Wis. 29/D3

Madras, India 89/C3
Madre de Dios (riv.),
    S. America 47/D5
Madrid (cap.), Spain 64/C1
Madurai, India 88/B4
Magadan, U.S.S.R. 77/H3
Magdalena (riv.), Col. .. 44/B2
Magdeburg,
    Germany 58/B1
Magellan (str.),
    S. America 51/B5
Maggiore (lake),
    Europe 69/C3
Magwe, Burma 90/A1
Maiduguri, Nigeria 107/D3
Main (riv.), Germany 59/B2
Majorca (isl.), Spain 65/D2
Majunga, Madagascar.. 113/D2
Makassar (strait),
    Indonesia 98/B3
Makgadikgadi (salt pan),
    Botswana 112/B3
Malacca (strait), Asia .. 98/A2
Málaga, Spain 64/B2
Malakal, Sudan 109/C4
Malatya, Turkey 83/C2
Malay (pen.), Asia 98/B2
Malmo, Sweden 57/B3
Małopolska (hills),
    Poland 74/B2
Mamoré (riv.), Bolivia .. 48/B3
Managua (cap.), Nic. 38/C2
Managua (lake), Nic. 38/C2
Manaus, Brazil 48/C2
Manchester, England 55/C3
Manchester, N.H. 23/B3
Mand (riv.), Iran 87/C3
Mandalay, Burma 90/A1
Manila (cap.), Phil. 96/B2
Manila (bay), Phil. 96/A2
Manizales, Colombia 44/A2

Mannheim, Germany 59/B2
Manta, Ecuador 46/A2
Maoke (mts.), Papua
    N.G. 99/C3
Maputo (cap.),
    Mozambique 105/D5
Maraba, Brazil 49/C2
Maracaibo, Venezuela ... 44/B1
Maracaibo (lake), Ven. 44/B1
Maracay, Venezuela 44/C1
Marajó (isl.), Brazil 49/D2
Marañón (riv.), Peru 46/B3
Maraş, Turkey 83/C2
Marcy (mt.),
    New York 24/E1
Mar del Plata, Arg. 51/C3
Margarita (isl.), Ven. 45/C1
Margherita (mt.),
    Africa 110/C2
Marie Byrd Land (reg.),
    Antarctica 114/B9
Mariscal Estigarribia,
    Paraguay 50/B2
Maritsa (riv.), Europe .. 73/B1
Markham (mt.),
    Antarctica 115/A6
Marmara (sea),
    Turkey 82/A1
Marne (riv.), France 62/D2
Marquette, Michigan 29/E2
Marrakesh, Morocco 106/B1
Marseille, France 63/D4
Marshall (isls.),
    Pacific Is. 102/C2
Martaban (gulf),
    Burma 90/A2
Martha's Vineyard (isl.),
    Massachusetts 23/B4
Martigny, Switzerland 68/B2
Masbate, Phil. 96/B2
Masbate (isl.), Phil. 96/B2

Maseru (cap.), Lesotho 112/B3
Massif Central (plat.), France 63/C3
Masurian (lakes), Pol. .. 75/C1
Matadi, Zaire 110/B3
Matagalpa, Nicaragua ... 38/C2
Matamoros, Mexico 37/C2
Matanzas, Cuba 40/A2
Mato Grosso (plat.), Brazil 49/C3
Matsuyama, Japan 94/B2
Matterhorn (mt.), Switzerland 68/B3
Maturín, Venezuela 45/C1
Maui (isl.), Hawaii 20/C3
Mauna Loa (mt.), Hawaii 20/D3
Mawson (sta.), Antarctica 115/C3
May (cape), N. J. 25/D4
Mayagüez, P. Rico 41/C2
Mazatenango, Guatemala 38/B2
Mazatlán, Mexico 36/B2
Mbabane (cap.), Swaz. 113/C3
Mbandaka, Zaire 110/B2
McKeesport, Pa. 25/B3
McKinley (mt.), Alaska 20/B3
McMurdo (sound), Antarctica 115/B6
McMurdo (sta.), Antarctica 115/B6
Mead (lake), U.S. 34/D2
Mecca (cap.), Saudi Arabia 80/B2
Mechelen, Belgium 61/B2
Medan, Indonesia 98/A2
Medellín, Colombia 44/A2
Medford, Oregon 32/B3
Medina, Saudi Arabia 80/A2
Mediterranean (sea) 52/C4

Mekong (riv.), Asia 79/E4
Melaka, Indonesia 91/B3
Melanesia (reg.) 102/B3
Melbourne (cap.), Victoria, Australia .. 101/D4
Melo, Uruguay 50/C3
Melville (isl.), N. Terr., Australia 100/B1
Memphis, Tennessee 26/A3
Menderes (riv.), Turk. .. 82/A2
Mendocino (cape), California 34/A1
Mendoza, Argentina 50/B3
Mergui, Burma 90/A2
Mergui (arch.), Burma.. 91/A2
Mérida, Mexico 37/D2
Mérida, Venezuela 44/B1
Meridian, Mississippi 26/A3
Mersin, Turkey 82/B2
Mesa, Arizona 35/E3
Meshed, Iran 87/C2
Mesopotamia (reg.), Iraq 86/B2
Messina, Italy 67/C3
Meta (riv.), Colombia.... 44/B2
Metz, France 62/D2
Meuse (riv.), Europe 61/B2
Mexicali, Mexico 36/A1
Mexico (gulf), N. Amer. 17/E3
Mexico City (cap.), Mexico 37/C3
Miami, Florida 27/C5
Michigan (lake), U.S. 21/E1
Micronesia (reg.) 102/B2
Middlesbrough, England 55/C3
Midland, Texas 30/B2
Midway (isls.) 103/D1
Milan, Italy 66/B1
Miles City, Montana 33/F2
Milk (riv.), N. America.. 33/E1
Millinocket, Maine 22/C2

Milwaukee, Wisconsin .. 29/D3
Mindanao (isl.), Phil. 97/B3
Mindanao (sea), Phil. .. 97/B4
Mindoro (isl.), Phil. 96/A2
Mindoro (strait), Phil. ... 96/A2
Minneapolis, Minnesota.. 28/C2
Miño (riv.), Europe 64/B1
Minorca (isl.), Spain 65/E1
Minot, N. Dakota 28/A1
Minsk, U.S.S.R. 76/B3
Mirnyy (sta.), Antarctica 115/C4
Miskolc, Hungary 71/D1
Mississippi (delta), La. 31/E3
Mississippi (riv.), U.S. .. 21/D2
Missoula, Montana 33/D2
Missouri (riv.), U.S. 21/D1
Misurata, Libya 108/A1
Mitchell (mt.), N.C. 26/C3
Mitú, Colombia 44/B2
Mo, Norway 56/B2
Mobile, Alabama 27/A4
Mobutu Sese Seko (lake), Africa 110/C2
Mogadishu (cap.), Somalia 111/E2
Mohawk (riv.), N.Y. 24/D2
Mojave (desert), Calif. .. 34/C3
Molodezhnaya (sta.), Antarctica 115/C2
Molokai (isl.), Hawaii .. 20/C3
Moluccas (isls.), Indon. 99/C3
Mombasa, Kenya 111/E3
Mona (passg.), W. Indies 41/C2
Monroe, Louisiana 31/E2
Monrovia (cap.), Lib. 107/A4
Mons, Belgium 61/A2
Montego Bay, Jamaica .. 40/B2
Montería, Colombia 44/B1
Monterrey, Mexico 37/C2
Montes Claros, Brazil 49/D3

Montevideo (cap.),
    Uruguay 50/C3
Montgomery (cap.),
    Alabama 27/B3
Montpelier (cap.), Vt. .. 22/A2
Montpellier, France 63/C4
Montréal, Québec 19/E2
Montreux, Switzerland .. 68/A2
Moosehead (lake),
    Maine 22/C2
Morava (riv.), Europe .. 71/C1
Morava (riv.), Yugo. 72/B1
Moray (firth), Scotland.. 54/C2
Moro (gulf.), Phil. 97/B4
Moscow (cap.), U.S.S.R. 76/B3
Mosel (riv.), Europe 59/A2
Mosquito Coast (reg.),
    Cent. America 39/D2
Mosul, Iraq 86/B2
Moulmein, Burma 90/A2
Mount Desert (isl.),
    Maine 22/D2
Mozambique (chan.),
    Africa 105/D5
Mtwara, Tanzania 111/D4
Mui Bai Bung (pt.),
    Vietnam 91/B3
Mukden, see Shenyang
Mulhacén (mt.), Spain .. 64/C2
Mulhouse, France 62/D3
Muncie, Indiana 29/E3
Munich, Germany 59/B2
Münster, Germany 58/A2
Muonio (riv.), Europe .. 56/C2
Murat (riv.), Turkey 83/D2
Murcia, Spain 65/C2
Mures (riv.), Romania.. 72/B1
Murmansk, U.S.S.R. 53/D1
Murray (riv.),
    Australia 101/C3
Muscat (cap.), Oman 81/B2

Muskogee, Oklahoma 31/D2
Myitkyina, Burma 90/A1
Mysore, India 88/B3

N

Nablus, Jordan 84/A1
Nacala, Mozambique .. 113/D2
Naga, Phil. 96/B2
Nagasaki, Japan 94/A2
Nagoya, Japan 95/B2
Nagpur, India 89/B2
Naha, Ryukyu Is. 95/C2
Nairobi (cap.), Kenya.. 111/D3
Nakhon Ratchasima,
    Thailand 90/B2
Nakhon Si Thammarat,
    Thailand 91/A3
Namakzar-e Shahdad
    (dry lake), Iran 87/C2
Nam Dinh, Vietnam 90/B1
Namib (des.), Namibia 112/A2
Namibe, Angola 112/A2
Namur, Belgium 61/B2
Nanchang, China 93/C2
Nancy, France 62/D2
Nanjing, China 93/C2
Nanning, China 93/C2
Nantes, France 62/B3
Nantucket (isl.), Mass. .. 23/C4
Naples, Italy 67/C2
Napo (riv.), S. Amer. 46/C2
Narbada (riv.), India 88/B2
Narew (riv.), Poland 75/C1
Narvik, Norway 56/B2
Nashua, New Hampshire 23/B3
Nashville (cap.), Tenn. .. 26/B3
Nassau (cap.), Bahamas 40/B1
Nasser (lake), Africa .. 109/C2
Natal, Brazil 49/E2

Natchez, Mississippi 27/A4
Nazareth, Israel 84/A1
N'Djamena (cap.),
    Chad 104/C3
Ndola, Zambia 112/B2
Neblina (mt.), Brazil 48/B1
Negev (reg.), Israel 84/A2
Negrais (cape), Burma.. 90/A2
Negro (riv.), Argentina.. 51/B3
Negro (riv.), S. America 42/B2
Negros (isl.), Phil. 97/B3
Neisse (riv.), Europe 58/C2
Neiva, Colombia 44/B2
Nelson (riv.), Manitoba 18/D2
Netanya, Israel 84/A1
Neuchâtel, Switzerland .. 68/A1
Neuchâtel (lake), Switz. 68/A2
Neutral Zone, Asia 80/B2
New Albany, Indiana 29/E4
New Amsterdam, Guy. .. 45/D2
Newark, New Jersey 25/D3
New Bedford, Mass. 23/B4
New Britain, Conn. 23/A4
New Britain (isl.), Papua
    New Guinea 102/B3
Newcastle, New South
    Wales 101/D3
New Castle, Pa. 24/A3
Newcastle upon Tyne,
    England 54/C3
New Delhi (cap.), India 88/B2
Newfoundland (isl.),
    Newfoundland 19/F2
New Guinea (isl.) 99/C3
New Haven, Conn. 23/A4
New London, Conn. 23/A4
New Orleans, Louisiana.. 31/E3
Newport, Rhode Island .. 23/B4
Newport News, Va. 26/D2
New Providence (isl.),
    Bahamas 40/B1

New Schwabenland (reg.),
  Antarctica 115/B1
New Siberian (isls.),
  U.S.S.R. 77/H2
New York, New York 25/E3
Niagara Falls, New York 24/B2
Niamey (cap.), Niger .. 107/C3
Nicaragua (lake), Nic. .. 38/C3
Nice, France 63/D4
Nicobar (isls.), India 89/D4
Nicosia (cap.), Cyprus.. 82/B2
Nicoya (pen.), C. Rica .. 38/C3
Niger (riv.), Africa 104/C3
Niigata, Japan 95/B2
Nijmegen, Neth. 60/B2
Nile (riv.), Africa 104/D3
Nîmes, France 63/D4
Niobrara (riv.), U.S. 28/A3
Nis, Yugoslavia 72/B1
Niterói, Brazil 49/D4
Nordvik, U.S.S.R. 77/F2
Norfolk, Nebraska 28/B3
Norfolk, Virginia 26/D2
Norfolk (isl.),
  Australia 102/C4
Norilsk, U.S.S.R. 77/E2
Norman, Oklahoma 30/C2
Norrkoping, Sweden 57/B3
North (cape), Norway .. 56/C1
North (isl.), N.Z. 101/E3
North (sea), Europe 52/C3
North Atlantic Ocean 14/G2
Northern Marianas (isls.),
  Pac. Is. 102/B2
Northern Territory,
  Australia 100/B2
North Magnetic Pole 18/C1
North Pacific Ocean 14/B2
North Platte, Nebraska... 28/A3
North Platte (riv.), U.S. 33/F3
North Pole 16,78

Northwest Territories,
  Canada C-E1/18-19
Norvegia (cape),
  Antarctica 114/B12
Norwegian (sea), Eur. .. 52/B1
Norwich, England 55/D3
Nottingham, England 55/C3
Nouakchott (cap.),
  Mauritania 107/A3
Nouméa, New Cal. 102/C3
Novaya Zemlya (isls.),
  U.S.S.R. 76/C2
Novi Sad, Yugoslavia 72/A1
Novokuznetsk, U.S.S.R. 76/E3
Novolazarevskaya (sta.),
  Antarctica 115/B1
Novosibirsk, U.S.S.R. 76/E3
Nubian (des.), Sudan .. 109/C2
Nueces (riv.), Texas 30/C3
Nuevo Laredo, Mexico .. 37/B2
Nullarbor (plain),
  Australia 100/B3
Nuremberg, Germany 59/B2
Nyasa (lake), Africa .. 105/D4

O

Oahu (isl.), Hawaii 20/C3
Oakland, Calif. 34/B2
Oak Ridge, Tenn. 26/B2
Oaxaca, Mexico 37/C3
Ob (riv.), U.S.S.R. 76/D2
Odense, Denmark 57/A3
Oder (riv.), Europe 74/A1
Odessa, Texas 30/B3
Odessa, U.S.S.R. 76/B3
Ogbomosho, Nigeria 107/C4
Ogden, Utah 35/E1
Ogdensburg,
  New York 24/D1

Ohio (riv.), U.S. 21/E2
Ojos del Salado (mt.),
  S. America 50/B2
Okeechobee (lake), Fla. 27/C5
Okhotsk (sea), U.S.S.R. 77/H3
Okinawa (isl.),
  Ryukyu Is. 95/C2
Oklahoma City (cap.),
  Oklahoma 31/C2
Oland (isl.), Sweden 57/B3
Olavarría, Argentina 51/B3
Olomouc, Czech. 71/C1
Olsztyn, Poland 75/C1
Olt (riv.), Romania 72/B1
Olten, Switzerland 68/B1
Olympia (cap.), Wash. .. 32/B2
Olympic (mts.), Wash. .. 32/B1
Olympus (mt.), Greece.. 73/B1
Omaha, Nebraska 28/B3
Oman (gulf), Asia 81/B2
Omdurman, Sudan 109/C3
Omsk, U.S.S.R. 76/D3
Oneida (lake), N.Y. 24/D2
Ontario (lake),
  N. America 21/F1
Oporto, Portugal 64/A1
Oradea, Romania 72/B1
Oran, Algeria 106/B1
Orange (riv.), Africa .. 105/C5
Orebro, Sweden 57/B3
Orense, Spain 64/B1
Orinoco (delta), Ven. 45/C1
Orinoco (riv.), S. Amer. 44/C2
Orkney (isls.), Scotland 54/C2
Orlando, Florida 27/C4
Orléans, France 62/C3
Orontes (riv.), Syria 83/C2
Oruro, Bolivia 48/B3
Osaka, Japan 94/B2
Oshkosh, Wisconsin 29/D2
Oslo (cap.), Norway 57/B3

Osnabrück, Germany 58/B1
Ostend, Belgium 61/A2
Ostersund, Sweden 56/B2
Ostrava, Czechoslovakia 71/C1
Ottawa (cap.), Canada ..19/E2
Ouagadougou (cap.),
    Burkina Faso 107/B3
Oulu, Finland 56/C2
Oviedo, Spain 64/B1
Owensboro, Kentucky 26/B2
Owyhee (riv.), U.S. 32/C3
Oxford, England 55/C4
Oyapock (riv.),
    S. America 45/D2
Ozark (mts.), U.S. 21/D2

P

Padre (isl.), Texas 31/C4
Padua, Italy 66/B1
Paducah, Kentucky 26/A2
Paektu (mt.), Asia 94/A1
Pagadian, Phil. 97/B4
Pago Pago, Am. Samoa 103/D3
Pakse, Laos 90/B2
Palau (isls.),
    Pac. Is. 102/A2
Palawan (isl.), Phil. 97/A3
Palembang, Indonesia 98/B3
Palermo, Italy 67/C3
Palma, Spain 65/D2
Palmas (cape), Liberia 107/B4
Palmer (sta.),
    Antarctica 114/C10
Palmer Land (reg.),
    Antarctica 114/B10
Pampas (plains), Arg. .. 50/B3
Pamplona, Spain 65/C1
Panamá (cap.), Pan. 39/E3

Panamá (canal),
    N. America 39/E3
Panamá (gulf), Panama 39/E4
Panama City, Florida 27/B4
Panay (isl.), Phil. 97/B3
Pantelleria (isl.), Italy .. 67/C3
Paraguay (riv.),
    S. America 50/C2
Paramaribo (cap.),
    Suriname 45/D2
Paraná, Argentina 50/B3
Paraná (riv.), S. Amer... 43/C3
Parintins, Brazil 49/C2
Paris (cap.), France 62/C2
Parkersburg,
    W. Virginia 26/C2
Parma, Italy 66/B1
Parral, Mexico 36/B2
Parry (chan.), N.W.T.,
    Canada 18-19/C-D1
Pasadena, Calif. 34/C3
Passero (cape), Italy 67/C3
Pastaza (riv.),
    South America 46/B2
Pasto, Colombia 44/A2
Patagonia (reg.), Arg. .. 51/B4
Paterson, New Jersey 25/D3
Patna, India 89/C2
Patos (lagoon), Brazil .. 49/D5
Patras, Greece 73/B2
Pau, France 63/B4
Paysandú, Uruguay 50/C3
Peace (riv.), Canada 18/C2
Pecos (riv.), U.S. 30/B3
Pecs, Hungary 71/C2
Peloponnesos (pen.),
    Greece 73/B2
Pelotas, Brazil 49/C5
Pendleton, Oregon 32/C2
Pennine Alps (mts.),
    Europe 68/B2

Pennine Chain (mts.),
    England 55/C3
Penobscot (riv.), Maine 22/C2
Pensacola, Florida 27/B4
Peoria, Illinois 29/D3
Perm, U.S.S.R. 76/C3
Perpignan, France 63/C4
Persian (gulf), Asia 80/B2
Perth (cap.),
    W. Australia 100/A3
Pescara, Italy 66/C2
Petra (ruins), Jordan 84/A2
Phan Rang, Vietnam 91/B2
Philadelphia, Pa. 25/D3
Philippine (sea) 102/A2
Phnom Penh (cap.),
    Cambodia 91/B2
Phoenix (cap.), Arizona 35/D3
Phoenix (isls.),
    Kiribati 103/D3
Piedras Negras, Mexico .. 36/B2
Pierre (cap.), S. Dak. 28/A2
Pietermaritzburg,
    S. Africa 113/C3
Pikes Peak (mt.), Colo. 35/F2
Pilcomayo (riv.),
    S. America 50/B2
Pilica (riv.), Poland 75/C2
Pinar del Río, Cuba 40/A2
Pindus (mts.), Greece 73/B2
Pine Bluff, Arkansas 31/D2
Piraeus, Greece 73/B2
Pisco, Peru 47/B5
Pittsburgh, Pa. 25/B3
Pittsfield, Mass. 23/A3
Piura, Peru 46/A3
Plateau (sta.), Antarc. 115/B2
Platte (riv.), Nebraska .. 20/D1
Plattsburgh, New York .. 24/E1
Pleven, Bulgaria 72/B1
Ploiesti, Romania 72/B1

Plovdiv, Bulgaria 73/B1
Plymouth, England 55/B4
Plzen, Czechoslovakia ... 70/B1
Po (riv.), Italy 66/B1
Pocatello, Idaho 33/D3
Poinsett (cape),
    Antarctica 115/C4
Pointe-Noire, Congo 110/B3
Polillo (isls.), Phil. 96/B2
Polynesia (reg.), ... 103/D2-3
Pomerania (reg.),
    Europe 74/A-B1
Ponape (isl.), Pac. Is. .. 102/B2
Ponce, P. Rico 41/C2
Pontiac, Michigan 29/F3
Pontianak, Indonesia 98/B2
Pontic (mts.), Turkey 83/C-D1
Poopó (lake), Bolivia.... 48/B3
Popayán, Colombia 44/A2
Popocatépetl (mt.),
    Mexico 37/C3
Pori, Finland 57/C2
Port-au-Prince (cap.),
    Haiti 40/B2
Port Elizabeth,
    S. Africa 112/B4
Portland, Maine 23/B3
Portland, Oregon 32/B2
Port Moresby (cap.),
    Papua New Guinea 99/D3
Pôrto Alegre, Brazil 49/D4
Port of Spain (cap.),
    Trinidad and Tobago.. 41/D3
Pôrto Nacional, Brazil ... 49/D3
Porto-Novo (cap.),
    Benin 107/C4
Pôrto Velho, Brazil 48/B2
Port Said, Egypt 109/C1
Portsmouth, England 55/C4
Portsmouth, N.H. 23/B3
Port Sudan, Sudan 109/C3

Potomac (riv.), U.S. 25/C4
Potosí, Bolivia 48/B4
Potsdam, Germany 58/C1
Poughkeepsie, N.Y. 24/D3
Powder (riv.), U.S. 33/F2
Powell (lake), U.S. 35/E2
Poznań, Poland 74/B1
Prague (cap.), Czech. 70/B1
Presque Isle, Maine 22/C1
Prescott, Arizona 35/D3
Pretoria (cap.),
    S. Africa 112/B3
Prince Rupert, Br. Col. .. 18/B2
Providence (cap.),
    Rhode I. 23/B4
Provo, Utah 35/E1
Prut (riv.), Europe 72/B1
Przemyśl, Poland 75/C2
Puebla, Mexico 37/C3
Pueblo, Colorado 35/F2
Puerto Barrios, Guat. 38/B2
Puerto Cabezas, Nic. 39/D2
Puerto Carreno, Ven. 44/C2
Puerto Maldonado, Peru 47/D5
Puerto Montt, Chile 51/A4
Puerto Princesa,
    Phil. 97/A3
Puget (sound), Wash. 32/B2
Pulangi (riv.), Phil. 97/C4
Punjab (reg.), Asia 88/B1
Puno, Peru 47/D5
Punta Arenas, Chile 51/A5
Puntarenas, Costa Rica .. 38/C3
Purus (riv.), S. Amer. .. 48/B2
Pusan, S. Korea 94/A2
Putumayo (riv.),
    S. America 46/C2
Pye, Burma 90/A2
Pyongyang (cap.),
    N. Korea 94/A2
Pyrenees (mts.), Europe 52/B3

Q

Qamdo, China 92/B2
Qandahar, Afghanistan . 88/A1
Qara (riv.), Iran 86/B2
Qazvin, Iran 86/B2
Qingdao, China 93/D2
Qiqihar, China 93/D1
Qishm (isl.), Iran 87/C3
Qom, Iran 86/C2
Québec (cap.), Québec .. 19/E2
Queen Charlotte (isls.),
    Br. Columbia 18/B2
Queen Elizabeth (isls.),
    N.W.T., Canada 18/C1
Queen Maud (range),
    Antarctica 114/A8
Queen Maud Land (reg.),
    Antarctica 115/B1
Quelimane, Moz. 113/C2
Quetta, Pakistan 88/A1
Quezaltenango, Guat. 38/A2
Quezon City, Philippines 96/B2
Quincy, Illinois 29/D4
Qui Nhon, Vietnam 91/B2
Quito (cap.), Ecuador.... 46/B2

R

Rabat (cap.), Morocco 106/B1
Rabaul, Papua
    New Guinea 102/B3
Race (cape), Newf. 19/F2
Racine, Wisconsin 29/D3
Radom, Poland 75/C2
Rainier (mt.), Wash. 32/B2
Raleigh (cap.),
    N. Carolina 26/D3
Ramadi, Iraq 86/B2

Rangoon (cap.), Burma 90/A2
Rapid City, S. Dak. 28/A2
Ras Aser (cape),
    Somalia 111/E1
Rasht, Iran 86/B2
Reading, Pa. 25/D3
Recife, Brazil 49/E2
Red (riv.), Asia 90/B1
Red (riv.), U.S. 20/C2
Red River of the North
    (riv.), N. America 28/B1
Red (sea) 80/A2; 109/C2
Redding, Calif. 34/B1
Regensburg, Germany ... 59/C2
Reggane, Algeria 106/C2
Reggio di Calabria, Italy 67/C3
Regina (cap.), Sask. 18/C2
Reims, France 62/D2
Rennes, France 62/B2
Reno, Nevada 34/C2
Republican (riv.), U.S. .. 28/B3
Resistencia, Argentina .. 50/B2
Reuss (riv.), Switz. 69/C1
Revillagigedo (isls.),
    Mexico 36/A3
Reykjavík (cap.), Ice. 56/A2
Rhaetian Alps (mts.),
    Europe 69/D-E2
Rhine (riv.), Europe 52/C3
Rhodes (isl.), Greece 73/B2
Rhodope (mts.), Europe 72/B1
Rhône (riv.), Europe 63/D3
Ribeirão Prêto, Brazil 49/C4
Riberalta, Bolivia 48/B3
Richmond (cap.), Va. .. 26/D2
Riiser-Larsen (pen.),
    Antarctica 115/C2
Rijeka, Yugoslavia 72/A1
Riobamba, Ecuador 46/B2
Rio Branco, Brazil 48/B2
Rio de Janeiro, Brazil 49/D4

Río Gallegos, Argentina   51/B5
Rio Grande (riv.),
    N. America 17/D3
Río Grande de Santiago
    (riv.), Mexico 36/B2
Río Muni (prov.),
    Equat. Guinea 110/B2
Rivera, Uruguay 50/C3
Riyadh (cap.),
    Saudi Arabia 80/B2
Roanoke, Virginia 26/C2
Roanoke (riv.), U.S. 26/D2
Rochester, Minnesota 28/C2
Rochester, New York 24/C2
Rockford, Illinois 29/D3
Rockhampton, Queens. 101/D2
Rock Island, Illinois 29/D3
Rock Springs, Wyoming.. 33/E3
Rockville, Maryland 25/C4
Rocky (mts.), N. Amer. 16/C2
Rome, Georgia 26/B3
Rome (cap.), Italy 67/C2
Rome, New York 24/D2
Ronne (ice shelf),
    Antarctica 114/B10
Roosevelt (isl.), Ant. .. 114/A7
Roraima (mt.),
    S. America 45/C2
Rosa (mt.), Europe 66/A1
Rosario, Argentina 50/B3
Roseau (cap.), Dom. 41/D3
Ross (ice shelf), Ant. .. 114/A7
Ross (isl.), Antarctica.. 115/B6
Ross (sea), Antarctica ..114/B7
Rostock, Germany 58/C1
Rostov, U.S.S.R. 76/C3
Roswell, New Mexico 35/F3
Rotterdam, Neth. 60/B2
Rouen, France 62/C2
Roxas, Phil. 97/B3
Royale (isl.), Michigan.. 29/E1

Rub' al Khali (des.),
    Arabia 80/B2
Rudolf (Turkana) (lake),
    Kenya 111/D2
Rügen (isl.), Ger. 58/C1
Ruhr (riv.), Ger. 58/A2
Ruse, Bulgaria 72/B1
Rutland, Vermont 23/A3
Ruvuma (riv.), Africa.. 111/D4
Rysy (mt.), Europe 75/C2
Rzeszów, Poland 75/C2

S

Saale (riv.), Ger. 58/B2
Saane (riv.), Switz. 68/B2
Saarbrücken, Ger. 59/A2
Sabadell, Spain 65/D1
Sabine (riv.), U.S. 31/D2
Sable (cape), Florida 27/C5
Sabzevar, Iran 87/C2
Sacramento (cap.), Cal. 34/B2
Sacramento (riv.), Cal. 34/A1
Saginaw, Michigan 29/E3
Sahara (desert),
    Africa 104/B-D2
Saigon (Ho Chi Minh
    City) Viet. 91/B2
Saint Cloud, Minnesota .. 28/C2
Saint Croix (riv.),
    N. America 22/D2
Saint Croix (riv.), U.S. 29/C2
Sainte-Marie (cape),
    Madagascar 113/D3
Saint Étienne, France 63/D3
Saint George's (chan.),
    Europe 55/B4
Saint John (riv.),
    N. America 22/C1
Saint John's (cap.),
    Ant. & Barb. 41/D2

Saint John's (cap.),
    Newfoundland 19/F2
Saint Joseph, Missouri ... 28/C4
Saint Lawrence (gulf),
    Canada 19/E2
Saint Lawrence (riv.),
    N. America 19/E2
Saint Louis, Missouri 29/D4
Saint-Louis, Senegal 107/A3
Saint Lucia (isl.) 41/D3
Saint Moritz, Switz. 69/D2
Saint Paul (cap.), Minn. 28/C2
Saint Petersburg, Florida 27/C5
Saint Vincent (cape),
    Portugal 64/A2
Saint Vincent (isl.) 41/D3
Saipan (isl.), Pac. Is. .. 102/B2
Sakarya (riv.), Turkey .. 82/B1
Sakhalin (isl.), U.S.S.R. 77/H3
Salado (riv.), Argentina 50/B2
Salamanca, Spain 64/B1
Salekhard, U.S.S.R. 76/D2
Salem (cap.), Oregon 32/B2
Salerno, Italy 67/C2
Salina, Kansas 28/B4
Salisbury, Maryland 25/D4
Salisbury (Harare) (cap.),
    Zimbabwe 113/C2
Salmon (riv.), Idaho 32/D2
Salong, Phil. 97/B3
Salonika, Greece 73/B1
Salt (riv.), Arizona 35/E3
Salta, Argentina 50/B2
Saltillo, Mexico 36/B2
Salt Lake City (cap.),
    Utah 35/E1
Salto, Uruguay 50/C3
Salto Grande (falls),
    Colombia 44/B3
Salton Sea (lake), Calif. 34/C3
Salvador, Brazil 49/E3

Salween (riv.), Burma.... 90/A2
Salzburg, Austria 70/B2
Samar (isl.), Phil. 96/C2
Samar (sea), Phil. 96/C2
Samarra, Iraq 86/B2
Sambre (riv.), Europe.... 61/B2
Sam Rayburn (res.),
    Texas 31/D3
Samsun, Turkey 83/C1
San (riv.), Poland 75/C2
San'a (cap.),
    Yemen 80/B3
Sanandaj, Iran 86/B2
San Angelo, Texas 30/B3
San Antonio (cape),
    Argentina 50/C3
San Antonio, Texas 30/C3
San Blas (cape), Florida 27/B4
San Carlos, Phil. 97/B3
San Cristóbal, Venezuela 44/B2
San Diego, Calif. 34/C3
Sandy Hook (pen.), N.J. 25/E3
San Felipe, Colombia 44/C2
San Fernando de Apure,
    Venezuela 44/C2
San Francisco, Calif. 34/B2
San Joaquin (valley),
    Calif. 34/B2
San Jorge (gulf), Arg. ... 51/B4
San Jose, Calif. 34/B2
San José (cap.), C. Rica 39/D3
San Juan, Argentina 50/B3
San Juan (cap.), P. Rico 41/C2
San Juan (riv.),
    Cent. America 39/C3
San Juan (riv.), U.S. 35/E2
San Julián, Argentina 51/B4
Sankt Gallen, Switz. 69/D1
San Lorenzo (cape), Ec. 46/A2
San Lucas (cape),
    Mexico 36/A2

San Luis Potosí, Mexico . 36/B2
San Matías (gulf), Arg. 51/B4
San Miguel, El Salvador.. 38/B2
San Pedro Sula, Hond. .. 38/C2
San Salvador (isl.),
    Bahamas 40/B1
San Salvador (cap.),
    El Salvador 38/B2
San Sebastian, Spain 65/C1
Santa Ana, El Salvador .. 38/B2
Santa Barbara, Calif. 34/C3
Santa Barbara (isls.),
    Calif. 34/B3
Santa Clara, Cuba 40/B2
Santa Cruz, Bolivia 48/B3
Santa Fe, Argentina 50/B3
Santa Fe (cap.), N. Mex. 35/F3
Santa Maria, Brazil 49/C4
Santa Marta, Colombia... 44/B1
Santander, Spain 64/C1
Santiago (cap.), Chile .. 50/A3
Santiago, Dom. Rep. 41/C2
Santiago de Cuba, Cuba 40/B2
Santiago del Estero,
    Argentina 50/B2
Santo Domingo (cap.),
    Dominican Rep. 41/C2
Santos, Brazil 49/D4
São Francisco (riv.),
    Brazil 49/D3
São Luis, Brazil 49/D2
Saône (riv.), France 62/D3
São Paulo, Brazil 49/D4
São Roque (cape),
    Brazil 49/E2
Sapporo, Japan 95/C1
Saragossa, Spain 65/C1
Sarajevo, Yugoslavia 72/A1
Saratov, U.S.S.R. 76/C3
Sardinia (isl.), Italy 66/B2
Sasebo, Japan 94/A2

Saskatchewan (riv.),
     Canada 18/C2
Saskatoon, Saskatchewan 18/C2
Sault Sainte Marie, Mich. 29/E2
Sava (riv.), Yugoslavia.. 72/A1
Savannah, Georgia 27/C3
Savannah (riv.), U.S. 26/C3
Savannakhet, Laos 90/B2
Schaffhausen, Switz. 69/C1
Schefferville, Quebec 19/E2
Scheldt (riv.), Europe .. 61/A2
Schenectady, New York.. 24/E2
Schouwen (isl.), Neth. .. 60/A2
Schwyz, Switzerland 69/C1
Scilly (isls.), England 55/B4
Scott (sta.), Antarctica 115/B6
Scottsbluff, Nebraska 28/A3
Scranton, Pa. 24/D3
Seattle, Washington 32/B2
Sebago (lake), Maine 23/B3
Sebha, Libya 108/A2
Sefid (riv.), Iran 86/B2
Seistan (reg.), Asia 87/D2
Selvas (forest),
     Brazil 48/B-C2
Semois (riv.), Europe 61/B3
Sendai, Japan 95/C2
Senegal (riv.), Africa .. 107/A3
Seoul (cap.), S. Korea .. 94/A2
Seraing, Belgium 61/B2
Setúbal, Portugal 64/A2
Severn (riv.), U.K. 55/C4
Severnaya Zemlya (isls.),
     U.S.S.R. 77/F1
Seville, Spain 64/B2
Seyhan (riv.), Turkey.... 82/C2
Sfax, Tunisia 106/D1
Shackleton (ice shelf),
     Antarctica 115/C4
Shan (plat.), Burma 90/A1
Shanghai, China 93/D2

Shannon (riv.), Ireland.. 55/A3
Shantou, China 93/C2
Shari (riv.), Africa 108/A3
Sharon, Pa. 24/A3
Shasta (mt.), Calif. 34/B1
Shatra, Iraq 86/B2
Shebbelle, Wabi (riv.),
     Africa 109/D4
Sheffield, England 55/C3
Shenyang, China 93/D1
Sheridan, Wyoming 33/F2
Shetland (isls.), Scotland 54/C1
Shikoku (isl.), Japan 94/B2
Shiraz, Iran 87/C3
Shire (riv.), Africa 113/C2
Shizuoka, Japan 95/B2
Shkoder, Albania 73/A1
Shreveport, Louisiana 31/D2
Shwebo, Burma 90/A1
Sian, see Xi'an
Siberia (reg.),
     U.S.S.R. 76-77/D-J2
Sibuyan (sea), Phil. 96/B2
Sicily (isl.), Italy 67/C3
Sicuani, Peru 47/D5
Sidi Bel Abbes, Algeria 106/C1
Sidley (mt.), Antarctica 114/B8
Sidra (gulf), Libya 108/A1
Siena, Italy 66/B2
Sierra Madre (mts.),
     Phil. 96/B1
Sierra Madre del Sur (mts.),
     Mexico 37/C3
Sierra Madre Occidental
     (mts.), Mexico 36/B2
Sierra Madre Oriental(mts.),
     Mexico 37/B2
Sierra Morena (mts.),
     Spain 64/B2
Sierra Nevada (mts.),
     Spain 64/C2

Sierra Nevada (mts.),
     U.S. 34/B2
Sierre, Switzerland 68/B2
Silesia (reg.), Poland.. 74/A-B2
Sinai (pen.), Egypt 109/C2
Singapore (cap.), Sing. .. 91/B3
Sinuiju, N. Korea 94/A1
Sion, Switzerland 68/B2
Sioux City, Iowa 28/B3
Sioux Falls, S. Dakota.... 28/B3
Sittwe, Burma 90/A1
Sivas, Turkey 83/C2
Sjaelland (isl.), Den. 57/B3
Skagerrak (str.), Europe 57/A3
Skelleftea, Sweden 56/C2
Skopje, Yugoslavia 73/B1
Słupsk, Poland 74/B1
Snake (riv.), U.S. 20/B1
Snowdon (mt.), Wales .. 55/C3
Socotra (isl.),
     Yemen 81/B3
Sofia (cap.), Bulgaria 72/B1
Solomon (isls.) 102/B3
Solothurn, Switzerland .. 68/B1
Songhua (riv.), China .. 92/B1
Songjin, N. Korea 94/A1
Songkhla, Thailand 91/B3
South (isl.), N.Z. 101/E3
Southampton, England .. 55/C4
South Atlantic Ocean 14/H6
South Bend, Indiana 29/E3
South China (sea), Asia 79/E4
South Magnetic Polar Area,
     Antarctica 115/C5
South Orkney (isls.) .. 114/C11
South Pacific Ocean 14/C6
South Platte (riv.), U.S. 35/G1
South Polar (plat.),
     Antarctica 115/A1
South Pole, Antarctica.. 115/A3
South Shetland (isls.) 114/C10

Soya (cape), Japan 95/C1
Spartanburg, S. Car. 26/C3
Split, Yugoslavia 72/A1
Spokane, Washington 32/C2
Springfield (cap.), Ill. .. 29/D4
Springfield, Mass. 23/A3
Springfield, Missouri 28/C4
Springfield, Ohio 29/E3
Srinagar, Jam. & Kash. .. 88/B1
Stamford, Conn. 23/A4
Stanley (falls), Zaire 110/C2
Stavanger, Norway 57/A3
Stewart (isl.),
    New Zealand 101/E4
Stockholm (cap.),
    Sweden 57/B3
Stoke-on-Trent, Eng. 55/C3
Strasbourg, France 62/D2
Stuttgart, Germany 59/B2
Subotica, Yugoslavia 72/A1
Süchow, see Xuzhou
Sucre (cap.), Bolivia 48/B3
Sudan (reg.), Afr. .. 104/B-D3
Sudbury, Ontario 19/D2
Sudeten (mts.), Europe.. 70/B1
Suez (canal), Egypt 109/C1
Sukarnapura,
    Indonesia 99/D3
Sulu (arch.), Phil. 97/B4
Sulu (sea), Asia 97/A-B3
Sumatra (isl.), Indonesia 98/A2
Sumba (isl.), Indonesia.. 98/B3
Sumbawa (isl.), Indon. .. 98/B3
Sunda (isls.), Indonesia.. 98/A3
Sundsvall, Sweden 57/B2
Superior (lake),
    N. America 29/E2
Superior, Wisconsin 29/D2
Surabaja, Indonesia........ 98/B3
Surigao, Phil. 97/C3
Surin, Thailand 91/B2

Susquehanna (riv.), U.S. 25/C3
Suva, Fiji 103/C3
Sverdlovsk, U.S.S.R. 76/D3
Sydney (cap.), N.S.W. 101/D3
Syracuse, New York 24/C2
Syrian (desert), Asia 83/C3
Szczecin, Poland 74/A1
Szeged, Hungary 71/C2
Szombathely, Hungary.... 71/C2

T

Tablas (str.), Phil. 96/B2
Tabora, Tanzania 111/D3
Tabriz, Iran 86/B2
Tacloban, Phil. 97/C3
Tacna, Peru 47/D6
Tacoma, Washington 32/B2
Taegu, S. Korea 94/A2
Taejon, S. Korea 94/A2
Tagus (riv.), Europe 64/B2
Tahiti (isl.), Fr. Poly. .. 103/E3
Tahoe (lake), U.S. 34/C2
Taipei (cap.), Taiwan .. 93/D2
Taitao (pen.), Chile 51/A4
Ta'izz, Yemen Arab Rep. 80/B3
Taiwan (isl.), China 93/D2
Taiwan (strait), China .. 93/C2
Taiyüan, China 93/C2
Tajumulco (vol.), Guat. 38/B2
Tak, Thailand 90/A2
Taklamakan (desert),
    China 92/B2
Talara, Peru 46/A3
Talca, Chile 50/A3
Tallahassee (cap.), Fla. 27/C4
Tamanrasset, Algeria .. 106/C2
Tampa, Florida 27/C4
Tampere, Finland 57/C2
Tampico, Mexico 37/C2
Tana (lake), Ethiopia.. 109/C3

Tana (riv.), Europe 56/C2
Tana (riv.), Kenya 111/D3
Tanezrouft (des.),
    Africa 106/C2
Tanga, Tanzania 111/D3
Tanganyika (lake),
    Africa 105/D4
Tangier, Morocco 106/B1
Tapajós (riv.), Brazil 49/C2
Tarabulus, Lebanon 82/C3
Taranto, Italy 67/D2
Taranto (gulf), Italy 67/D3
Tarapoto, Peru 46/B3
Tarija, Bolivia 48/B4
Tarn (riv.), France 63/C4
Tarnów, Poland 75/C2
Tashkent, U.S.S.R. 76/D3
Tasman (sea) 101/D4
Taurus (mts.), Turkey .. 82/B2
Tavoy, Burma 91/A2
Tawitawi (isl.), Phil. 97/A4
Tegucigalpa (cap.),
    Honduras 38/C2
Tehran (cap.), Iran 87/C2
Tehuantepec (isth.),
    Mexico 37/C3
Tel Aviv-Jaffa, Israel...... 84/A1
Temuco, Chile 51/A3
Tennessee (riv.), U.S. 26/B3
Teresina, Brazil 49/D2
Terre Haute, Indiana 29/E4
Texarkana, Arkansas-
    Texas 31/D2
Texoma (lake), U.S. 31/C2
Thailand (gulf), Asia 91/B3
Thames (riv.), England.. 55/C4
Thun, Switzerland 68/B2
Thunder Bay, Ontario 19/D2
Thur (riv.), Switzerland 69/C1
Thurston (isl.),
    Antarctica 114/B9

Tianjin, China 93/C2
Tian Shan (mts.), China 92/B1
Tiber (riv.), Italy 66/C2
Tiberias, Israel 84/A1
Tiberias (lake), Israel .. 43/A1
Tibesti (mts.), Chad ... 108/A2
Tientsin, see Tianjin
Tierra del Fuego (isl.),
    S. America 51/B5
Tigris (riv.), Asia 80/B2
Tijuana, Mexico 36/A1
Tilburg, Neth. 61/B2
Timbuktu, Mali 107/B3
Timisoara, Romania 72/B1
Timmins, Ontario 19/D2
Timor (isl.), Asia 99/C3
Timor (sea) 100/B1
Tinaca (pt.), Phil. 97/C4
Tirane (cap.), Albania .. 73/A1
Tisza (riv.), Hungary 71/D2
Titicaca (lake), S. Amer. 42/B2
Toamasina, Madagascar 113/D2
Tobago (isl.), Trinidad
    & Tobago 41/D3
Tocantins (riv.), Brazil.. 49/D2
Tokyo (cap.), Japan 95/B2
Toledo, Ohio 29/F3
Toledo, Spain 64/C2
Toledo Bend (res.), U.S. 31/D3
Tombigbee (riv.), U.S. .. 26/A3
Tonkin (gulf), Asia 90/B1
Tonle Sap (lake), Camb. 91/B2
Toowoomba, Queens. .. 101/D3
Topeka (cap.), Kansas .. 28/C4
Torbat-e Heydariyeh,
    Iran 87/C2
Torne (riv.), Europe 56/C2
Toronto (cap.), Ontario 19/E2
Torrens (lake),
    S. Australia 100/C3
Torreón, Mexico 36/B2

Torres (strait) 101/C1
Toruń, Poland 74/B1
Toubkal (mt.), Mor. .. 106/B1
Touggourt, Algeria 106/C1
Toulon, France 63/D4
Toulouse, France 63/C4
Tournai, Belgium 61/A2
Tours, France 62/C3
Townsville, Queens. 101/D2
Toyama, Japan 95/B2
Trabzon, Turkey 83/C1
Transvaal (reg.),
    S. Africa 112/B3
Transylvanian Alps (mts.),
    Romania 72/B1
Traverse City, Michigan.. 29/E2
Trent (riv.), England..... 55/C3
Trento, Italy 66/B1
Trenton (cap.), N.J. 25/D3
Tres Marías (isls.),
    Mexico 36/B2
Trieste, Italy 66/C1
Trinidad (isl.), Trinidad
    & Tobago 41/D3
Trinity (riv.), Texas 31/C2
Tripoli (cap.), Libya.... 108/A1
Tripolitania (reg.),
    Libya 108/A1
Tromso, Norway 56/B2
Trondheim, Norway 56/B2
Troy, New York 24/E2
Troyes, France 62/D2
Trujillo, Peru 46/B4
Tsinan, see Jinan
Tsingtao, see Qindao
Tsitsihar, see Qiqihar
Tuamotu (arch.),
    Fr. Polynesia 103/E3
Tucson, Arizona 35/E3
Tucumán, Argentina 50/B2
Tulcán, Ecuador 46/B1

Tulsa, Oklahoma 31/D1
Tumbes, Peru 46/A2
Tumen (riv.), Asia 94/A1
Tunis (cap.), Tunisia.. 106/D1
Tunja, Colombia 44/B2
Turin, Italy 66/A1
Turkana (lake), Kenya 111/D2
Turneffe (isl.), Br. Hon. 38/C1
Tuscaloosa, Alabama 26/B3
Tuz (lake), Turkey 82/B2
Twin Falls, Idaho 32/D3
Tyrrhenian (sea), Eur. .. 67/B2
Tzepo, see Zibo

U

Ubangi (riv.), Africa.... 110/B2
Ucayali (riv.), Peru 46/C3
Uele (riv.), Africa 110/C2
Ufa, U.S.S.R. 76/C3
Ujung Pandang, Indon. .. 98/B3
Ulaanbaatar (cap.),
    Mongolia 93/C1
Ulan-Ude, U.S.S.R. 77/F3
Uliastay, Mongolia 92/B1
Umea, Sweden 56/B2
Ungava (pen.), Québec .. 19/E1
Uppsala, Sweden 57/B3
Ural (mts.), U.S.S.R. 53/E2
Ural (riv.), U.S.S.R. 76/C3
Urfa, Turkey 83/C2
Urmia, Iran 86/B2
Urmia (lake), Iran 86/B2
Uruguay (riv.),
    S. America 43/C3
Ürümqi, China 92/B1
Ushuaia, Argentina 51/B5
Uster, Switzerland 69/C1
Usti nad Labem, Czech. 70/B1
Usumacinta (riv.),
    Central America 38/B1

Utica, New York 24/D2
Utrecht, Neth. 60/B1
Utsunomiya, Japan 95/C2

V

Vaal (riv.), S. Africa .. 112/B3
Vaasa, Finland 56/C2
Vaduz (cap.), Liecht. ... 69/D1
Valdés (pen.), Argentina 51/B4
Valdivia, Chile 51/A3
Valdosta, Georgia 27/C4
Valencia, Spain 65/C2
Valencia, Venezuela 44/B1
Valencia (gulf), Spain .. 65/D2
Valera, Venezuela 44/B1
Valladolid, Spain 64/B1
Valparaíso, Chile 50/A3
Van (lake), Turkey 83/D2
Vancouver, Br. Col. 18/A2
Vancouver, Washington.. 32/B2
Vancouver (isl.), B.C. .. 18/B2
Vanern (lake), Sweden....57/B3
Varanasi, India 89/C2
Vardar (riv.), Yugo. 73/B1
Varna, Bulgaria 72/B1
Vasteras, Sweden 57/B3
Vattern (lake), Sweden.. 57/B3
Vechte (riv.), Europe 60/C1
Venezuela (gulf),
    S. America 44/B1
Venice, Italy 66/C1
Veracruz, Mexico 37/C3
Verde (cape), Senegal.. 107/A3
Verkhoyansk, U.S.S.R. .. 77/G2
Verona, Italy 66/B1
Versailles, France 62/C2
Vesteralen (isls.), Nor. .. 56/B2
Vestfjord (fjord), Nor. .. 56/B2
Vesuvius (vol.), Italy 67/C2
Vevey, Switzerland 68/A2

Vicksburg, Mississippi .. 26/A3
Victoria (cap.),
    Br. Columbia 18/B2
Victoria (falls), Africa 112/B2
Victoria (cap.), B.C. 18/B2
Victoria (lake), Africa 105/D4
Victoria Land (reg.),
    Antarctica 115/B6
Vienna (cap.), Austria.. 71/C1
Vienne (riv.), France 63/C3
Vientiane (cap.), Laos .. 90/B2
Vigan, Phil. 96/B1
Vigo, Spain 64/A1
Vila (cap.), Vanuatu .. 102/C3
Vilcanota (mt.), Peru 47/D5
Viña del Mar, Chile 50/A3
Vincennes (bay),
    Antarctica 115/C4
Vinh, Vietnam 90/B2
Vinson Massif (mt.),
    Antarctica 114/B10
Visayan (sea), Phil. 97/B3
Vistula (riv.), Poland 74/B1
Viterbo, Italy 66/B2
Vitoria, Spain 64/C1
Vladivostok, U.S.S.R. .. 77/G3
Vlone, Albania 73/A1
Vltava (riv.), Czech. 70/B1
Volga (riv.), U.S.S.R. .. 53/D3
Volgograd, U.S.S.R. 76/C3
Volta (riv.), Ghana 107/B4
Vosges (mts.), France.... 62/D3
Vostok (sta.), Antarc. 115/B4

W

Waal (riv.), Neth. 60/B2
Wabash (riv.), U.S. 29/E4
Waco, Texas 31/C3
Waddenzee (sound),
    Neth. 60/B1

Wad Medani, Sudan 109/C3
Wakayama, Japan 94/B2
Walbrzych, Poland 74/B2
Walcheren (isl.), Neth. .. 60/A2
Walla Walla, Wash. 32/C2
Walvis Bay, S. Africa .. 112/A3
Warsaw (cap.), Poland.. 75/C1
Warta (riv.), Poland 74/B2
Warwick, Rhode I. 23/B4
Wash, The (est.), Eng. .. 55/D3
Washington, D.C. (cap.),
    U.S. 25/C4
Washington (mt.), N.H. 22/B2
Waterbury, Conn. 23/A4
Waterloo, Iowa 28/C3
Watertown, New York .. 24/D2
Watcrville, Maine 22/C2
Wau, Sudan 108/B4
Weddell (sea),
    Antarctica 114/B11
Wellington (cap.),
    New Zealand 101/E3
Wenzhou, China 93/D2
Weser (riv.), Germany.. 58/B1
West (ice shelf),
    Antarctica 115/C3
West Bank (reg.) 84/A1
Western Ghats (mts.),
    India 88/B3
West Frisian (isls.),
    Neth. 60/B1
West Indies 40-41
West Palm Beach, Fla. .. 27/D5
Wettingen, Switzerland .. 69/C1
Wheeling, W. Virginia.... 26/C1
White (mts.), N.H. 23/B3
White (riv.), Vermont .. 23/A3
White (sea), U.S.S.R. 76/B2
Whitehorse (cap.),
    Yukon 18/B1
White Nile (riv.), Afr. 104/D3

Whitney (mt.), Calif. 34/C2
Wichita, Kansas 28/B4
Wichita Falls, Texas 30/C2
Wiener-Neustadt,
    Austria 70/B2
Wiesbaden, Germany 59/B2
Wight, Isle of (isl.),
    England 55/C4
Wilkes-Barre, Pa. 24/D3
Wilkes Land (reg.),
    Antarctica 115/B5
Willamette (riv.), Oreg. 32/B2
Willemstad (cap.),
    Neth. Antilles 41/C3
Williamsport, Pa. 24/C3
Wilmington, Delaware .. 25/D4
Wilmington, N. Carolina 26/D3
Windhoek (cap.),
    Namibia 112/A3
Windsor, Ontario 19/D2
Windward (isls.),
    W. Indies 41/D3
Windward (passage),
    W. Indies 40/B2
Winnipeg (cap.), Man. .. 18/D2
Winnipeg (lake), Man. .. 18/D2
Winnipesaukee (lake),
    New Hampshire 23/B3
Winston-Salem, N. Car. .. 26/C2
Winterthur, Switz. 69/C1
Wisconsin (riv.), Wis. .. 29/D3
Włocławek, Poland 74/B1
Wolin (isl.), Poland 74/A1
Wollongong, N.S.W. 101/D3
Wonsan, N. Korea 94/A2

Worcester, Mass. 23/B3
Wrocław, Poland 74/B2
Wuhan, China 93/C2
Wurzburg, Germany 59/B2

X

Xiamen, China 93/C2
Xi'an, China 93/C2
Xingu (riv.), Brazil 49/C2
Xinjiang (reg.), China .. 92/B1
Xuzhou, China 93/C2

Y

Yakima, Washington 32/B2
Yakutsk, U.S.S.R. 77/G2
Yalu (riv.), Asia 94/A1
Yaoundé (cap.), Cam. 110/B2
Yaqui (riv.), Mexico 36/B2
Yarmuk (riv.), Asia 84/A1
Yaroslavl, U.S.S.R. 76/C3
Yavarí (riv.), S. Amer... 46/C3
Yazd, Iran 87/C2
Yellow (Huang) (riv.),
    China 93/C2
Yellow (sea), Asia 93/D2
Yellowknife (cap.),
    N.W.T., Canada 18/B1
Yellowstone (riv.), U.S. 33/F2
Yenisey (riv.), U.S.S.R. 76/E2
Yining, China 92/B1
Yokohama, Japan 95/B2
Yonkers, New York 25/E3

York, England 55/C3
York, Pa. 25/C4
Yucatan (pen.), Mexico 37/D2
Yukon (riv.), N. Amer. 18/A1
Yuma, Arizona 34/D3
Yumen, China 92/B2
Yurimaguas, Peru 46/C3
Yverdon, Switzerland 68/A2

Z

Zabrze, Poland 74/B2
Zacapa, Guatemala 38/B2
Zagreb, Yugoslavia 72/A1
Zagros (mts.), Iran 86/B2
Zahedan, Iran 87/D3
Zambezi (riv.), Africa.. 105/D4
Zamboanga, Phil. 97/B4
Zanjan, Iran 86/B2
Zanzibar, Tanzania 111/E3
Zanzibar (isl.), Tanz. .. 111/E3
Zarqa (riv.), Jordan 84/A1
Zermatt,
    Switzerland 68/B2
Zhengzhou, China 93/C2
Zibo, China 93/C2
Zielona Gora, Poland 74/A2
Zomba, Malawi 113/C2
Zonguldak, Turkey 82/B1
Zug, Switzerland 69/C1
Zugspitze (mt.), Europe 59/B3
Zürich, Switzerland 69/C1
Zürich (lake),
    Switzerland 69/C1